Conquering Your
Financial Stress

BRUCE EATON

Conquering Your Financial Stress

The Five-Point Plan
for Generating *True* Wealth

TIMES BUSINESS

RANDOM HOUSE

This publication is designed to provide accurate and authoritative information in regard to the subject matter covered. It is sold with the understanding that the author and publisher are not engaged in rendering financial, legal, accounting, and other professional services. If expert assistance is required, the services of a professional should be sought.

The author and publisher specifically disclaim any liability or loss that is incurred as a consequence of the use and application, directly or indirectly, of any information presented in the book.

Copyright © 1998 by Bruce Eaton

All rights reserved under International and Pan-American Copyright Conventions. Published in the United States by Times Books, a division of Random House, Inc., New York, and simultaneously in Canada by Random House of Canada Limited, Toronto.

Library of Congress Cataloging-in-Publication Data

Eaton, Bruce.
    Conquering your financial stress : the five-point plan for generating true wealth / Bruce Eaton.
        p.   cm.
    Includes bibliographical references and index.
    ISBN 0-8129-6376-8
    1. Finance, Personal.   2. Life style.   3. Quality of life.
I. Title.
HG179.E234   1998
332.024′01—dc21   97-33697

Random House website address: www.randomhouse.com

Printed in the United States of America on acid-free paper

9 8 7 6 5 4 3 2

First Edition

Dedicated to the memories of
Laura Eaton Langejans and David Wheeler,
and to the future of Alexander Warfield Eaton

Acknowledgments

WRITING A BOOK may seem a solitary task—especially at 5 A.M. in the middle of February—but every author is surrounded by many people who make his or her work possible. Three people in my life deserve special acknowledgment:

Working with my agent, Anne Zeman, has fulfilled a longtime wish. The entire journey of taking an idea and turning it into a book is infinitely smoother when you have unwavering confidence in, and total respect and admiration for, your guide. Every writer should be as fortunate as I, to feel they are in such good hands. Also, thanks are due to her Irving Place Inc. partner, Kate Kelly.

I am forever grateful to Karl Weber, my first editor at Times Business Books, who appreciated the potential of the central concept of the book—reducing financial stress—and gave me both the direction and the latitude to develop it as fully as possible while keeping an eye on the deadline.

In acknowledging one's spouse, a writer must include a phrase such as "without whom this book would not exist." I could express such sentiments in one-hundred-foot-high concrete letters stretching around the equator and it would still be an understatement. My wife, Linda, has given me an extraordinary amount of support and encouragement. Without her love, patience, insight, strategic prodding, and judgment, this book would still be a cardboard box full of clippings and scribbled thoughts waiting for the arrival of "someday." Her presence is on every page.

In addition, hearty shouts of "Thanks!!" to . . .

John Mahaney, my editor at Times Business Books, and his assistant, Luke Mitchell, for smoothly taking over the helm and for their continuing guidance.

Mary Beth Roche and Will Weisser of Times Books Publicity, for all of their efforts on behalf of the book.

Margaret Wilson, for providing immeasurable assistance throughout the writing of the book. (Thanks, Marg!)

All of the people who graciously agreed to be interviewed for the book. They have served as an inspiration to me and, undoubtedly, to many others. A special tip of the hat to Tony Strusa.

Dr. Jamie Shiffner, for the key concept that enabled me to get out of a rut and sprint to the finish line.

The many wonderful people I've met from the Franklin Covey Company over the years, whose interest in my work has been both flattering and invigorating.

David Midland and Kathleen Rooney, for making my experience as Jazz Producer for Artpark a dream come true.

A loose band of literary confederates—Errol Somay, Mark Peel, Ruth Fecych, Parke Puterbaugh, and Ivan Wong—for treating me as if I were a writer, long before I could even claim to be one.

Peter Labonne and Shelley Valachovic, for keeping me perpetually off-center.

Paul Dodd and Peggi Fournier of 4D Advertising for ushering me onto the information superhighway with the care of school crossing guards.

Bruce Moser, Doug Dombrowski, and the staff of Could Be Wild Promotions, for showing me how things really happen.

My friends and relations who had the good manners to whisper "What's taking him so long?" out of earshot—or so they thought.

My brother, Murray Eaton, for helping develop the concept of "chud."

My parents, David and Eleanor Eaton, who—like many of their generation—provided their children with an extraordinary range of opportunity with everyday means.

Thank you to God for an astonishing world.

Bruce Eaton
January 1998

Contents

Conquering Your
Financial Stress

Introduction:
True Wealth

I SPENT MUCH of the summer of 1978 driving around Buffalo, New York, in a rusty Ford Maverick talking to people about their money. As a fledgling stockbroker, my charge was to sign up new clients. Nobody was exactly knocking down my door, so it was up to me to turn the slightest indication of interest—perhaps an unwitting response to a mailer offering "free" information—into a face-to-face meeting.

Salespeople are forever urged to focus on the big fish and not to waste time on the small fry. Truth be told, I'd talk to anyone who would talk to me—whether they had $1,000 or $100,000 to invest, whether they lived in the shadow of the steel plant or overlooking the eighteenth green. In the space of one week, I met with two prospective clients whose lives were so different from appearances and expectations that my entire worldview was forever turned upside down.

The first prospect looked like the plum—an anesthesiologist I'll call Dr. Knock. Doc Knock lived in a swanky new development and was eager to set up an appointment. But soon after I entered the oversized foyer of his mini-manse, my envisioned plum of an account shriveled into a sour prune.

Dr. Knock half greeted me from where he lay on the family room couch, distractedly watching television as two kids slugged away at each other in hopes of winning adult attention. The doc's buffed-up wife never introduced herself, but glared at me with a neurotic intensity that left no doubt that I was The Enemy: someone with the potential to divert precious dollars from her visions of Tara.

After a seeming eternity of fragmented conversation, the doc allowed during a commercial break as to how he might be able to come up with $2,000 to invest, but only if I could double it in three months to help pay some bills. "No can do," I replied and headed into the night, pondering the doc's misguided existence.

The second prospect was a couple, Frank and Mary Kasprzyk (not their real names)—an auto plant worker and his wife—who lived in a modest neighborhood and wanted to sell 100 shares of stock in Ford Motor. I could have taken their order over the phone easily, but decided to go see them anyway. It was while sitting at the Kasprzyks' kitchen table that the seeds for this book were planted.

The Kasprzyks had only a small amount of business for me, but they had saved over $150,000 (quite a sum then), mostly in bank CDs, some in company stock. As I dutifully pitched them on investment alternatives, Frank listened politely and then shot down the entire bundle of trial balloons with irrefutable common sense that had nothing to do with the merits of any specific investment.

"I don't want to bother with that stuff. Here, let me show you what I like to do," Frank explained as he led me on a tour of his property. In his basement was a woodworking shop where he spent the winter months making furniture. The yard was accented by beautiful flower beds. Behind the garage was a neatly tended vegetable garden. "Every minute I spend monkeying around thinking about some investment is time I can't be doing any of this."

What Frank meant was that the return he realized from pursuing activities he loved with an uncluttered mind was worth more than an extra ½ percent return from his CDs and a cluttered desk (the one thing any investment can guarantee you is more paper).

Later, over homemade dessert, Frank and Mary talked with pride about their two children, who had graduated from college, with appreciation about opportunity that had allowed them to live very different lives than they could have had in the native Eastern Europe they had fled as teenagers, and with contentment about an unpretentious life that mirrored their good nature.

Beyond their bank balance, the Kasprzyks were truly wealthy in ways that the Knocks couldn't even recognize. I felt embarrassed for even attempting to invade and mess around with Frank and Mary's joyous—and financially stress-free—daily life.

I drove away knowing that the Kasprzyks had life nailed across the boards—financially and nonfinancially—and that *I wanted to be just like them.* The particulars of their lives might be impossible to replicate, but I had the feeling that if I could just approach *my* life from *their* perspective, then I'd be on the right track. The only glitch was that I didn't have a clue how to go about it.

Twenty years later, I'm happy to say that I now see life in much the same way the Kasprzyks do. And although my life is quite different from theirs, I'd like to believe that my overall sense of well-being and lack of financial stress are comparable. The key question: How did I get from cluelessness to contentment?

After meeting the Kasprzyks, I began to identify other individuals whose daily lives appeared to be free from financial stress. Almost immediately I noticed people like the Kasprzyks in all walks of life. When I moved to New York City in 1981 to work on Wall Street—surrounded by even greater extremes in income, character, and behavior—any lingering preconceptions I had about the relationship between stress and money were blown away.

I hadn't yet sought to isolate the common elements among the lives of people who live free from financial stress. But looking back now, I can see that many of my pivotal decisions were influenced by the outlook and habits of the people whom I admired. And long after making these decisions—in true cart-before-the-horse fashion—I figured out some key lessons that helped me get closer to the Kasprzyks' state of mind. Let me tell you the highlights of these pivotal decisions, and the lessons I derived from them.

In 1985, an idea popped into my head that inspired me to say, "Hey, someone ought to write a book about it." Unlike what often happens with so many "good ideas," I actively pursued this one. Three months later, I sold the proposal for my first book to a major publisher. Two years later, I was on the business best-seller list.

The decision to take the risk of trying something new transformed me from a frustrated corporate staffer into an entrepreneur—and uncovered and led to the development of some talents I never knew I had.

The lesson: *Risk is worth taking when it can make a substantive and positive difference in the fabric of your day-to-day life.*

I also made the most important decision of my life in 1985: to marry my wife, Linda. When her job was relocated to central New Jersey, we found ourselves looking for housing amid an ultrahot real estate boom. Our real estate agent scolded us when we admitted to having cold feet about putting our every last dime into a cheesy condo in a cornfield. "Prices have gone up 10 percent a year since World War II—always have, always will," she said with the same certainty some people now apply to the stock market.

A few minutes applying our common sense to a calculator was enough to convince us that we would be foolish to buy just because everyone else was. Amid the frenzy, few had stopped to consider that with each upward surge in prices, the pool of qualified buyers shrank—and in fact was already about dried up. (Prices soon dropped precipitously.) We rented—and avoided being tied to an upside-down mortgage in an area we soon decided we'd rather leave behind.

The lesson: *Common sense is usually a better friend than the hottest trend.*

Like a lot of people, Linda and I unwittingly subscribed to the "when you make more, you get to spend more" credo. But not long after making the decision not to buy property, we thought: "Hey, maybe just because we make more money doesn't obligate us to spend it all." Duh. So as our incomes rose, we maintained our same lifestyle instead of ratcheting up our spending.

By the end of the 1980s, we found ourselves growing tired of Wall Street and yearning for a more manageable place to live. So we packed up and moved to Buffalo, New York—just like that! Some of our cohorts thought we'd lost our minds, but many of the best things in our lives can be traced to that single decision—made possible by the financial cushion we'd built up.

The lesson: *Living below your means increases your means.*

Special bonus lesson: *It's your life, so why not write the script?*

Very few couples share identical attitudes and habits when it comes to money—a primary reason why money is the number one source of marital conflict. Linda and I are no different—we began our relationship with widely disparate financial perspectives. After several years together, we faced a financial crisis so great that I believe it would have destroyed most marriages.

How did our relationship not only survive, but emerge even stronger? We made a commitment to identify, forge, and reinforce as much agreement in principle as possible on the financial issues that we—and most families—face. By agreeing, for example, that staying out of debt is more desirable than almost anything you can get into debt for, we avoid much of the spending squabbles that have the potential to flare into all-out war.

The lesson: *If you agree in principle, you won't fight over the principal.*

I've had a passion for music since earliest memory. I was elected president of my high school student council in the late '60s, when student governments were trying to become more "relevant." What was relevant to me, however, was that our school dances were lame. I hired a popular area band for triple the fee we were used to paying a local combo to fumble through "In-A-Gadda-Da-Vida." For the first time since anyone could remember, the school gym was packed for a dance. I had found something that to this day I truly love—booking and presenting music.

In the early '70s, I served as chairman of the concert committee at college. Our small school didn't have the big budget of neighboring universities, so our forte became booking unknown acts who eventually went on to great success, including Billy Joel and Bruce Springsteen (their combined concert fees: $2,500).

By graduation, I had no doubt that I wanted to be in the music business. So off I went to New York City—résumé in hand—and back I came with the cold realization that I lacked the sharp interpersonal elbows to work my way out of a mail room. After a while, I buried my dream and went out and got a job.

But, just as in a cheap horror movie, the dream never died. It was always lurking in the shadows. And however much I liked my work, there was always the nagging feeling that what I was doing was second choice. Nothing could replace the thrill of making the connection between artist and audience.

Over the years, I'd become a serious jazz fan. And one day in 1990, I was sitting around with some friends complaining about the lack of live jazz in Buffalo. It was a replay of countless previous conversations, but this time I told myself, "Quit talking and start doing." So I began writing letters and proposals, making phone calls, and setting up meetings until I was offered the chance to produce jazz concerts for a regional arts complex.

A year later, I was able to say to a packed house, "Ladies and gentlemen, please welcome, in his first-ever area appearance, Tommy Flanagan." (Tommy is a pianist who for me virtually defines the art of jazz.) As the Jazz Producer for Artpark in Lewiston, New York, for five years, I had the thrill and privilege of presenting dozens of the greatest jazz musicians in the world.

Although I've scaled back my work with music—by choice—it remains an active part of my life. But having made what I really wanted to do most a part of my life, whatever I do in life from here on out, it will be without the feeling that it's a substitute. As disconnected as it might seem, I doubt that I would have been able to completely pour myself into writing this book had I not also introduced audiences to the music of Bobby Watson, Leon Parker, and Joe Lovano.

The lesson: *Life offers a lot of different ways to do what you love.*

Ten years after meeting the Kasprzyks, I began in earnest to try to figure out their secret: jotting down ideas, clipping articles that somehow seemed relevant. At first, I thought strictly in terms of personal finance. After all, there's nothing more to financial stress than money and investments, right? Wrong. But it wasn't until I stepped back from the financial trees that I could start to see the forest.

As I was trying professionally to solve the riddle of the Kasprzyks, I was grasping personally for a solution to a far more urgent problem. In the early '90s, my sister, Laura, began a valiant fight with breast cancer. If only to quell my feelings of helplessness, I read everything I could put my hands on about every possible treatment—from the conventional to the furthest-out alternative.

Somewhere in my ruminations, several parallels between the traditional medical industry and the financial industry became apparent. Not wanting to throw a blanket indictment over many good people, I'll just say this: Both industries are unable and/or unwilling to treat the client as a whole. Soon after, I "resigned" from my self-image as a financial industry insider and began to work on this book in earnest.

When I first took full measure of all the factors that play a role in fighting financial stress, I was overwhelmed by the challenge of giving them a sense of order and relative weight. But the more I sat down and talked with people—rather than just observing them at arm's length—the more clearly the key components of a financially stress-free life came into focus.

By now, my work and my life have become intertwined. As I've learned how others have created True Wealth—the absence of financial stress—in their lives, I've simultaneously applied their common wisdom and perspective to my life. The result, in the words of bluesman Willie Dixon: "I live the life I love, and I love the life I live."

So here you are, with the finished book in your hand. And you may be asking yourself: "Who is this guy? Does he actually follow his own advice—walk it like he talks it? Is this really something I can do?"

Actually, I'm probably a lot like you. I have my concerns about the future. I have bills to pay. I'd like to save more. And, yep, I experience stress. But here's where I—and my family—may be different from you:

We believe that what the future holds is more dependent on who we are and what we do than on precisely how much money we have.

It's easier for us to pay the bills that have to be paid—mortgage, utilities, health insurance, and so on, because we don't have a lot of bills for things we didn't really have to have.

We've increased our savings rate severalfold. Knowing that we have the tools and the intent, we know that saving even more is not only doable, it's going to get done.

The stress we feel in our daily lives isn't caused by money. Rather, it's the natural by-product of our efforts to shape and direct our lives in ways that accurately reflect that which we value most. It's good stress.

One last important point: I think that people are often hesitant to take control of their lives out of fear that somehow they'll end up looking or being "different" from everyone else. "Keeping up with the Joneses" might be a cliché, but it's also one of the most powerful, conscious or unconscious, forces in society.

So I'd like to reassure you, not only from my observations but also my personal experience, that people who live free from financial stress are not a bunch of sprout-munching ascetic fringe dwellers. Whatever your livelihood, they're your fellow coworkers. Wherever you live, they're your neighbors.

My wife and I live in a standard-issue, twenty-five-year-old colonial with aluminum siding in a typical ex-burb neighborhood. We drive the most common car in America. Our vocations are right in the mainstream. Linda works for the largest corporation in her field. I work with some of the biggest names in my field. If you saw us walking through an airport, you probably wouldn't give us a second glance.

From all outward appearances, we're right-down-the-middle normal. All we're doing that's different is thinking like the Kasprzyks. You already know and admire people just like them. If they can live without financial stress, you can too. Read on, and discover how.

True Wealth:

What It Is, Where to Find It

The Truth About Money and Stress

I T'S THE LAST quiet night of the year.

What started as a quick initial tabulation of your holiday bills has sprouted into a carpet of charge slips, checkbooks, monthly statements, personal finance magazines, and investment sales literature spread out on the floor in front of you. As your past money missteps carom into everything you've put off for another day, your personal financial stress Super Collider revs up inside you. The pressure rises every time your eyes catch a word like *investment* . . . *future* . . . *retirement* . . . *savings* . . . *college.* You stare at all the scrubbed and happy faces on the brochures—with smiles that say, "It's so easy"—and want to swat them.

Overpowered, you fall back in your chair and drift off to sleep. You begin to dream. . . .

You're standing on the steps of a brightly lit house buzzing with a New Year's celebration. The front door suddenly flies open, an arm pulls you in, and the voice of the hostess welcomes you.

"You've got financial stress? Come on in and join the party! Everyone's here!

"Over in the corner, that's Don 'Darth' Downsizer introducing Skip Wadsworth IV to Joe Sixpack. They'll see each other again in the unemployment line on Monday.

"And you already know the Bickersons. Steer clear—they're at each other's throats about money again. Looks like their wedding videos are headed for the Dumpster. And they haven't even paid off the honeymoon.

"Do you know the Carps? Wonderful people—if they'd just stop talking about how they don't have it as good as their parents. I don't remember Fred and Esther ever living in a colonial-style airplane hangar.

"Isn't it nice to see the Smith family? . . . three generations—Leo, Steve, and Zack—all together. Let's listen in."

Leo: "I grew up in the Depression, fought the Big One, worked forty years without a gripe, and now some punk bureaucrat is trying to stick me with a copayment."

Steve: "Well, I'm paying out the nose to support the government's pyramid schemes, keep a roof over my head, and send Junior here to college to learn the things he should've learned in high school."

Zack: "You older dudes can gripe all you want, but you've trashed the planet, spent our future, and didn't leave nuthin' for us but the words 'temp' and 'part-time.' "

"Oops! Let's leave them to work it out.

"Looking for a comfortable place to park for a while? Sorry, but the worn-out Barcalounger has been put out on the curb—just like the cozy job with a thirty-year guarantee that your dad used to enjoy. Maybe you can commiserate about it in the kitchen with the Voters. Every year they have a new slogan—you know, like 'It's the economy, stupid' or 'Government's too big, but give me my check.' Let's see what's on their mind this year. 'Let's start another party,' is it? Good luck.

"Okay, everyone! It's time to play some games! First we're going to play Pin Your Future on a Good Mutual Fund. You did bring your meager savings for the year, didn't you? Then go ahead, pick one. There are only eight thousand to choose from. But if you get the right one, you'll be clipping coupons when you retire . . . and not for dinner at Denny's. So keep trying!

"Be sure to give me your resolutions so we can tally them up for the Number One Resolution for the New Year. Let's see what we have here. . . .

"Quit smoking. What, again?

"Lose weight. Borrrrring.

"Stay home and watch 'Dick Clark's New Year's Rockin' Eve.' You mean you're not having fun?

"And here's our winner, everyone: The number one resolution for the coming year is 'Get my finances under control.' Wahoooo! We're gettin' down now. . . ."

As the revelers whoop it up, you struggle to find the door. In a flash, you're awake. . . .

So now you're sitting there with a head-pounding, gut-wrenching hangoverlike feeling that you just *know* has everything to do with money. And what's the chance of making it go away? According to what you've read and heard, slimmer than slim.

If you want to retire, you'll need more money than everything you've earned in your lifetime—total. If you want a bigger house in a neighborhood outside the jurisdiction of a teenage gang, you'll need to sign away every dollar you'll make before you retire. If you want to send your kids to college, you'll need an amount equal to the GNP of an Eastern European country you don't even know exists. And this is on top of the bills for straightening out Josh's teeth and then sending him to hockey camp to get them knocked out.

To find a job to pay for all of this, you'll have to have enough technical expertise to run everything in sight, eight free arms to actually do it, and a callous enough heart to make the rest of us work for minimum wage. No wonder you have financial stress.

As you reach for the television remote, you tell yourself, "If there was anything I could do to make even a little bit of my financial stress go away, I'd do it, but . . ."

Don't touch that dial. Let's get on the case.

THE NINE SYMPTOMS OF FINANCIAL STRESS

If you visit your doctor and tell him, "Gee, Doc, I feel really awful. I know there's something wrong with me," he's going to ask you about your symptoms. He'll look you over, perform some tests, make a diagnosis, and prescribe a course of action. So what are your symptoms?

If you put your financial stress under a Stress-o-Scope, you're going to find one or more of these nine common identifiable symptoms and some possible indications:

FINANCIAL STRESS SYMPTOM #1: **You need a new job . . . yesterday.** The symptom with the fastest-growing rate of occurrence.

- You've got a pink slip in your hand.
- As you watch your coworkers being tossed overboard, you're counting on being the last person on the deck.
- The last thing you learned at work was how to transfer a call on the new phone system.
- You've heard the plant is shutting down but won't believe it until you see the padlocks.
- Your career growth is strictly a function of longevity—when someone asks, "Still workin' at Nudd-Tech?" you get queasy.

○ You're working for a psychotic tyrant (as opposed to a typical manager who doesn't do things exactly the way you would or fully recognize the scope of your genius).

○ The only reason you haven't quit your job is because of a little voice in your head that asks, "But what else can you do?"

FINANCIAL STRESS SYMPTOM #2: **You don't have enough money to pay your bills.** The indications for this symptom fall on a sliding continuum from being "a little short this month" to being completely buried.

○ Paying your monthly bills has become an eternal juggling act.
○ You are constantly dipping into your savings to pay your bills.
○ You're going into debt to pay your bills.
○ You're going into debt to pay off debt.
○ The dial-a-bankruptcy lawyer in the television ads you used to make jokes about is starting to look like a pretty good guy.

FINANCIAL STRESS SYMPTOM #3: **You can't control your spending.** This symptom is thriving in an atmosphere of easy credit and where delayed gratification is often measured in seconds.

○ You have a continually evolving universe of things that, if they were yours, would make your life "perfect."
○ Your house is cluttered with barely used stuff.
○ You don't realize you've bought something until you're out the door of the store.
○ Shopping is an activity of first choice rather than necessity—your car heads to the mall on automatic pilot.
○ You slip your purchases into the house and hide the receipts so you can pretend they were already there.

FINANCIAL STRESS SYMPTOM #4: **You're constantly fighting with your spouse or partner about money.** An eternal symptom—Adam and Eve may even have argued about the cost of hiring a landscape architect for the Garden of Eden.

○ If you didn't have arguments about money, you wouldn't have a reason to communicate.
○ Your relationship is one long steel-cage wrestling match over: Whose fault it is that you don't have enough money to spend right now: "If you hadn't bought that boat . . ."

How to spend what money you do have: "I've been playing with the same clubs since college, and you just changed curtains last year."

How to spend money you don't have yet: "Our tax refund is not going for something we don't need and I don't want."

How to spend money that isn't yours and in all likelihood never will be: "If we won the ten million, there's still no way we're giving a dime to your sister."

FINANCIAL STRESS SYMPTOM #5: **You're leaving the back door open to financial disaster, and deep down you know it.** Even in a world where people take every risk imaginable and expect bullet-proof immunity, this symptom can't be contained.

○ You've ignored an IRS audit notice, hoping you'll get lost in the bureacratic shuffle.
○ You have plenty of losing lottery tickets but no insurance.
○ You've bet the farm on someone else's horse—and it's headed for the glue factory.
○ You're engaging in stupid behavior that's going to get you tossed out of your house.

FINANCIAL STRESS SYMPTOM #6: **You can't part with money, even if it's for your own darn good.** The opposite of being unable to control spending, this single symptom can act like a permanent case of ultrabad breath, keeping family, friends, and associates at bay.

○ When you go out for lunch with eight other people, you insist on figuring out your share right down to the penny.
○ You'll drive five extra miles to avoid a twenty-five-cent toll.
○ You'll avoid going to the doctor or filling a prescription because you don't think your condition is life-threatening.
○ Your whole day is ruined by a two-dollar service fee you don't think you should have to pay.
○ Your rule for spending money is "Cheaper is better."
○ You complain about people mooching off the government but will angle for every piece of change you can keep from the IRS— even if it means ignoring the law.

FINANCIAL STRESS SYMPTOM #7: **The words "future" and "savings" turn your stomach into a knot and shut your brain down.** This symptom thrives on the belief that "things were never this bad."

○ You'd rather look at autopsy photos than an article about retirement.

○ Your only active savings plan is your "Buy ten, get one free" punch card from the local pizzeria.

○ You embrace predictions of ecological or nuclear disaster as a rationale for not making plans.

○ You've said "Wait till next year" more often than the Boston Red Sox.

○ Your ace in the hole is that "your ship is going to come in."

○ You've redefined the future to mean next Monday.

FINANCIAL STRESS SYMPTOM #8: **You're overwhelmed and intimidated by the prospect of making an investment decision.** Odds are that your parents or grandparents didn't have this problem.

○ You've had excess funds sitting in a checking account for the past year.

○ You'd rather go to the dentist than to a stockbroker, er, excuse me, financial consultant.

○ You find investment literature harder to crack than a Sanskrit translation of *Ulysses*.

○ You feel more confident about predicting the winner of the Super Bowl than choosing an investment.

○ You've narrowed your investment choices down to three but can't figure out how all of them can simultaneously claim to rank as number one.

○ If you wanted a part-time job, you tell yourself, it wouldn't be junior portfolio manager.

FINANCIAL STRESS SYMPTOM #9: **You're losing money on the investments you've already made.** This symptom can be either real (you're down big time, pal) or a case of relative performance envy (you're up, but not as much as the next guy).

○ When you ask your broker, "What's going on here?," you get a rambling monologue that includes "I'll have to call research" and "Long term still looks good."

○ You have no idea why you own the investment other than that it was supposed to go up.

○ You're losing sleep because you don't own the hottest mutual fund.

○ Your investment headed south right after you bought it and hasn't been seen since.

○ You finally own an investment in the Top Ten. Unfortunately, it's a percentage loser.
○ That fabulous business opportunity you sank your life savings into has turned out to be a black hole.

THIS IS THE PART WHERE THE TEST ISN'T

"So how bad is my financial stress, Doc?" You want to know, right?

This is where you'd usually take a test, score your answers, and find out how you rate on a scale from 0 points: "You have achieved a state of bliss reserved for yogis and saints," to 100 points: "You are in great danger of spontaneously combusting."

We're going to skip the test and here's why.

First of all, you must be experiencing financial stress to some degree or you wouldn't have picked up this book. If that's good enough for you, that's good enough for me.

Second, when you read through the nine symptoms of financial stress, you *knew* which ones were really grinding you. You don't need a pencil and paper to trace the dots and make the connection.

And third, *your symptoms aren't that important.*

"Yow! How can you say that, Doc?! I'm hurtin'!" you cry.

Because once your symptoms have been identified, they can not only distract you from reducing your financial stress, they can send you off in an entirely wrong direction.

Let's go back to the doctor's office. You walk in with a burning, throbbing sensation in your abdomen. Suppose the doctor examines you, hands you a bottle of antacid, and sends you on your way. He doesn't advise you that a cup of coffee doesn't qualify as breakfast or that chicken wings and pizza aren't a balanced diet. He doesn't tell you to exercise or practice relaxation techniques. But, hey, you don't care—you've got some strong medicine that will make the pain go away and that's what counts. Right?

You know the answer: wrong. Until you address the root causes of your physical distress—not just the symptoms—you can swill down all the chalky liquid with the minty fresh taste you want and lurking right beneath that soothing protective coating will be a legion of stress massing for your next order of nachos.

This is true for any number of maladies—from allergies to back pain. Many of the common remedies are doomed to fail because they point people in the wrong direction: looking for solutions by covering up the symptoms. They take a Band-Aid approach to what is often a code-red problem.

As a society, we're starting to recognize the pitfalls of cosmetic change versus core change. Witness the increasing emphasis on preventive medicine. Yet we're still taking cosmetic approaches to financial stress with remedies that, at best, are marginally effective and, at worst, create even more stress.

The two most frequent prescriptions for money woes come from two diametrically opposed camps in a scene reminiscent of the long-running Miller Lite beer commercial. On one side there's a group shouting "Make more!!" and on the other side everyone's chanting "Need less!!" As different as they are, they have one thing in common: They're both wrong.

THE WEALTH WIZARDS: "MAKE MORE!!"

The most commonly prescribed remedy for financial stress is "more money."

Prodded or irritated by a financial stress symptom, we have an impulsive—almost instinctual—reaction: A check filled out with the right numbers would make all of this go away.

If I had a higher-paying job, I'd be able to save a little.

If I could just get out from under these bills, I could stay on top of things.

If this investment hits, I'm all set.

If we had more in the bank, we could both get what we want and not have to argue about all of this.

Where does this impulse come from? There are those who would say that man is an animal driven by greed and envy and that money—like booze to a barfly—fuels his out-of-control behavior. Let this wobbly warthog loose in the consumer jungle, and look out!

I believe that it's inaccurate—and counterproductive—to consider extreme human behavior the norm. Sure, there are some outright swine mixed in with the human race who'd trip their grandmothers and trample a toddler to make a buck. But, on the whole, our general condition is much more benign: Man is like a squirrel scampering around gathering nuts, frequently getting too wrapped up in the process to think about where he's stashing them or how his efforts are adding up. The squirrel starts off thinking "More is good" and, without even realizing it, gets whipped into a nut-chasing frenzy.

Fanning and feeding off our "make more" impulse are the wealth wizards—get-rich gurus with their own personal double-secret formula for getting rich in a flash, over a lifetime, or even while you sleep. If you need to hitch a ride to Easy Street, they're headed that way. And through a stroke of good fortune, they're willing to let *you* hop on board (along with anyone else who has the fare).

Wealth wizards ply their trade in three general areas:

1. *Investments.* After the longest bull market in stock market history, investment wealth wizards are multiplying faster than rabbits with calculators. With the 10 Percent Mantra ("Stocks will return 10 percent until the end of time") as their bottom line, the ranks of investment wizards have grown as large as the Red Army. And when they tweak the numbers, the returns soar.

Why settle for 10 or 20 percent when you can get 300 or even 3,000 percent returns? With their "If you had invested $1,000 in Investment X when I told you to, you'd be rich" come-ons, investment wizards would have you believe that lightning can strike not just twice, but whenever they snap their fingers. Blammo! Another pile of loot!

Investment wizards don't just deal in stocks. You'll find them touting coins, art, real estate, pork belly futures, china plates with drippy pictures of wide-eyed waifs . . . you name it. But all investment wizards have one thing in common: Each self-proclaimed Number One Guide to the Good Life has figured out what none of his or her compatriots has been able to—the key to surefire all-profit no-can-lose investing.

2. *Business and Career Opportunities.* Opportunity wizards not only have the inside track to wealth, they're going to have you riding in the breakdown lane at 100 mph. Wearing special infrared goggles that make super-wealth opportunities stand out like skyscapers in the Sahara, opportunity wizards have a singular response for skeptics: Why?

Why labor like a mere mortal when there are scores of people waiting to sell you their house or car for pennies? Why take your licks at the office when you can make a bundle licking envelopes at home? Why hang around the coffee cart when your block doesn't have a gourmet coffee shop? Why comb the "help wanted" section for a job opening when you can place ads and get money in the mail?

In other words, why do you insist on being a schlub when a helping hand is so close?

3. *Wealth Alchemy.* Wealth alchemists specialize in "making more" through means that would have been described in less-informed times as hocus-pocus.

Walk into any New Age bookstore and right in the middle of every possible road map to spiritual enlightenment you'll find books on how to get more money flowing from the cosmos right to your wallet. If you can free up your vibrations and visualize the keys to Fort Knox in your hand, you can psychically channel a bundle without breaking a single law. Evidently money gathered in this fashion is purer than money you just plain work for.

Want something a little more concrete? With a single weekend seminar you can double your personal effectiveness (translation: more bucks). Don't have time for a seminar? Then bungee jump over a shark tank for an instantaneous unleashing of the Super You.

The wealth wizards can make any of us feel a little anxious. What if we are traveling an inferior road in life for no good reason? But on the other hand, what if we do reach for the brass ring and it turns out to be soap on a rope? But trying to sort through the individual messages of the wealth wizards is actually a minor cause of financial stress compared to the underlying message shared by every one of them: The solution to your financial stress is more money.

MORE MONEY ≠ LESS STRESS

The truth is that "make more" is not an effective antidote to financial stress. And that's not just some clench-jawed neo-Marxist wannaspoil-the-party wishful thinking. Here are three reasons why:

1. There Is No Correlation Between Money and Happiness

The fundamental precept behind "make more" is that "more is good" because "more makes you happy." Most people spend their lives equating money with well-being—believing that happiness is achieved by addition.

In reality, happiness cannot even be quantified, let alone be determined by the presence of any one thing or things in your life. There's not a secret bank account, executive home, or personal driving machine in the world that, if it were yours, would enable you to say, "I have achieved well-being."

In his terrific book *The Pursuit of Happiness,* psychology professor David G. Myers examines a broad range of existing studies on the relationship between money and happiness. The overwhelming conclusion: Once you get above a subsistence level—adequate food, clothing, and shelter—any significant relationship between money and happiness ends.

Examining the relationship between income and happiness for *Forbes* magazine, Dan Seligman arrived at a similar conclusion: ". . . the bottom line, according to those who have studied the question, is that typically only 1% to 2% of people's differences in happiness is attributable to their differences in income."

"More" is a mirage, always in the distance no matter how much ground we cover. Whether they earn $15,000 or $150,000, a preponderance of people believe that if their incomes were 10 percent higher, they'd have it made. But we know from experience that this isn't the case. You get the raise, your spending habits ratchet up, and before too long, you're looking for more.

The confounding thing is that we all know that money can't buy happiness from our own experiences. Yet we act as if there's an "I know, but . . ." microchip in our brains that tells us to ignore what we know, on a rational level, is true. If we hear that Fred makes more money than Fran, we automatically think that Fred is "doing better," even though concrete observation shows us that Fred is on the fast track to being a miserable ol' coot as well as a regional manager, while Fran gracefully traverses life's path in and out of the workplace. We willfully ignore the overwhelming evidence.

More money won't make you happier, it will only change the scenery. It doesn't matter whether you're sitting on worn-out beanbag chairs or a brand-new Ethan Allen love seat, if you and your spouse are duking it out, you're going to be miserable. If all the car loans in the country were magically paid off, the proud new owners would likely find themselves another ditch to park in.

One need only look at the experience of lottery winners to understand that more money can be a godsend, handy, convenient, no big deal, troublesome, or an outright curse. A good number of winners blow through their winnings even faster than they get them and end up flat broke with a trail of busted relationships, sipping sorrow from a spoon instead of champagne from a glass. But others use their prize to enhance, but not radically alter, their current paths in life. And therein lies a critical point.

The only thing for certain about more money is, well, that it's more money. And even that is written in sand as often as it's written in stone. But although there's no significant correlation between money and happiness, there is a critical relationship between your current level of financial stress and how you'd handle more money.

When your life is relatively stress-free financially, you've already got a pretty clear idea about how you'd turn extra cash into an enrichment. But if you're under financial stress and more money does come your way, you'll get temporary relief at best. (You'll learn why this is the case in the pages ahead.)

Only if you get your financial stress under control at your current income will "more" do you real lasting good. And there are two potential bonuses along the way to reducing your financial stress at your current income level:

○ You may discover that you really don't need more.
○ You may very well end up with more.

2. "More Money" Distracts Us from
Realistic Solutions and Delays Meaningful Action

Solutions fall into two categories: self-generated and off the shelf.

The seeds to self-generated solutions lie in the determination to make a change and get things done. You roll up your sleeves and dig into a course of action. Through trial and error you refine and adapt your growth, building on your successes, often discovering entirely unexpected branches in your life. You end up exactly where you want to be—and find often that it's a place you didn't even know existed when you began.

Self-generated solutions are often misconstrued as fate or luck rather than the result of the forces of cause and effect working together in unseen ways. Unfortunately, we're standing at Point A—Unacceptable Reality—and we often can't imagine what Point B—A Better Place—is, let alone how to get there. We don't have the patience for self-generated solutions. Instead, we head for the drive-through window for a fast solution right off the menu.

Off-the-shelf solutions are the opportunity-in-a-box variety—a neat prepackaged one-decision solution to whatever's bugging you. Need to lose weight? Buy a Gut-Be-Gone or a Jogmeister. Need to jump-start your income? Get an MBA, or sell *your* friends on the idea of selling *their* friends on the idea of selling something that no one ever gets around to selling.

The wealth wizards are among the most forceful and visible purveyors of opportunities in a box—often to the point where you believe that if you have a financial question, you need to deal with them for the answer. But once you start sorting through the options, you quickly encounter some stumbling blocks: How do you separate hype and outright hucksterism from the legitimate opportunities? Is that hot career going to stay hot and—just as important—will you warm to it? And if all these investment systems work, how come most professionals underperform the market most of the time?

Life shouldn't be a big game of Eenie-Meenie-Minie-Moe where you hope that you land on something that's better than where you are right now. But if you believe that "make more" is the immediate answer to your financial stress, that's the game you'll be playing. And all the while, you stare at endless shelves of dazzling prefab off-the-shelf solutions, you could be generating your own solutions.

One key to conquering financial stress is to take the specific actions that will conquer *your* financial stress, not someone else's. The best solutions to your financial stress can be found in your own backyard. In all likelihood they're going to be more accessible, more reliable, less expensive—or even free. And they'll be easier to use than whatever's being hawked across the street by the wealth wizards.

3. "Make More" Solutions Can Be Fraught with Financial Stress

Chasing after "make more" solutions not only can waste your time—a valuable commodity in and of itself—but can cost you enough cash to make your present financial stress seem like a picnic in the park. For every McDonald's franchise, there are hundreds of businesses that worked only on paper. There's nothing like losing your entire savings to make you wish that there were such a thing as a "do over" in real life and not just on the playground.

It should be no surprise that part of the universe of "make more" solutions is a petri dish for fraud and deception. The grass may look greener on the other side, but that lush appearance could be a thin coating of slime. And if you think that you're too smart to be conned, you need only consider the recent case of New Era Funding—a philanthropic scam that left dozens of colleges and nonprofit institutions (i.e., smart folks) out millions of dollars. Or any story in your local paper that includes the quote "It seemed too good to be true, but everyone recommended him and he was such a nice guy."

Equally as dangerous as preplanned fraud and deception, if not more so, is the phenomenon of mass delusion: A certain outcome is so desirable for everyone concerned that no one pauses to consider that it might not happen or—even worse—ignores in-your-face evidence that real life isn't following the "make more" script. For Exhibit A I'd suggest the billions of dollars that Ma and Pa Investor lost in limited partnerships in the '80s.

Before leaving our first look at "make more," one point can't be emphasized enough: *This book is about reducing financial stress, not making more money.* I recognize that you can't disconnect that "I know, but . . ." chip in your brain in the time it takes to read a few pages, but if you can consciously set aside your "make more, right now" hopes, you'll put yourself at the foot of a much clearer path to a less stressful life.

THE NEW FRUGALISTS: "NEED LESS!!"

Scolding us to "need less" are the New Frugalists, those penny-pinching funsters who believe that financial stress is caused by an evil conspiracy (one that's eluded even Oliver Stone) that traps us into wasting our lives earning and spending money. Their defense against the oppressive Almighty Dollar: Save up every cent, cash everything in, drop out, live a simple life, and save the planet.

The New Frugalists are in many ways children of the '60s—in spirit, if not in fact—perhaps even ex-hippies whose first attempts to live an idyllic counterculture existence didn't pan out. Long ago they discovered that living under a geodesic dome didn't guarantee harmony among the inhabitants or vanquish that annoying need for money to keep the Magic Bus on the road. Now, a generation later, weighed down by careers, kids, and mortgages, the rough edges of their memories smoothed over by listening to too much Jerry or Yanni, they're ready for another crack at proving that Castro is an economic genius.

"What's wrong with voluntary simplicity [to use the preferred phraseology of the New Frugalism]?" you might ask. Isn't there an awful lot of waste in the world? Yes. Couldn't everyone from the federal government on down benefit from learning how to get by with less? You bet. Don't we spend a great portion of our lives working to make a living? Sure do. Isn't community service a noble and worthy pursuit? Undoubtedly. Shouldn't we be careful with the environment? Absolutely. Then what's the problem?

The problem with the New Frugalism is that it throws out the baby with the bong water.

If you're working too hard at a job you don't like to buy stuff you don't need that doesn't make you happy anyway, that's a problem all right—your problem. You're making the choices, not society, the economy, or money itself. But it's more convenient to ascribe your problems to a big, eight-legged bogeyman (capitalism, progress, technology, money, consumerism, mean spirits, greed, and pollution) and take a self-righteous copout than it is to self-generate real solutions.

WHY "NEEDING LESS" MAY NOT MEAN "LESS STRESS"

A scaled-down lifestyle might be just what the doctor ordered, if in fact the change of course is directed toward a self-generated vision. But if you're just throwing in the towel, you're making a decision based on some notions at the foundation of the New Frugalism that are flat-out wrong. The most prominent of them are:

1. *Money is evil.* New Frugalists treat money as if hidden in the engraving on a dollar bill—akin to a backward message from Satan on a heavy metal record—is the line "Covet me, worship me, waste me, devote your life to me." But money doesn't make people do bad things any more than Ozzy Osbourne makes stupid teenagers do stupider things.

In reality, money is a blank slate. It's what you make of it. There's nothing inherently positive or negative about money. The problem is that loathsome behavior centered on money is often louder—and deemed more newsworthy—than all of the good things that money does. A brutal holdup or a Wall Street insider trading scandal is front-page news. There's never a headline that declares "Millions Use Money to Buy Food." A sports franchise that leaves town in the middle of the night will get the fans jawing that money is ruining sports. Yet without money, there'd be no players' strikes or Steinbrenner types to gripe about. Okay, maybe money *is* ruining sports.

Think of the things in your life you couldn't do without money. Look in your community and note all of the infrastructure, services, and good deeds that are made possible by money. Do you think that all of it could be possible through the miracle of barter? Get real. Money may not be a panacea, but it certainly is a handy tool.

When someone starts running down the rich because all they care about is ripping off the little guy so they can afford their big houses and fancy cars, he's letting his own negative emotions (a little envy or jealousy, have we?) blind him to the facts. Or maybe he doesn't know the real facts.

Extensive research has revealed that the average millionaire in this country made his fortune through his own business (creating jobs for others, no doubt) and lives well below his means, exhibiting a lifestyle that is virtually indistinguishable from his nonmillionaire neighbors.

Implying that wealthy people are coldhearted crooks has about as much validity as saying that people who live in poor neighborhoods are violent slobs. Again, bad behavior is simply louder than good.

Ironically, New Frugalists who believe that money is evil and have set a pious limit on their own wealth have no qualms about setting wealth limits for you and everyone else. And they see no irony in asserting that they know best how your extra cash should be redistributed. In other words, your money is bad; but if you let a New Frugalist dole it out to his pet causes, then it's good.

2. *Progress is bad.* Some of the New Frugalists are neo-Malthusian Luddites (often with laptops, mind you) who believe that growth and progress are bad.

They yearn for the days when health care didn't cost you an arm or a leg—unless you had a simple infection. There were no cars polluting our cities—just a foot of horse dung on the streets. There were no big faceless corporate employers to sap you of your vitality and leisure time—maintaining adequate food, clothing, and shelter took care of that for you. You didn't have to slave your entire life to afford a comfortable retirement—your life expectancy even at the turn of the century was less than fifty years.

One target of all of the railing against progress is the consumer-driven world we live in. The Frugalists pine for the days when every consumer good in the world could be found in a single Sears catalog. There's more than a kernel of truth in the assertion that—as a society—we're losing our bearings in a blizzard of mass-produced junk that distracts us from more satisfying pursuits.

As a parent, I wish I didn't have to battle to keep the Atomik Karate Kats or the latest Disney marketing vehicle out of range of my son's consciousness. But I'm also thankful for all of the consumer products that make my life easier or more enjoyable. I'm willing to put up with Sega Genesis as long as I get to have an automatic coffeemaker. And I won't attempt to abridge your right to own a Salad Shooter.

The problem with Consumer World isn't its existence; it's our inability to manage it. We've made Mickey Mouse a villain only through our collective inability to use rodent traps. Show me a Frugalist who rails against progress and I'll show you someone who wouldn't want to give up his high-tech mountain bike or the fax machine that allows him to telecommute. They have no problem with the fruits of growth they deem acceptable. They just don't believe we're capable of making choices as wise as theirs.

3. *Work is bad and a waste of time.* A sound bite of the New Frugalism is "making a dying"—the idea being that any- and everything we do for money is a waste of our precious lives.

One manifesto of the New Frugalism, *Your Money or Your Life,* even derides "the false assumption that what we do to put food on the table and a roof over our head should also provide us with our sense of meaningful purpose and fulfillment" and asserts that "you may love your work, you may hate it—it doesn't matter."

If you're thinking "Oh, yes it does, pal," I'm with you. Given the choice to make—and everyone has the choice—I'd much rather love my work. And yes, getting paid to communicate ideas gives me a great sense of purpose and meaning, right along with putting a heap of Oatios in my son's cereal bowl.

Allow me to blunt this fuzzy Utopian gibberish with a three-word quote from economist Hans Sennholz: "Man must work."

Most of us recognize that we have a basic need for at least one member of a family to be in the economic arena on a continuing basis. And as long as you have to work, why condemn yourself to stress by approaching your job with the attitude that work is a waste of time and killing you to boot? Talk about a self-fulfilling prophecy!

Without any sense of irony, *Your Money or Your Life* urges readers to work at their paid jobs for "the highest remuneration possible" yet save their "love and enthusiasm" for the rest of their work. With a sourpussed sense of entitlement like that, no wonder frugalists don't like the idea of work: They've totally cut themselves off from the biggest potential benefits of work—both financial and nonfinancial.

Some of the New Frugalists are akin to the birds who live on the backs of hippos, flitting around while the beast does the heavy lifting. Their lives are made possible, ironically, through the largesse (stock purchase programs, severance packages, or simply paying a substantial salary despite their indifferent attitudes) of the dreaded employers that once enslaved them.

With a downscaled existence powered by their financial solar cells, they're able to tinker with their computers or browse through a bookstore in the morning and then do volunteer work in the afternoon before walking home to watch a nature documentary on public television (made by someone who undoubtedly didn't hate her work). But this smacks of a certain smug elitism. Because for them to enjoy this lifestyle, the rest of us have to show up—whether it's at the utility company, bookstore, school, or television station.

It is the very progress and technology that Frugalists frequently decry that has freed them from having to toil in the fields, chop down trees, and tend livestock. But it hasn't freed any of us from our basic need to support ourselves and our families, and there's no getting around it: That demands work. Working in a cubicle on the fortieth floor of an office building fills the same basic need in our life as clearing the rocks off the back forty. It is inherently no less meaningful or important.

I think these words by Hans Sennholz set the record straight on the role of work as well as any: "There is no more abiding happiness than the knowledge that you are free to do, day by day, the best work you can do, thereby supporting yourself and the people you love. Perfect freedom is reserved for the man who lives by his own work and is happy in that work. If you love the labor of your job or profession, apart from any pride of success or recognition, you are truly chosen."

4. *Simple is always better.* Frugalists worship simplicity—jettisoning the clutter and commitments from their lives until a ringing phone never interrupts endless placid moments of idle contemplation.

But do you really want to, say, have only barely enough plates and utensils for household members so that "uninvited visitors just can't come for a casual visit for any great length of time without some hard planning," as is suggested in *Living the Simple Life*? This sounds like life inside some cult compound. Heaven forbid you should actually *want* to have a bunch of people you enjoy over for a long and lively evening of food and conversation without asking them to bring their own forks.

You probably do have a bunch of junk you should get rid of, but the simple life can also turn into a boring or isolated routine. Just as there's nothing wrong with money, there's nothing wrong with an action-packed life. Simple does not mean superior.

5. *Getting the absolute most for your money is the same as getting the most out of life.* Another central characteristic of the New Frugalism is a J. Paul Getty–like fixation with squeezing the most out of every penny. This bent on total maximization totters between two pitfalls.

One pitfall is that being frugal becomes an end unto itself—your entire existence revolves around getting by for less, not on where you want to go. Another pitfall is that your life becomes crowded with clutter that you can't bear to throw out because you might need it for something someday. Fall into either trap and you risk certification as a kook—whether you're making tomato juice from fast-food ketchup packets and water or tripping over boxes of empty "perfectly good" jars in your garage.

It takes a certain type of person to relax about something while at the same time being totally obsessed or preoccupied with it. If you don't have a pet named Kerouac, recycling your sandwich bags and keeping track of each red cent as it enters or leaves your hands until you've accumulated your holier-than-thou determination of what's "enough" is as sure a path to Misery as to anywhere else.

WHEN MORE—OR LESS—REDUCES STRESS

A crucial point needs to be made here. There are plenty of people who have reduced their financial stress by making more money—and plenty who have done it by needing less. The key is not what they specifically did that worked, but *why* it worked.

During a three-year period in my life when my income doubled, my financial stress was reduced not so much by the money, but rather because of the things I was doing that had led to more money. Making more worked because of the way it had come about, not because of the money itself.

The same is true for "needing less." In the introduction to *The Tightwad Gazette,* Amy Dacyzyn relates how she got started on the path to becoming a frugal guru. She had her own dream—buying a big house in the country on one income—and self-generated her solution. She was moving toward something—not just rejecting an unhappy life that caused her stress—discovering ideas along the way and, not insignificantly, having a lot of fun with them (humor is often found to be lacking among frugalists). It's not what she did that is important, but why she did it.

The key to conquering your financial stress can't be found by aping someone else's program or actions. You're going to have to determine your own path. What we're going to zero in on is how to set that path. But first we have to clear some brush away and set our bearings.

FORGET ABOUT MONEY—IT'S THE STRESS THAT'S GOT TO GO

Concentrate on the phrase *financial stress* for a moment.

In all likelihood, your mind gravitated to the word *financial.* That's indicative of how we see the relationship between money and stress. We think that because we have problems that involve money in some way—how we earn, spend, or invest it—that money itself is the root cause of our stress and at the same time holds the key to making the stress go away. We mistakenly think that money is the horse that's pulling a cart full of stress into our lives—and the same horse we expect to haul it away.

Our efforts are going to focus on the word *stress.* Because *that's* what you can do without. If you're not going to disappear into the backwoods and live completely off the land, money is going to remain an integral part of your life. You might as well accept it. What we want to do is to sort out the tangled web of money and stress and, once we've clearly identified the causes of our stress, take action that will get rid of it.

There's a good and simple reason why money and stress have become so intertwined. Money plays such a pivotal role in the flow of modern life that, no matter where problems have their origin, they can quickly get translated into financial terms. For example, if you and your spouse agree on how important it is to redo the bathroom and just how and why it needs to be redone, I guarantee you won't be heading to divorce court over the cost of sink fixtures.

Money isn't causing the stress, it's just shifted the spot where its pointy little head pops up. The stress that starts in the difference between your respective visions and priorities—and your inability to resolve them—is most readily defined and visible in dollars and cents. It's useful to understand how this came to be.

A MARRIAGE MADE IN MODERN TIMES: HOW DID STRESS AND MONEY GET SO ATTACHED?

Travel back in time for a moment. If you were a caveman, a peasant in medieval times, a settler on the Great Plains, or an immigrant at the turn of the century, your daily routine would focus on an immediate and broad challenge: physical survival. You'd roll out of bed in the morning, stroll outside your shelter, and get going on whatever would help you make it until tomorrow. Most, if not all, of your time and effort would go directly toward meeting your basic needs. Instead of being stressed about the cost of new sink fixtures or an unexpected plumbing repair, you'd be stressed about having enough drinking water.

Through cumulative progress over time—including the development of agriculture, industrialization, and technological advancements—few of us today focus on the direct and broad tasks of survival. Today we have jobs (string them together and presto! a career!) that enable us to concentrate on specialized activities that by themselves are as life-sustaining as the atmosphere on Pluto. The money we get paid then enables us to go out and get just about anything we truly need—and some chunk of what we want. Money is what makes it possible for Todd the Snack Food Marketing Specialist to get a potato for dinner from Farmer Ted and for Farmer Ted to enjoy a bag of potato chips with his lunch.

What this transformation from localized subsistence economies to a highly specialized and complex global economy has done is transfer a lot of stress from direct-results life-sustaining activities to the continual stream of financial transactions in our lives. To wit:

We don't have the stress of finding and chopping up enough firewood to heat our homes for an entire winter. We do have the stress of paying the utility company for being able to wear a T-shirt around the house in the middle of January.

We don't have the stress of watching a swarm of bugs eat our crops or a dust storm blow them away. We do have the stress of paying for the dinner we charged two months ago or the microwavable stuffed potatoes when it'd have been cheaper to buy a five-pound bag.

We don't have the stress of bouncing around in a horse-drawn wagon at 7 mph for weeks on end to get across country. We do have the stress of trying to figure out the cheapest airline fare to Orlando and having enough money at the end of the trip to bail our car out of the airport parking lot.

We don't have the stress of trying to build a house from scratch out of sod, rocks, or trees. We do have the stress of budgeting for a new roof with a twenty-five-year guarantee when what we really want is a deck.

We may have stress, but the simple fact is that we have no real reason to hold a things-have-never-been-worse Mope-a-thon. Everyone before us from Pioneer Pete and Isabel Immigrant had a lot of serious stress: life-threatening, physically taxing, hardscrabble stress that would make life in a run-down trailer with cold running water and a television set seem like unimaginable luxury.

Anyone who thinks that today's financial stress is the biggest monster ever to plague civilized man need only consider going back to the days when stress had more to do with staying alive than paying a phone bill.

This is not to say that your financial stress isn't a real and legitimate part of your everyday life. It most certainly is. It's simply going to be a lot easier to deal with effectively if you treat stress as a phenomenon common to everyday life and not some massive truckload of woe that modern civilization has conspired to dump in your driveway, blocking your path to anywhere you want to go. Stress has always been a part of life and always will be. Ours has more numbers attached to it. Our stress has become "financialized."

Far from being an obstacle, the financialization of stress can actually work to your advantage. If all of the stress in your life seems to come back to dollars and decimals, your ability to resolve that quandary to your satisfaction will have far-reaching benefits. When you reduce your financial stress, you'll actually be reducing your stress across the board throughout your life.

LIFE BEYOND FINANCIAL STRESS: THE ADVENTURE

Financial stress rarely enters your life and announces that it's here to stay. It subtly builds over months and even years, so that you gradually accept the symptoms of your financial stress as part of the terrain. Then one morning you open your eyes, and bang! it hits you. You're boxed in like a laboratory rat. You're surrounded by a barrier of financial stress that virtually defines your daily life.

What's worse, your stress symptoms have mapped out a Kafka-meets-Catch-22 defense strategy to prevent you from tackling them. You can't even think of changing jobs because you need to pay your bills and you need to pay your bills because you don't have much in savings and you don't have much in savings because you can't think about the future right now because there's one more thing to buy and if you'd only made that investment when you should have . . .

What compounds your stress is that you can see what lies beyond your stress barriers: life's open field of discovery, opportunity, challenge, and fulfillment. Perhaps you see work that runs on passion, a household budget that doesn't run on fumes, an interest or activity that doesn't siphon buckets of cash, a relationship that doesn't run aground on debt, investments that don't run your life, and a future that you can't wait to turn into today. In short, the life you'd really like to live.

If I had to choose one word to describe life beyond financial stress it would be *adventure*. An adventure is *an exciting and remarkable enterprise whose growing sense of reward along the way mutes the attendant risks.* Let's examine the key words and phrases one by one:

Exciting. Exciting means that life grabs you by the lapels and compels you to be engaged in the moment—the here and now—and holds your attention as you eagerly anticipate what lies ahead. You're not just drifting on autopilot, the days floating by.

Remarkable. Remarkable signifies that there's a depth to your daily experience—it's more than just a superficial passing of the time. What you do soaks into your being and becomes a part of you—the difference between viewing a painting by a master for the first time, knowing that it might take a lifetime to absorb what's in front of you, and watching a cheesy action flick that you'll forget before the picture fades.

Enterprise. Enterprise stresses that there's an organic continuity in your actions. You're building on your previous steps, all the while adapting to observations and events. If you trace the development of your accomplishments to date, you'll discover that an unpredictable chain of events, in retrospect, looks like a perfect plan.

Growing sense of reward along the way. A true adventure provides a continually unfolding sense of reward—neither immediate gratification nor a pot of gold at the end of the rainbow. The reward is not just material, but emotional and mental as well.

Mutes the attendant risks. Risk is part and parcel of life. Yet somehow we've embraced the concept that life should be risk-free, that we're entitled to lifetime employment regardless of circumstance, investments that never lose, health that costs us nothing to maintain in effort or money, children who excel in every way, and happiness without chancing—let alone experiencing—failure. And when reality doesn't meet our expectations, we ditch our marriage partners, hire sue-on-sight lawyers, or whine for a government bailout to make our lives conform to our expectations.

THE STRESS OF AVOIDING RISK

It is impossible to factor the risk out of life.

One reason that we're so anxious to avoid risk is that we lump risk and stress together—we think the more risks we take in life, the more stress we'll have. This is nonsense.

If anything, one reason we have stress in our lives is that we don't take enough risks. And no, I'm not talking about putting more money in the stock market. The mass stampede into mutual funds coincides with the mass acceptance of stocks as the safest of all investments.

The risks we don't take enough of include sticking our neck out and not being afraid of failure, developing our abilities and broadening our horizons without the guarantee of immediate reward, or starting something and seeing it through. The risk of looking up when others are looking down. The risk of being true to ourselves and our ideals. The risk of saying "It's up to me. I'm in charge."

There are just as much risk and far more stress potential in trying to avoid these risks or pretending they don't exist. Let's take a look at a common case.

Ron has worked for an aerospace company for twenty years without so much as a hint of layoffs. But nothing stays the same forever, and now that cutbacks are imminent, he snaps at the grave injustice, "Where else am I supposed to find a twenty-two-dollar-an-hour job with a high school education?"

What's happened is that Ron's inability to take risk has created far more stress than he ever bargained for. Presumably there may have been some time during two decades to get more than a high school education or develop a skill in an unrelated area. That might have meant giving up the low-stress activity of *Monday Night Football* in exchange for an activity with a risk of failure: serious learning. But it would have been precisely this activity that would have helped inoculate him from the stress that's now poisoning him from head to toe. In a rapidly changing world, Ron, like thousands of others, ignored the reality that his job might not last a lifetime and chose not to take risks that might have kept financial stress at bay.

The sooner you embrace the concept of risk, rather than run and hide from it, the sooner you can start to reduce your financial stress. Only when all of the potential risks are on the table can you ask yourself these three questions:

- ○ Which of these risks can I readily reduce?
- ○ Which of these risks can I rationally ignore?
- ○ Which of these risks can I best overcome through self-generated positive actions and experience?

In other words, manage some risks the best that you can and then set out on the adventure.

WHAT IF YOUR LAST NAME ISN'T COUSTEAU?

Reducing your financial stress is in many ways related to your ability to maintain a sense of adventure in your approach to life. And you don't have to be Jacques Cousteau to have it be part of your life.

The spirit of adventure isn't found in some faraway land, on the open sea, or hanging from a rope on the side of a mountain. The beginning of every adventure is in the mind. It is an approach to living. Is working a drag or an adventure? Is living at the end of the twentieth century—and on the edge of the millennium—a scary prospect or an adventure? Is commitment a ball and chain or an adventure? Is learning a chore or an adventure? Is community involvement an obligation or an adventure? Is living within your means a burden or an adventure?

No matter who you are and where you are in life, I believe that you have the opportunity to change any and all of your answers to *adventure*. And we're going to talk a lot about how to create the adventures that reduce financial stress.

THE MOMENT OF TRUTH

At some point your life started getting boxed in by financial stress. By the time you realized what was happening, the wall seemed built to last a thousand years.

Now you're wondering: Is there really a life for you beyond financial stress, or is it just an illusion fueled by wishful thinking? Can you really make a difference, or is anything you do going to be like spray-painting a bald spot—it looks like hair only because you wish it were hair? Do you just have to accept financial stress as a given in your life—a quid pro quo for the Internet and dual air bags? Or can you get beyond your financial stress barriers?

This is the moment of truth. As the author, this is the point where I either have to look you in the eye and tell you with total honesty, "Yes, you can conquer your financial stress," or put on my shades and push the snake oil.

I believe that you *can* reduce financial stress—without becoming a millionaire or living like a monk—and by using your current life right where you are as the starting point. And that's not just because I've done it.

You're going to meet people throughout this book who are living proof that you can live your life unencumbered by financial stress.

Many of them are the very individuals whose examples I've followed in my own life and whose lives collectively serve as the foundations for this book. It's important to stress that I haven't had to go out and beat the bushes or conduct a nationwide search to find rare specimens of financially stress-free lives. They're everywhere.

The truth is, I don't have to tell you that it's possible to live free from financial stress because you know people who are doing it—relatives, friends, neighbors, and coworkers. What you can't quite figure out is *how* they do it. That's the ground we're going to cover in the chapters ahead.

Before we head out on this adventure, let's pause for a moment and fix our sights. Remember, you can't stay parked in your easy chair and expect to shoo your stress away with a mutual fund prospectus. You're going to have to get up, get moving, and climb over your stress barriers to get to your life beyond financial stress. But in what general direction are you going to head? And what will serve as your beacon high above the daily hubbub and the humdrum to guide you and help you stay on course?

The answers lie in a definition of wealth that's above and beyond the familiar "make more or need less" terrain.

THE NORTH STAR: TRUE WEALTH

True Wealth is *the action-created absence of stress related to money, regardless of your income or assets.*

This definition is your guiding light to leaving your financial stress behind. It will take you past your stress barriers to life's open field of discovery, opportunity, challenge, and fulfillment. And when you've done that, it won't matter how much money you make or don't make, or how much you have or don't have. There will be so many more good things happening in your life that the sheer positive momentum will overpower your financial stress. You'll have every sound reason to feel that there's more to life than money, even if there's more money in your life.

Let's look at True Wealth across the economic spectrum. You can be pulling down six or seven figures and drop dead from financial stress—ask any Manhattan cardiologist. Working on Wall Street, I encountered human crankshafts who consumed more and more trophy goods and would seize up at the slightest decrease of cash intake.

Yet don't think for a moment that you can't live a stress-free life when you're sitting on a bundle. I know of an entrepreneur who started a business in a garage and ten years later *gave away* millions of dollars. I can assure you that this individual has True Wealth far beyond his financial fortune.

What about the broad middle? With $40,000, the average income for a family of four, your financial life can be anything from smooth to crazy. Again, I'm not talking about having either 3,000 square feet of living space or a tub of homemade granola in the kitchen. But rather living *your life* in a way that isn't unduly hampered by financial stress.

And the bottom of the income scale? The couple I know with the least financial stress lives on less than $10,000 a year. I know recent college dropouts working for relative peanuts who have little financial stress. And, yes, you can have no money and a ton of stress.

The truth is, money is merely a tool, and frequently one that's not pivotal, in creating or relieving financial stress. It is one resource among many—a resource that can be molded and shaped to fit your life, not someone else's. What determines the role of money in your life—and indeed your level of True Wealth—is action. Your action.

2

What Do People
with True Wealth
Have in Common?

N OW IT'S TIME to ask the $399,000 ($64,000 adjusted for inflation) question: "What do people with True Wealth have in common?"

In this chapter you're going to meet individuals and couples who are representative of the range of backgrounds of people with True Wealth. Jonas Gadson is a motivational speaker with blue-collar beginnings. Earl and Michiko McElfresh run a map company in the small city that has been home to their families for a century. Diana Nicols passed on the opportunity to go to medical school and became a police officer. Ed and Bonnie Hearn live right in the middle of the corporate fast lane without losing control of their lives. Muzaffar Afzal drives a cab in New York City—halfway around the globe from his native Pakistan. So what can Muzaffar, Ed and Bonnie, Diana, Earl and Michiko, Jonas—and everyone else with True Wealth—possibly have in common?

EDUCATION: CAN TRUE WEALTH BE TAUGHT?

There's no doubt that—as a general rule of thumb—the higher your level of formal education, the higher your income. One estimate is that a college degree can mean an extra $600,000 in income on average over a lifetime. Another current estimate is that the average college graduate will earn 60 percent more over her lifetime than a high school graduate.

But, aha! Caught you! That is, if you just jumped to the conclusion that formal education is a common element of True Wealth. For while if you learn more, you might very well earn more, there is no diploma that protects you from financial stress.

In reality, *people with True Wealth come from every possible educational background.* Just as with income, once you get above a subsistence level of education—reading, writing, arithmetic, and critical thinking—there is little relationship between financial stress and formal education.

Tragically, a subsistence education is no longer guaranteed by a high school—and, in some cases, college—diploma. This is one of the two or three most critical problems our country faces. The basic skills of today's high school senior might not compare favorably to those of an eighth grader at the turn of the twentieth century. But presumably he or she feels better about knowing less! Recently the Lincoln Electric Company in Ohio was unable to fill 200 factory positions from over 20,000 applicants. The sticking point? A basic knowledge of high school algebra—rather than, one might assume, an expertise in recycling.

On the other hand, *all* of the people I've met who have True Wealth have a broad view of education that extends beyond formal boundaries and they are continually proactive in their pursuit of knowledge and skills. This is the real relationship between education and True Wealth. Let's meet one of these individuals.

Jonas Gadson is poised to become one of the top motivational speakers in the country. Known as "Mr. Enthusiastic," the message on his answering machine alone will pump you up. But equally inspirational as one of Jonas's speeches is his personal story: how he set his own course for learning that has taken him far beyond even his own initial expectations.

Now in his early forties, Jonas went directly from high school in South Carolina to working on an assembly line in a manufacturing plant in Rochester, New York. By 1975, he had settled into a similar position with Eastman Kodak. As the years rolled along, Jonas felt increasingly bogged down by the repetition of his work.

"In 1980, I woke up to the fact that no matter who I worked for, I couldn't expect Corporate America to do for me the things I needed to do for myself. College isn't for everyone, but learning is. You can't control your job security—you *can* create skill security."

Jonas began an intensive and self-directed program of self-improvement—absorbing videos, tapes, and books on his own time and attending evening classes on a consistent basis. By 1989 he had the confidence to pursue his vision: becoming a motivational speaker.

Long involved with charity work, Jonas had helped raise over a million dollars for Rochester's underprivileged. But all of his speaking experience was within the church. "I had to start over and learn how to deliver my message in a way that would permit me to speak anywhere—in front of any audience. So I began my journey."

Jonas joined the National Speakers Association and Toastmasters International—winning contests and becoming an area governor in the organization. Seeking out the best speakers in the business for advice, he spoke at every opportunity—and with experience came recognition. The requests for his presentations began to grow—from inner-city churches to elite private schools and corporate boardrooms.

Jonas now makes over one hundred speeches a year around the country—his signature speech is "How to Fly like an Eagle with Wings like a Wimp." He now has his own weekly radio show, "Partners for Purposeful Living." In the works: a video, a book, and expanding his show to a daily broadcast.

"I'm investing in my dreams," Jonas explains. "Money is a tool. Unfortunately, too many people love money and use people, instead of loving people and using money. I tell entrepreneurs that if they're getting into business just to make money, I'll save them the trip—they won't make it. You've got to love something so much that you'll do it for free—and that's what will make you good enough to get paid."

All the while preparing himself for future opportunities as a public speaker, Jonas had become a specialist in quality control at Kodak. "One day the company initiated a diversity training program. I knew that the program was perfect for me to use my skills and that I was more than ready to make a positive difference. I said, 'Let me try.' People looked at me like I was crazy—they had no idea what I was working on outside the plant."

Jonas shattered the preconceived mold for a corporate trainer—on his way to becoming the 1995–96 Eastman Kodak Trainer of the Year. Over 5,000 of his fellow employees from sixty-nine countries and from janitors to vice presidents have benefited from the knowledge and skills he developed bit by bit on his own time, turning spare hours into ability.

When Jonas puts his charge into his audiences and brings them to their feet, I guarantee you that no one hesitates or sits on his hands while pondering Jonas's background. He's great at what he does—and that's what really counts. And the key to his success is his vision of his classroom—all of life, twenty-four hours a day—and truly believing his motto: "Since greatness is possible, being excellent is not enough."

EDUCATION IS WHAT YOU ACTUALLY LEARN, HOWEVER YOU LEARN IT

Reality can fly in the face of everything we've been told about the importance of getting a good education. The key word here is *good*—and good is getting harder to find. With high school students not testing in the sciences as well as students in countries that didn't exist six years ago, and "college" students taking courses to learn how to read and write, education is no longer a uniformly consistent experience. Still, college students expect to earn more—whether or not they learn more.

The deterioration of the educational system has coincided with the rise in our unwavering belief that education is a commodity that can be purchased off the shelf with a 100 percent money-back guarantee. But a lot of formal education is like a cheesy kitchen appliance that comes in a big bright box. The box says it will slice, dice, shake, bake—you name it, anything you need it to do. The reality is that the content may not be all that useful and before long it's on the shelf gathering dust. This explains, in part, why the income disparity among people with the same amount of advanced education is growing.

So let's back up and look at what makes up an education. There are three levels of education:

○ *Basic Skills:* Reading, writing, arithmetic, and critical thinking.
○ *Worldview:* An understanding of the world around you and its history. This level includes the arts and sciences—the traditional liberal education.
○ *Specialized Skills and Knowledge:* Areas of specific expertise, whether they be auto mechanics, Sanskrit, saxophone, or computer animation.

If you look at these three areas as if you were farming, your basic skills would serve as the bedrock and your worldview would be the topsoil. From this plot you'd grow some specialized skills. Obviously, the more solid your basic skills and the richer your worldview, the easier it will be to grow specialized skills and knowledge. And today more than ever, you want to have more than just one "plant" to live on for your whole life.

Earl (mid-forties) and Michiko (late thirties) McElfresh are the owners of the McElfresh Map Company, which specializes in historical base maps of American battlefields. Friendly and self-assured, Earl and Michiko are a couple who seem so comfortable with each other that their personal partnership was destined to be. Their professional partnership, however, is an entrepreneurial adventure that took them both by surprise.

As Earl puts it, he was "born a vice president" of the insurance company founded by his grandfather in 1919. Acquaintances since childhood, Earl and Michiko married after meeting up in New York City. Earl represented the family business to accounts in the region. With a degree in accounting, Michiko worked for a Big Six firm.

By the early 1990s, Earl and Michiko found big-city life with two small children to be a stressful proposition. They moved back to Olean, their hometown in upstate New York, and began to assume an active role in the day-to-day management of the family insurance business. Unexpectedly, the table turned upside down—the major insurance company they represented abruptly terminated its relationship with the firm. Within weeks it became obvious that what had seemed like a lifetime situation had come to an end. The answer to the question "What do we do now?" came from an unlikely source: Earl's hobby.

A Civil War buff, Earl had developed—beginning in the margins of high school notebooks—a unique approach to mapping Civil War battlefields: showing the physical characteristics— from specific crops to roads and rocks—of a battlefield as they were on the day of the battle. With Earl as historian and cartographer and Michiko as business manager, the McElfresh Map Company was launched.

Started on a shoestring, the company's first foray into the marketplace was "a disaster." But what kept the adventure alive—and mitigated the stress—was that "there were always promising things coming out of the failures." Drawn and water-colored by hand, their maps are valued by experts for their accuracy and are spectacular works of art to even the casual eye. A boxed set of maps of Gettysburg, sold in bookstores coast to coast, proved to be a breakthrough. When the History Book

Club ordered the McElfresh's first non–Civil War map—the Battle of Little Big Horn—the company had reached a new level.

While experiencing the demands and challenges faced by any business start-up, the McElfreshes feel the rewards have outweighed the risks.

Earl says, "Before we started the business, the thought often crossed my mind that there was more within me than was being tapped. These maps will be around forever—you can't put a price tag on that."

Michiko explains, "I used to walk past a machine shop every day. It made me really want to own a business that made something that you could actually hold in your hand." She was able to realize her dream using the knowledge and resources she already possessed.

You can't put a price tag on the formal training Earl needed to create his maps—he doesn't have any. "I was invited to speak at a symposium and they asked for my academic credentials. They were taken aback that I'm self-taught—no history studies, no art or drafting studies, nothing. Just a degree in English." He's since lectured at the Smithsonian Institution, the University of London, and the National Archives.

The McElfreshes are proof that, in relation to financial stress, it is more useful to think in terms of the broader ideals of learning and knowledge rather than simply formal academics. Knowledge can be gained in a classroom, through self-education, or through experience, or any combination thereof.

A degree can't replace knowing what you want to do and figuring out how to do it—which is how immigrants can land in the middle of an alien culture and make quick and tremendous strides toward making their dreams come true. And why you know something—what was the driving force behind the learning process—can be as important as how you learned it. What it says on your degree—if you even have one—is no substitute for actually knowing something and knowing what to do with it.

All this is not to downplay the role of formal education in a low-stress life. To quote the motto of the legendary Faber College, from the movie *Animal House:* "Knowledge is good." Only a fool would deny that the classroom—when it's an arena for serious and rigorous learning rather than a feel-good playpen—is the foundation of a good education. Certainly none of us would want to fly in a jet airplane that was designed by self-trained engineers or be operated on by a self-taught surgeon. But only a fool would contend that a self-taught skilled craftsman isn't on equal ground with a garden-variety "now what?" college graduate.

If you don't believe that people with True Wealth come from every imaginable educational background, try this experiment. Make two lists: on one, list everyone you know with a lot of financial stress and on the other, everyone with little financial stress. Now, next to each name write his or her educational background. In each column, you're going to find that the level and type of education are going to be all over the map.

We leave the education category with an important clue: *People with True Wealth like to learn.* But that doesn't mean you should close the book and just go out and start hoovering all the information you can get your hands on. There has to be the right rhyme and reason to your efforts. We still have to uncover what ultimately will direct our efforts toward True Wealth.

IN SEARCH OF THE MAGIC PROFESSION

Is there such a thing as a magic profession that guarantees True Wealth?

One common illusion is that the more glamorous your job—glamour being a by-product of a few people getting a lot of attention—the lower your financial stress. If you're lucky enough to be a video director, swashbuckling technology honcho or honchette, power forward in the NBA, or just famous for being famous, you've got the corner table in the restaurant of life. What could be better than doing something *anyone* would love to do and getting paid for it while the rest of us have to rely on tricking ourselves into actually liking our work?

Yet the evidence is everywhere that working in a "glamour" profession isn't necessarily a ticket to True Wealth. If you've ever worked in such a profession, or know anyone on the inside, you don't need to be convinced that financial stress is as pervasive as the worship of celebrity.

Interestingly—but perhaps not surprising for baby boomers—when adults who seek career counseling are asked what they would be if they could be anything in the world, the number one answer is "rock star." So let's take a short quiz:

   1. The Beatles broke up primarily because:
     (a) John kept sticking used bubble gum in George's sitar.
     (b) Ringo took a new job on the Island of Sodor.
     (c) they couldn't agree on how to handle their millions.

2. Right at this moment, that new band whose hit CD you just love is:
   (a) relaxing around a pool before their next sold-out gig.
   (b) laying down some groovy new riffs in the studio.
   (c) screaming at a bunch of newly hired lawyers to fire their manager and audit their record company to find out why, after selling a million albums, they still owe their record company a million dollars.

3. Of these two individuals featured in the movie *Woodstock,* who had the least financial stress?
   (a) Jimi Hendrix
   (b) The Port-O-San man

The truth is that while Jimi Hendrix fumbled his way through a desultory "Purple Haze," not far from his mind—and certainly dampening his spirit—was the fact that he was getting ripped off at every turn by unscrupulous associates and yet had to keep working relentlessly to support a legion of leeches in order to have a nickel for himself.

The Port-O-San man had not only made it to middle age in good cheer but took pride in work that most of us would rank as a "least desirable profession." Think that this happiness is an anomaly? Meet Muzaffar Afzal.

Most of us would be terrified just to drive in New York City. Yet Muzaffar Afzal, in his early thirties, drives a taxi six nights a week with the grace and good cheer of a small-town shopkeeper. I had the good fortune to hail Muzaffar's cab on a rainy Friday evening in Manhattan at the end of what I thought was a long and exhausting day. His friendly greeting had the effect of whisking me to a calm tropical island. By the time we reached La Guardia Airport, I was invigorated by his spirit.

The secret to Muzaffar's enjoyment of his work is a simple understanding: "It is making my dreams come true." As a youth in his native Pakistan, he dreamed of coming to America: "My father owns a small auto parts business. I knew what opportunities there were in Pakistan, and I saw what my relatives who had migrated to the U.S. had been able to accomplish. I'd go to sleep at night and pretend I was going to wake up in America."

In 1986, Muzaffar arrived in this country using his cousin's passport. With a few dollars in his pocket and a few English words in his vocabulary, he hit the ground running. "My initial goal was to never be a burden to anyone—to maintain my self-respect."

After a series of odd jobs, he began working at a 7-Eleven. Ironic that while the only thing some people find in convenience-store work is comedy fodder, Muzaffar found dignity. "It was a great teacher," he relates. "It taught me how to act in business in America." He applied for his green card. "When it arrived in the mail, it was one of the proudest moments of my life."

Muzaffar moved to New York City—"the gateway of opportunity"—in 1990 and began driving a cab. He's now saved nearly enough money to buy his own cab medallion. After getting married, he plans to move somewhere in the middle of the country, buy a house, and raise a family. "I will be a citizen in time to vote in the next election," he says with pride. His long-range objectives: "This is a society for literate people. I want to study history and literature. And spread peace wherever I go."

As he told me his story, the phrases "convenience store" and "cab-driver" kept replaying in my mind and along with them the idea that opportunity is only as great as your broader sense of purpose.

ADVENTURE AMID THE STRESS: THE CHOICE IS YOURS

What makes a given profession an adventure for some and a high-stress paycheck for others? It depends not on the profession, but on why you choose the work in the first place.

Some professions serve as a readily visible and all-too-frequently-coveted "opportunity in a box." How many people have become lawyers or teachers not for any particular love for the work but rather for the neat answer it provides to a lot of life's big questions, like, "What am I going to do to be a success or at least to avoid being a screwup?" And, if you were attracted to a government job solely for the security and lavish benefits, sooner or later you would end up feeling trapped and screaming for more. Walk past a picket line during any public employees' strike and you're going to hear some of the shrillest "gimmes" ever.

On the other hand, if your work is what you really wanted to do (as opposed to wanting a job), you don't feel trapped. You feel lucky that you're getting to do something you love for a living.

Diana Nicols, in her mid-twenties, looks as if she might be a photographer for *National Geographic*. A petite redhead, she enjoys the outdoors—spending her spare time camping, rock climbing, or bicycling. But when Diana gets ready to go to work, she doesn't strap on a camera. She wears a badge—and straps on a pistol holster.

"The whole time I was growing up I wanted to be a doctor—or at least I thought I did," Diana explains. During her senior year of college, when it came time to fill out the applications to medical school, she began to have doubts about her goal. "I'd accepted that that was what I was going to do for so long, I'd never questioned it," she says. "And when I did, I found I wasn't ready to make the huge commitment."

With a degree in human ecology (computer science and biology combined with the liberal arts) she returned to her home near Cooperstown, New York, to work in a rape crisis and domestic violence center and ponder her future. "I had liked school a lot but didn't want to go on until I knew what I wanted to do. There were a lot of possibilities—teaching, counseling, emergency medical response. I even thought about becoming a stuntwoman."

Then one day she saw a notice in the local paper for the civil service examination for police officers. "I paid the ten dollars to take the test without knowing much about the job. But the more I looked into it, the more I realized it was what I was looking for. Being a police officer wraps everything I wanted to do into one."

Diana is now in her third year as a full-fledged officer on the street in Oneonta, New York. Almost immediately after joining the force, her skills were tested to the maximum as she successfully defused a standoff with an armed gunman holding a hostage. "You can have a positive impact in a lot less dramatic ways too. I know that sometimes police officers can get cynical—you see a lot of people not at their best—so I'm adamantly trying not to get that way. The key for me is to try to make a difference when people are suffering. If a mother and her five-year-old son get in a car accident, I can't change that. But I can make them less apprehensive about what's going to happen next."

Having refused her Generation X membership card, Diana says, "I can think of only one or two of my friends from high school or college who are doing something related to their studies or even doing something they want to do.

"Sometimes when I'm out on patrol I run into some old friends. They're kind of surprised at what I'm doing. I think it took people a while to realize I was really serious. What's important is that every day I'm doing something I really want to do—that's more important to me than money. I can't imagine leaving."

Diana often goes back to a question posed by her father: "Do you think happiness is based more on circumstances or disposition?"

Many of us rationally believe it is the latter, but then wait for a change in circumstances to improve our disposition. People with True Wealth rely on their dispositions to improve their circumstances. What we'll be looking to uncover is the specific factors in their dispositions that fight off financial stress.

To again quote Hans Sennholz: "There is no work so crude that you cannot improve it, no work so dull that you cannot enliven it, no work so base that you cannot ennoble it." Which is why the tollbooth collector who approaches his work with zeal has as good a chance at True Wealth as a bond trader—no more, no less.

There is no magic profession—just magic motivations.

DOES A DOLLAR BILL HAVE A HAPPY FACE?

Once you're above the poverty level, there is no meaningful correlation between income and True Wealth.

Here's how I discovered this firsthand.

In 1983 I joined the training staff of a major brokerage firm at their Wall Street headquarters. When I accepted the position, I was keenly aware of two circumstances. The first was that I enjoyed teaching and had displayed a raw talent for it going way back to high school. The second was that training was not a place where it was possible to cash in on the Wall Street bonanza—it was a modest flat-fee position in the Land of Big Bonuses. After a while, I forgot the second circumstance. Like some of my cohorts, I began to feel cheated by the injustice of it all. Here we were, entrusted with the dissemination of priceless knowledge and vital, career-making skills, and yet we were rewarded with relative scraps.

At my year-end review my manager, whom I respected tremendously, asked what I thought could be done to improve my job. "Why, more money, of course," I replied. "A higher salary grade and a bonus." He stopped me in my tracks. However fair or unfair the situation was, he advised, it wasn't going to change appreciably no matter how much emotional energy I devoted to it. I'd be far better off accepting my compensation as a given and finding added rewards elsewhere in my work.

It would have been easy to think, "Yeah, buddy, that's easy for *you* to say," but for once I listened. I took my eye off the dollar sign and

dug into my work—tackling new subjects, finding ways to collabo-
rate with other departments in the firm. In time I went from feeling
broke to feeling rich—on the same salary. A year later, I walked out
the door with a contract for my first book. With some good advice
and a change in perspective, I'd discovered some abilities that were far
more rewarding than a bonus check.

Returning to the bottom line: Once you're out of poverty, there's little or no relationship between True Wealth and income. And to any
degree that high-income individuals feel less stress in their lives compared to low-income individuals, a good chunk of the difference can
probably be attributed to their actions and attitudes that precede the
money, not the money itself—or what it can buy.

IS TRUE WEALTH SOLD IN A STORE?

Some years ago I spent a summer afternoon with the heir to an
eight-figure fortune. When our mutual friend teased him that his
shirt pocket was adorned with a bush-league penguin instead of the
then de rigueur alligator, he replied, "People with real money don't
care about that stuff." Hardly a week goes by when that statement
doesn't come to mind—whether it's watching a family decked out in
the latest gear on a suburban shopping safari in search of—what
else?—more gear, or perusing an ad for some overpriced piece of designer ephemerality.

Which is not to say that people with substantial wealth are immune to financial stress—but that **the entire notion of *spending* your
money simply to give the appearance that you *have* money is absurd.**
If I'm not missing something . . . once you spend money, you *don't*
have it. This concept is not lost on Ed and Bonnie Hearn.

Ed and Bonnie Hearn are a baby-boom couple consciously
living below their means in the land of "executive living"—the
Princeton, New Jersey, area. Ed, an institutional investment broker, is the quintessential "good guy"—someone whose personality alone makes the world a better place. Pretty and energetic,
Bonnie looks after their two young children. A former professional pianist—playing at one time in the lobby of a famous
New York City hotel—Bonnie recently began teaching piano
part-time.

From all appearances, Ed and Bonnie appear to have avoided
the spend-till-you're-maxed-out lunacy that plagues many of
their contemporaries. Instead of being saddled with a potentially
upside-down mortgage on a half-furnished power house in the

Hunt Club at Provence Meadow Estates, they live in a comfortable house on which they made a 50 percent down payment. They drive two modest cars paid for in cash. They save at least 30 percent of their household income.

Are Ed and Bonnie a pair of like-minded bean-counting skinflints? Absolutely not. You won't find them cutting off their noses in order to cut corners. And, in fact, they aren't even of the same mind-set, having widely disparate backgrounds. Ed grew up with self-described "modest expectations"—never having been around material wealth. Bonnie grew up in a suburban bedroom community where "appearances were everything." What enables Ed and Bonnie to keep their spending—and emotions—in check is simply a willingness to recognize the dictates of common sense when they are spelled out in fifty-foot-high neon letters for all to see.

Bonnie explains: "The people we know who tried to 'have it all' in the eighties ended up getting wiped out. That's a lesson you shouldn't forget. But people do. Our neighbor was thinking of sending her husband to golf school for his birthday and casually remarked that maybe she should use the $2,500 to help pay down their Visa bill instead. Yow. I mean, buy him a book." The Hearns use their leisure time to enrich themselves and their children—reading, hiking on nature trails, going to museums—rather than enriching others.

As an institutional investment broker, how does Ed avoid the financial stress that afflicts so many of his compatriots? "I have the same attitude about money today as when I was in the navy making 5 percent of what I'm making now. It's not that important. Success to me is how you serve others—how you raise your family."

Another key to their restraint: "a healthy dose of fear." Ed relates that "We haven't been through tough times like our parents and grandparents, and we don't want to. My job won't last forever—it's the nature of the business. So I even go out on practice interviews to stay up on what's going on."

Ed and Bonnie understand that there's a big difference between being comfortable and being conspicuous—something understood by people who actually accumulate wealth, rather than just the trappings.

As previously noted, the typical millionaire owns a small business or factory. Looking at it another way, he made his good fortune outside the mainstream corporate structure, which often fosters an environment of consumer one-upmanship. Car numerology ("Will a

340XL make me appear $20,000 more successful than a 300ZX?"), the square footage of suburban housing on steroids, and all of the trimmings of the good life on a silver platter can eat through a paycheck faster than a beaver with the munchies. Our millionaire's annual income may actually have been less than his corporate counterparts'—he simply kept more of it.

Does this typical millionaire live a spartan secondhand life that would embarrass those more attuned to social perceptions? No. But he's probably not going to care if he's wearing a simple nylon jacket instead of a shearling bomber jacket. He may not take "power" vacations, although he almost certainly indulges some true passions in his life. And he's not going to care that you're stressed out about your mortgage when he could pay his off with a flick of the pen.

And what if you're not one of these low-profile millionaires? You can still think like one and be far better off for it. Remember: *You can spend money to look like you have it, or simply have it for something more important.*

Just as with money, consumer goods are best thought of as tools, not totems. The truth is that there's no pair of handmade Italian loafers that smooths the way to happiness—and no magic $1.99 pair of flip-flops. There is no correlation between True Wealth and what you own.

This brings us to the final stop on our financial trajectory: investing your savings, i.e., whatever's left over. Given its burgeoning prominence in our collective consciousness, investing deserves a detailed look.

TRUE WEALTH AND INVESTING: IT'S NOT WHAT YOU KNOW THAT COUNTS

In the past fifteen years, investing has somehow come to be regarded as the mystical summit activity of any accomplished and meaningful existence. Whether you've found a cure for cancer, run a homeless shelter, won an Olympic gold medal, worked your way from the mail room to the boardroom, or raised well-adjusted, productive children—your life isn't complete. Not unless, of course, you've found that perfect mix of information, investments, and strategies that will alchemize your modest savings into a winning lottery ticket, render you invisible to the IRS, and warrant a cover spread on the next issue of *Unlimited Moolah.*

This phenomenon has been driven by a premise that is just as stress-creating—and just as erroneous—as "make more" and "need less": the widespread belief that it's *what* you know that counts. The line of thinking is that your well-being somehow depends on your ability to make sense out of an ever-growing mountain of needless investments, confusing information, and contradictory opinions. And it's not enough to understand and be conversant, you have to find the combination that's just right for you.

Concurrent with the elevation of personal finance to the level of spiritual pursuit has been the proliferation of *financial "what"*—a staggering mass of investments, statistics, opinions, strategies, information, prognostications, pitches (and, uh, opportunities).

Let's examine "what"—the key word here. What is this "what" that we're supposed to care so much about and that is so vital to our well-being? That is supposed to hold the key to our happiness? An infinitesimal piece of the tip of the mountain of financial "what" might include:

"What" is a CMO? UIT? CUB? REIT? IPO? TIGR? LYON? The put-call ratio? The McClellan Oscillator? A 200-day moving average? Book value? Cash flow?

"What" do the latest housing start numbers mean? The drop in durable goods orders or the unemployment numbers? A rise in the yen or wholesale inflation?

"What" does Mr. Expert say about the market? What does Ms. Expert say? Who's right? What's the best investment right now? And which one is about to nose-dive?

If you're not up for sorting it all out yourself, thankfully there's a legion of camouflaged salespersons, and all are ready to offer you their unique brands of what: "This is exactly 'what' you should do with your money right now. Really. No, I've thought about it and I'm serious, even though we're all just kind of guessing."

One thing is for certain: No doomsayer will ever be able to forecast a shortage of financial "what." So what does all of it mean for you?

If you buy into the conventional wisdom, it should mean an awful lot. As the mass of financial "what" has expanded like some sci-fi blob to a size where it now qualifies for continent status, we've been told that the more financial "what" you can absorb and process, the better off you'll be. Of course, this will entail untold hours of sifting through confusing and contradictory material about investment vehicles and personal finance, the very same activity that revved up your financial stress Super Collider to start with.

Here's the key question: Do you have to absorb all this financial "what" to be able to ward off financial stress? The answer is a resounding "No!" (I heard that sigh of relief.) Here are the two solid reasons why not:

THE #1 REASON WHY IT'S NOT
WHAT YOU KNOW THAT COUNTS

Financial "what" does not exist to serve—it exists to be sold.

When I became a stockbroker in 1977, my firm bragged about its competitive edge: "We have over thirty products to offer our customers." By the time I left in 1985, the number had grown to *two hundred* and thirty. Today, it's anyone's guess: four hundred, five hundred—however many vice presidents need a reason to exist.

In 1985, there were approximately 1,500 mutual funds. Today, there are over 8,000 mutual funds, including 6,500 that invest primarily in stocks. To put that in perspective, there are only roughly 1,500 stocks traded on the entire New York Stock Exchange.

New investment products come into existence primarily for one reason: The purveyors think they can be sold with relative ease. Whether anyone *needs* them is secondary to the consideration of whether anyone will *buy* them.

The easiest product for Wall Street to sell is one that purports to take advantage of something that's already in the headlines. Stocks have been in a bull market for close to two decades? Start a fund! Rest assured that if the Martians landed on Earth tomorrow, the day after there'd be a mutual fund purporting to take advantage of the trend in interplanetary invasion.

Few new investment products anticipate a trend or actually serve as a truly useful tool to the average individual investor. For every worthwhile innovation like cash management accounts or index funds, there is far too much financial gadgetry cluttering the shelves—the equivalent of smokeless ashtrays, Chia pets, and electric shoe polishers.

And what about all of the analysis, opinions, and information? As public interest in all things financial has grown, so has an entire global round-the-clock media to cover the financial markets and personal finance. Your local newspaper or television news inevitably has a feature entitled "Your Money Matters" or "Dollars and Sense." Financial magazines and radio talk shows ("This is Biff calling from Cheektowaga. . . . I wanna talk about the new mutual fund rankings . . . cause, like, I had the 2001 Fund picked for only number four for the year, and then they get ranked number two. . . . I mean, like, no way.") have proliferated right along with funds. Cable television networks cover the action with the same intensity as a Super Bowl broadcast.

So is any of this "what" useful? Yes—but it's a fraction that's smaller than most would care to admit. Much of the pregame

("What's the market going to do?") and postgame ("What did the market do?") analysis falls into the category of following the herd and covering your tracks.

Far more useful is the general information on basic personal finance: choosing insurance, buying a home, avoiding rip-offs, gathering consumer tips, and the like. In this area, I believe the media on the whole perform a real service to the public. But because this information lacks the dynamics of the markets—and, let's face it, super-duper moneymaking potential—it often gets lost in the mass of financial "what."

A mass of "what" that exists to be sold—but not one you have to buy into.

REASON #2 WHY IT'S NOT WHAT YOU KNOW THAT COUNTS

Financial "what" doesn't help the experts themselves.

If financial "what" is so helpful, shouldn't the experts who immerse themselves in it for a living be so uncanny and on target in their money moves that they'd have cornered the market in True Wealth? A close look at the evidence reveals that the situation is closer to the cobbler with worn-out shoes.

Ask any stockbroker to rate her cohorts on their overall ability to manage their finances in a prudent and unstressful manner. Bask in the laughter.

Consider that Wall Street is almost the opposite of Lake Wobegon, where all the children are above average. Three quarters of professional money managers perform below average over any meaningful stretch of time. If you're in a business where you're continually graded in dollars and cents and you're scrambling to get at least a C, you've got a timeless recipe for financial stress.

Then there are bankers, those paragons of sound money practices who have an almost lemming-like knack for investing large sums of money in the worst possible investments at the worst possible time: oil and gas, real estate, currency futures, international development. If financial "what" conferred on its bearers any inherent insights, Ma and Pa Taxpayer wouldn't have gotten stuck with the hundreds-of-billions-of-dollars tab for the savings and loan debacle of the '80s. After all, the people who made those decisions were the "experts."

I've found that for people who have a practical low-stress perspective on investing, their investments are the punctuation at the end of a well-written chapter in their life, not the lead paragraph. In other words, how they handle their investments is a natural extension of how they live the rest of their lives. People with True Wealth invest without a lot of fuss and muss—and without a lot of financial "what." In fact, their investment choices often drive professionals crazy. The pros can look only at the dollars and cents, not the reality of the person's life.

HOWEVER YOU TRAVEL, WHEN YOU GET THERE, YOU'RE THERE

My local newspaper regularly features "financial makeovers" where an individual or couple submit their finances to a panel of experts. One recent case really caught my eye—and got my goat. The man in question was a bachelor in his late thirties and had an income in the high thirties. Through conscientious saving he had accumulated well over a half a million dollars. He was on track to retire with nearly two million dollars. Mr. Bachelor seemed to enjoy life, too—he had a hobby that actually earned him a few thousand dollars a year, and he traveled to Europe periodically.

So what financial deficiencies did Mr. Bachelor have? According to the experts, he didn't own enough stocks. And they unanimously believed he should buy a variable annuity (usually a high-commission contraption). It simply never occurred to them that if the guy was happy—and there was no indication to the contrary—it didn't matter that most of his money wasn't in stocks. The results spoke for themselves—and they basically told the pros to get lost.

Looking at it another way, however you travel to Pittsburgh, when you arrive, you're in the same place: Pittsburgh is Pittsburgh. But some car salesmen will keep on trying to sell you a car long after you've arrived by bus—refusing to believe that you've already arrived at your destination or that it was even possible. However more efficiently or quickly you might have traveled—at least in theory—the results completely negate any second-guessing.

A significant number of the people I've met with True Wealth have never made a single investment in the stock market. It's not out of ignorance, either. They know it's there. They know what it's done the past decade. They just don't care. And yet they've still been able to buy houses, plan their retirements, send their kids to college, or start businesses. They've covered the bases without playing the market game. How can that be?

The truth is that when it comes to fighting financial stress, *it's not what you know that ultimately counts.*

THE SEARCH CONTINUES . . .

We've looked at education, profession, income, possessions, and investments and come up with a few clues but no definitive answers. If we don't find any common elements to True Wealth on the financial trail, how about the other most obvious demographic categories? What if we throw age, sex, ethnicity, race, religion, or geographic location into the mix? What we'd find is what we already know from our own experience and observations: True Wealth cuts across every imaginable demographic category.

People with True Wealth come from every possible background. If you have any doubts—which, given the potential hot buttons, I'm sure some of you do—I'd suggest that you keep a high-stress/low-stress record of the people you encounter unfiltered by your preconceptions; and remember, we're not talking about how much money people have or don't have.

There are some things you can't change: your age, sex, race, and ethnicity. Life won't be played on a level playing field in your lifetime—if ever. Personal and institutionalized prejudices do exist—as do innumerable people who've overcome them. What's enabled them to counter any disadvantages is their ability to recognize this simple fact: The absolute surest way to be held back and restricted by unseen forces in life is to act as if you already are. In other words, if you don't like the role, refuse to play the part.

If demographics don't provide us with a picture of the experience of True Wealth, there's a good reason. Demographics might capture the surface and signposts of life, but what we're trying to understand is an internal ongoing state of experience and how it came to be.

THE SYMPTOMS OF TRUE WEALTH

What are the symptoms of True Wealth? That's simple, you think, the opposite of being in debt is not being in debt. Either I need a new job or I don't. But the mere absence of something doesn't fully describe the picture.

Remember that True Wealth is the *action-created* absence of stress related to money. An absence could be the result of an ongoing conscious effort to mask a static or long-ignored circumstance that could give way to financial stress at any moment. It's the difference between an actively maintained car and one that hasn't had an oil change since it left the dealer's lot. They both may be free from mechanical stress at a particular moment, but that doesn't reflect what's really going on under their hoods. The engine of the ill-maintained car could be one mile from a total seizure.

Trying to live in the neutral zone—where there's nothing bad happening at the moment, but not due to any particular effort on your part—leaves you defenseless against swift or unexpected change. You may have enough money to pay your bills this month, but your spending habits might be secretly brewing up a batch of future stress. You might feel that you don't need major medical insurance (as millions of above-average earners do), but that's only because you're not in the path of a speeding truck. If you're content with an as-luck-would-have-it absence of a stress symptom, be aware that change will likely occur in one direction—*toward* financial stress.

Let's then examine the opposite of each of the nine symptoms of financial stress—the symptoms of True Wealth:

FINANCIAL STRESS SYMPTOM #1: You need a new job . . . yesterday.
TRUE WEALTH: You enjoy your work and are creating opportunities ahead of immediate or apparent need.

FINANCIAL STRESS SYMPTOM #2: You don't have enough money to pay your bills.
TRUE WEALTH: You're living within your means through conscious, embraced choice.

FINANCIAL STRESS SYMPTOM #3: You can't control your spending.
TRUE WEALTH: You're focusing on what you can do with what you already have—not what you don't have.

FINANCIAL STRESS SYMPTOM #4: You're constantly fighting with your spouse or partner about money.
TRUE WEALTH: You're resolving your financial differences rationally, using a shared logical framework.

FINANCIAL STRESS SYMPTOM #5: You're leaving the back door open to financial disaster, and deep down you know it.
TRUE WEALTH: You're maintaining a financial foundation that can withstand a setback from any direction.

FINANCIAL STRESS SYMPTOM #6: You can't part with money, even if it's for your own darn good.
TRUE WEALTH: You treat money as a means to a desired end, not as an end in and of itself.

FINANCIAL STRESS SYMPTOM #7: The words "future" and "savings" turn your stomach into a knot and shut your brain down.

TRUE WEALTH: You're looking forward to tomorrow because of the things you're doing today.

FINANCIAL STRESS SYMPTOM #8: You're overwhelmed and intimidated by the prospect of making an investment decision.

TRUE WEALTH: Choosing an investment is no more confusing or anxiety-causing than ordering from a restaurant menu.

FINANCIAL STRESS SYMPTOM #9: You're losing money on the investments you've already made.

TRUE WEALTH: You've made investments that will grow with time and have your money ready and waiting when you need it.

Now that we have a clearer idea of True Wealth, let's get back to our question: "What do people with True Wealth have in common?" What we've just looked at are signposts of an ongoing state of experience. But these common signposts of True Wealth don't tell us how to get there and—most important—where the starting point is.

THE RAW MATERIAL OF FINANCIAL STRESS—AND TRUE WEALTH

Join me at an imaginary fork in the road where the paths to True Wealth and financial stress divide. We've defined True Wealth as the action-created absence of stress related to money. Isn't financial stress, therefore, the action-created *presence* of stress related to money (keeping in mind that inaction is a form of action)? And what determines our actions? The decisions we make, minute by minute, throughout each and every day.

Let's assume that a financial decision is any decision that touches in part on how you earn, spend, save, or invest money. One common misconception is that financial stress is strictly the product of "big" decisions—like that fateful day you bought a house based on the Realtor's formula of what you could afford.

Just as often, financial stress comes from the little decisions that grind away beneath the surface of everyday life until a salesclerk sniffs, "Your charge request has been denied." Buying more house than you can comfortably afford might seem like a single big decision, but there were hundreds of little decisions that led up to that horse-choking monthly nut.

And just as little decisions add up to big-time stress, it is a subtle day-by-day process that creates concrete and substantial change. True Wealth does not necessarily begin with a "magic bullet" decision that will vanquish stress from your life. And even then, the big decision has to be supported by little decisions or the result will be stress of a different nature. If, for example, you decide to quit your job or move from the city to the country, those big decisions on their own will accomplish little.

Your financial decisions are more frequent and cover a much broader range than you might at first think. You make numerous financial decisions throughout the day, consciously or unconsciously, and carry them out through action or inertia. You can't avoid making financial decisions. And if you don't like what your decisions are adding up to, the first step toward changing their direction is to be aware of their full range.

This doesn't mean you have to walk around all day checking off decision after decision: "Eat yogurt before expiration date? Check! Read five pages of *Think and Grow Rich*? Check!" But in order to be able to reevaluate your decisions, you must be conscious of what they are.

Here's an instructive exercise you can do with a pen and paper. Pretend that it's Monday morning and your alarm has just gone off. Now write down all of the financial decisions you're going to make over the first hour of the day.

What did you include? These could be just a few of the decisions:

What time did you actually get up? Are you going to have to scramble to get to work on time—struggling to catch up from the moment you jog through the door?

What did you eat for breakfast, if anything? You can't be at a high performance level on an empty tank. Are you going to wait to get to work to eat something? What does that cost add up to for a year?

What are you wearing to work? Scuffed and worn shoes? What if the new client you're meeting with is a former military officer and she thinks you're a slob?

Do you have to get your child ready for day care? Is that a luxury or a necessity? What decisions make it a necessity?

How are you getting to work? Are you driving a $359-a-month vehicle that's essentially a twice-a-day shuttle? How many more days are you going to make that decision?

These are all, at least in part, little financial decisions that add up to the bigger picture.

Little decisions have an advantage: On their own each one is manageable. You can decide to spend ten minutes each morning planning your day instead of idly watching a celebrity interview on a morning talk show. You can decide to drink a glass of water instead of spending yet another dollar on carbonated sugar water.

Little decisions also have a big disadvantage: There are a lot of them. If you want to effect meaningful change, it's difficult not to feel that you're a juggler with a thousand balls in the air. And before too long, you just want to give your arms a rest.

When you consider switching even one of your financial stress symptoms into the True Wealth column, it seems like a tall order. "Need to get my career revitalized? That's a full-time job in itself." If you think that tackling a handful of financial stress symptoms could entail micromanagement to an impossible degree, you're right. But people with True Wealth make the right decisions day in and day out, and they do it with an almost unconscious grace, without any fuss and frenzy or endless calculation. How can they do it?

If you're not aware of your decisions, you're even less aware of how you *make* decisions. For most people, decisions just happen, by golly. You walk into Super Electronic Warehouse to buy a microwave oven, page-worn *Consumer Reports* in hand, and walk out with . . . a satellite dish.

But over time your financial decisions fall into distinct patterns because they're all made within the same framework: your personal internal mechanism for making financial decisions. We're going to give this heretofore mysterious thing a name, shine a light on it, and explore how it works—and why it doesn't work.

MEET YOUR BUCK-O-MATIC

Think of yourself as having a little black box inside you that makes your financial decisions. We're going to call this contraption your "Buck-O-Matic."

Your Buck-O-Matic is a one-of-a-kind gizmo slapped together over a lifetime from a grab bag of components: your family, education, culture, and experiences. You begin building it before you can walk and keep adding to it until it is a complex, incomprehensible mechanism that can have more control over you than you have over it. It processes everything from hard-edged information to soft and fuzzy emotions and spits out decision after decision.

If you're wondering why your Aunt Edna will drive across town to save five cents on a can of cat food while your Uncle Edgar can drop a thousand dollars in Vegas without a blink, here's the culprit. Their Buck-O-Matics are wired to crank out decisions in entirely different directions.

It'd be wonderful if your Buck-O-Matic combined the best qualities of Peter Lynch and Henry David Thoreau with the efficiency and precision of a Macintosh. But in all likelihood it resembles a Rube Goldberg contraption, complete with a dazed squirrel on a treadmill. It can be a calculator powered by cold logic one moment and a coin toss run by fleeting whimsy the next.

Your Buck-O-Matic can work as fast as lightning or as slowly as a glacier, or not at all. Think about the times you've physically spent money without it registering in your mind until after you've left the store. And then there's that money sitting in your checking account waiting for the day you decide to find a better investment.

Right here there's a sign that says "Major Detour This Way," but we're going to blow right by it. What's the detour? Wallowing in the peculiarities and faults of your Buck-O-Matic, trying to re-create how it got that way in the first place ("My father gave me fifty cents for each A on my report card, and my mother would give me a dollar to leave her alone"), accepting yourself the way you are (and, yes, you are wonderful), typecasting yourself and then trying to work around it ("I'm a passive-compulsive horder, and so I shouldn't buy anything that's two for the price of one").

You have to ask yourself: "Am I looking for an excuse for my financial stress, or am I looking to get rid of it?"

Tinkering with your Buck-O-Matic is fruitless. It's a waste of time to spend years on an analyst's couch—literally or figuratively—trying to reconstruct how your Buck-O-Matic got built in the first place. Trying to work around your current decision-making framework or suppressing it won't work either. The situation is no different than with dieting. You can't keep off physically stressful pounds until you truly embrace a reality that excludes Twinkies as a food group.

If you really want to get rid of your financial stress, there's only one way: Replace what doesn't work with what does. To gain a better understanding of what does work, we need to first understand in a general sense what causes your Buck-O-Matic to make stress-creating decisions.

WHAT IS STRESS, AND HOW DO WE MAKE DECISIONS THAT CREATE IT?

So far we've bandied the word stress about without answering an obvious question: What is stress?

Incredible as it may seem, many popular books on stress don't even venture a definition. They just assume that when you see the word, you know the feeling, and that's sufficient. But as long as you don't have a clear idea of what causes stress in the first place, a visit from the Publishers Clearing House Prize Patrol will stay on your shortlist of viable solutions.

According to *Webster's* and stress researchers, stress is bodily or mental tension caused by:

- A constraining force or influence
- A lack of control
- The altering of an existent equilibrium

Let's examine these three causes one by one:

A constraining force or influence. How does it happen that no matter what you do, you feel as if you're butting your head against a brick wall? You set out to make a change in your life, full of the best intentions, and before you know it, you're a step back from where you started, your plans soon abandoned. And life goes on.

What is this invisible force that thwarts us at every turn? Imagine what would happen if you programmed your calculator with wrong numerical values. If six was nine and four was five, no matter how hard you tried to balance your checkbook, the calculations would come out wrong. Before long, you'd give up in frustration.

This is exactly what happens if your Buck-O-Matic is programmed with the *wrong meaning of money.* That wrong meaning—whether it's "Money is how society keeps score," "Money is a measure of my worth as a person," or "Money is power"—is a constraining force that will make True Wealth only a random possibility. If you make your financial decisions based on the true meaning of money (it's coming in the next chapter), however, you will be free to make decisions that add up to what you intend them to—a life free from financial stress.

A lack of control. How do you end up feeling that someone is running your life, but it sure isn't you? That you're allowed three decisions a day—black or brown shoes, mustard or mayo, and Letterman or Leno—and beyond that, you might as well be a puppet.

On first impulse it may seem that the "easy" decision is the stress-free decision. But if your Buck-O-Matic is geared toward easy decisions that don't require any extra effort, self-restraint, or risk, or that avoid conflict at any cost, you *surrender control* of your decisions. The path of least resistance is really a direct route to financial stress.

When Dudley kicks back every night with a video, he has made the easy decision: whether to rent *Lethal Influence* or *Die Fast Three.* But with each explosion or shoot-out, he is also surrendering control of his career. And yet he fails to see any irony in his constant carping about his company's failure to provide more opportunity. When Victoria makes the easy decision to buy a sweater on sale (she has one for each day of the month), she's surrendering control of her future—paying for her retirement—to politicians and taxpayers.

How does the avoidance of conflict create stress? When you continually avoid conflict by giving in to your spouse—the easy decision—instead of trying to truly resolve your financial differences, you're stockpiling financial stress for a major explosion.

One of life's great ironies is that it is the *slightly harder decisions that ultimately make life easier.* If you can reprogram your Buck-O-Matic to consistently make the decisions that keep you just ahead of the moment, you will regain control of your life.

The altering of an existent equilibrium. How do you end up feeling as though there's no balance to your life, that everything is totally out of whack? You mutter to yourself, "I can't believe I was put on the planet to work this job to pay these bills."

A common cry heard above the din of modern life is for more balance in our lives. But what is a balanced life? A balanced life is one where no one aspect of your life so dominates or is so neglected that it negatively impacts the rest of your life.

For many of us, the last time our lives came anywhere near being balanced was back in high school or college. You had time for family, friends, learning, work, play, community—everything. Then along came the "heavy" stuff: careers, bills, commitments, responsibilities. The question is: Can your life ever be balanced as an adult, or is it merely wishful thinking? The answer is yes, it can, if you start with an idea of what your balanced life would include—the counterweights to the heavy stuff—rather than just an idyllic longing for a simpler life.

Balance requires an equilibrium in your thought process—the ability to weigh today and tomorrow, one need or desire against your other needs and desires. No financial decision, no matter how small, takes place in a vacuum. If your financial decisions focus too much on today, your future will be nothing more than a hodgepodge of effect. And you won't be able to go back into the past and redo the cause, only cope with the stress. It will be impossible to maintain, let alone develop, an equilibrium in your life that will resist financial stress.

On the other hand, if you fit your decisions into a broader schema, you can make sure that your requirements for a balanced life are in place.

Now you're thinking, "If I can make decisions that are free from constraining influences, that give me more control over my life, and that create a greater sense of balance, then I'll be able to reduce my financial stress? C'mon, how simple can that be?"

Let's begin at the single point that makes all of these things possible and see where it takes us.

SO *THAT'S* WHAT PEOPLE WITH
TRUE WEALTH HAVE IN COMMON

What people with True Wealth have in common is *how they think about money.*

Not how much money they have.

Not how little they need.

Not what they know.

But rather, *how they think about money.*

People with True Wealth have a simple framework inside their Buck-O-Matics, making decisions that not only neutralize the causes of financial stress but also create its active, ongoing opposite: True Wealth. When this common mind-set is applied to the unique particulars of your life, it will create the same result. It is what makes it possible for people from every possible background to take the specific actions that will conquer their financial stress.

This common mind-set is no hot hunch or New Age noodling. Rather, it is an understanding of five basic components that work together to create True Wealth. We're going to examine each of these five components in depth. As we do, you'll see that they begin with the true meaning of money and are connected by a simple flow of logic that makes them easy to use. With even a little effort, they will become second nature. Just as important, they get rid of constraining influences, give you more control over your life, and enable you to gain a strong sense of balance in your life. And, best of all, no matter who you are, they work.

Now before we start to overhaul your Buck-O-Matic, we're going to spend just a little time polishing and reinforcing its casing.

A SHINY AND STRONG BOX FOR YOUR BUCK-O-MATIC

There are two factors that are going to greatly increase your ability to create True Wealth: your general level of optimism and your effectiveness at warding off Crisis Creep, the information malady that makes every problem in the world your very own.

The Role of Optimism in Reducing Stress

During a class discussion in ninth-grade English, a female class-mate turned to me half in tears and cried, "You're such a cynic!" (I think I had said something about girls reading only books that had a horse for the main character.)

Having been accustomed to being called a twerp, I liked my new handle. Before too long, I reveled in cynicism and its close relative—outright pessimism—as a defense mechanism in a world where girls were content to consider me a good friend and being short, slow, and puny kept me off the basketball team.

A large dose of attitude carried me through school with minimal trauma (growing another twelve inches helped too) but served me poorly in the real world. I still thought that optimists were a bunch of creepy extras from a Lawrence Welk television special who slept with coat hangers in their mouths to maintain their perma-smiles. To me it was cut and dried: Either you were an optimist or you had a grip on reality.

What I ignored was that optimists had more adventures. Pessimists were far less likely even to begin an adventure. And when they did, they spent most of the time looking for reasons to give up or turn back. Optimists accomplished more of whatever they undertook. They didn't just *act* happier; they *were* happier.

When my younger sister became ill with cancer, I began looking for a lot of answers. If you've been in a similar situation, you know such an event not only sends you to far corners looking for any way possible to help your loved one, but also causes you to reevaluate your own life. In my case, a pivotal tool for reevaluation was the book *Learned Optimism* by Martin E. P. Seligman, Ph.D.

Seligman's studies (he's the director of clinical training in psychology at the University of Pennsylvania) show that optimists are healthier and happier. They are able to overcome failure and frustration (both inevitable occurrences when you take risks) much more successfully than pessimists are. And, most encouraging, optimism can be learned. And pessimists don't have to completely throw in the towel. It turns out that a reasonable amount of healthy skepticism is—what else?—healthy.

The people I've met who have True Wealth are invariably optimists—although pessimists often confuse the benefits of optimism with "luck." You pessimists know who you are. If you can be honest with yourself, you'll admit that your pessimism prevents you from even trying to do things that would make your life better. As a learned optimist, let me tell you that it is worth the effort to shake off the grip that pessimism holds on your life.

Saying "No" to Crisis Creep

What were some of your mother's most repeated words of wisdom? When you told her that everyone stayed out past midnight, her standard response to your airtight argument was "You're not everyone." And guess what? She was right; you're not!

However, when you see broad trends and nationwide averages as being the markers for your life, you've opened the door to Crisis Creep—a condition where all of the problems and concerns in the world are absorbed into your life, even when they don't really exist. The result—a prevailing sense of futility that freezes you in your tracks. "What's the use of trying?" you ask yourself. "When the ozone layer disappears, it won't matter that I only have two hundred bucks in my IRA."

Day after day we're bombarded with crises. Turn on the nightly news and you're liable to hear about the latest alarming trend involving "millions of Americans." That many retirees have to eat pet food to get by. Yeesh. Crises pop up overnight. One day they're a bunch of numbers on someone's desk. The next day, from the mouth of Peter Jennings—a full-blown crisis springs! "By the year 2040, two out of every three Americans will work for Wal-Mart or McDonald's," predicts a concerned expert with an unseen agenda. Let's just go fill out an application and skip the wait.

If we're not careful, we become unwitting members of the Crisis-of-the-Month Club, passively accepting these crises as part of our outlook, never bothering to refuse delivery, not remembering that the last bunch of crises never came to pass. Remember when everyone fretted about the Japanese overrunning our economy?

What's worse is that while these secondhand, theoretical, or trumped-up crises take over, you ignore the very real crises in your own life. While Connie frets about foreigners taking away her job, her lack of action in boosting or broadening her skills is likely to create far more financial stress than Juanita or Ng.

Only your mother knows how truly special you are. But I do know this: There's no reason you have to see yourself as average or feel compelled to join a crowd. You may have been told that every second marriage ends in divorce—an express lane to financial stress—but in any given year, only a tiny fraction of marriages break up. There's plenty of room on the low-stress route. If credit card debt is at an all-time high—the average household is now over $6,000 in hock—there are still a lot of people with negligible balances.

If you want to make faster headway against your financial stress, you're best off consciously guarding against Crisis Creep. Unless your first name is Misery, don't let unwanted company in the door. Ignore the latest specimen of economic anguish or prediction of impending doom on the evening news. Financial stress isn't a statistic or a headline; it is an unwanted part of your life.

The only financial stress that counts at the moment is *yours*. That's what you want to get rid of.

So let's get started.

3

You Can't Buy
the Life That
Money Can't Buy

WHEN WE'RE admiring people with True Wealth, we often use the phrase "They have the life that money can't buy."

This statement is a revealing admission: When the evidence is plainly laid out before our eyes, we recognize that many of the things that really matter in life can't be bought. So what do we do? We turn right around and try to buy them anyway.

To many of us, money is no longer mere currency. It has become the primary—and in many cases, the only—current of change in our lives. We not only count on money to do everything it can do—put a roof over our head—but expect it to do everything it can't do—turn our children into responsible adults. We count on money to pay for the first date, and we expect it to guarantee love everlasting. The truth is we expect money to do just about everything but keep our belly buttons lint-free.

Why do we insist on trying to buy the life that we know money can't really buy? Because we're making our decisions based on the wrong meaning of money. Undoubtedly, you've been told that:

Money is power. And how rich were Gandhi and Martin Luther King, Jr.?

Money is love. Which is why Cupid ditched his bow and arrow for a gold card.

Money is a measure of your worth to others. Mother Teresa was a bust.

Money is how society keeps score. It sure is . . . of how much money you have.

All of these meanings of money are quite common—and quite wrong.

You may very well be unwittingly making your financial decisions based on an erroneous meaning of money simply because it's been passed along to you by your parents or because everyone else does. Your commitment to the meaning may be tenuous, indeed. The key—and possibly unpondered—question: Is there a meaning of money that will allow you to stay squarely in the mainstream of society and yet also allow you the flexibility to control your life? Fortunately, the answer is "yes."

People with True Wealth are able to create the kind of life that money can't buy because they make decisions based on the true—and quite practical—meaning of money. The understanding lies in the answers to two fundamental questions: (1) What is money? (2) What does the amount of money you make really mean?

WHAT IS MONEY?

Webster's defines money as "a means of exchange." We've heard that definition so many times that, just as with the word stress, we don't scratch beneath the surface when we hear it. When you swap a piece of paper with a picture of George Washington on it for a pack of gum, what's really being exchanged?

People who live beyond financial stress understand that *money is simply the means by which we exchange value.*

Out of all of the choices in the 7-Eleven, you value the pack of gum. The dollar you plop down on the counter represents the point where the value of the minutes you spent in a meeting, dealing with a customer, making a product, or writing a report is equal to the value of the materials used to make the gum and the time and effort of the dozens of people who transformed and transported those materials until they became that tasty wad between your teeth. Without money, no burst of flavor.

Money came into existence to serve a specific need—and it wasn't so that Thor the Hunter could prove he was a better person than Gonan the Gatherer. Whenever man bands together in a group, he starts swapping things—"goods and services" in economic lingo. Eventually direct barter proves too cumbersome and a means of exchange comes into existence—beads, coins, carved stones, cigarettes, paper, brass statues, you name it. This has happened over and over again throughout civilization.

Man has often been called an "economic animal" because of this innate swapping impulse. After all, you're unlikely to see young apes trading Pogs—unless they're in the back of your minivan and you're stuck in traffic. As work has become increasingly specialized and aimed less at directly meeting basic needs, the symbol of money—like King Kong rising above the New York City skyline—has loomed larger and larger in our lives. On bended knee we look up to money, fearing what might happen if we pause in our vigil.

The down-to-earth, practical meaning of money has become obscured by an overgrowth of cultural kudzu. Indeed, a huge part of our economy is based on meanings of money that have grown like scraggle bush on an otherwise healthy concept. So let's cut further through the brush.

WHAT'S IT WORTH TO YA?

With all of our preoccupation with the accounting of money—how much does something cost? how much do we have? how much are we getting paid?—we rarely think about the dynamics of value. In other words, who says what something is worth? How do the numbers end up on a price tag or on our paychecks?

There are two vantage points to value—analogous to the opposite ends of a giant telescope. At one end is the perspective of the marketplace—the big picture that includes the billions of people who make up our world economy, from your local sales territory to a factory on the other side of the world. At the other end is the very personal perspective of a single individual: you. The magnitude of the difference between these two perspectives is immeasurable; for while price is determined by the marketplace, value is created within an area no further than your arm's reach.

The price tag placed on value is determined in the marketplace—supply and demand. The price for some goods can be fairly consistent throughout a market—you might get a "deal" on a new car, but you're not going to get it for half price. There can also be a wide variance in the price placed on the exact same good: A Serge Aldente shirt might be valued at fifty dollars in a boutique and fifteen dollars in the outlet mall next door.

Many economists argue that value exists only in the mind of the marketplace. Whatever the marketplace says, goes. If you don't like the verdict, tough noogies. But before the market gets to be judge, *you* have to act. If you don't take the plunge, Judge Marketplace doesn't get to hold up the scorecard. In fact, if everyone spent the whole day doing nothing, Judge Marketplace would be unemployed right along with us.

From your perspective the market may determine price, but *you create the value.* Walt Disney had to create value—there certainly was no readily apparent megamarket for a charming animated mouse and his fun-loving pals—before the market could make him wealthy. The market wasn't clamoring for Velcro: Georges de Mestral had to create it before anyone could want it. And what about Earl and Michiko McElfresh? One would have surmised that the Civil War had been pretty much mapped over—until the McElfreshes created their brand of value.

So in terms of that which is most important, indeed the foundation of any economy, *you are the printing press. You generate value—* whether you're an entrepreneur generating value with an anticipation of a demand or an employee hired for your anticipated ability to contribute value to an organization.

One thing inherent in all of this is that life isn't fair. The numbers that the marketplace puts on value can often seem illogical, if not cruel. You might have a really great product and can't get arrested, yet down the street some guy is making a bundle selling fake beepers and car phones to wanna-be hoodlums. You might be a corporate Cal Ripken and not make the cutdown while some egregious toad hops right into a key management position.

Trying to make sense out of the marketplace can drive you nuts. On the one hand, you can try to reassure yourself that the marketplace is run by the impartial logic of supply and demand. And on the other, you can turn around and wonder what it is that Mr. Executive actually did to justify his $40 million payday ("It's the going rate," we're reassured) for selling off the company he helped run into the ground.

So let's resolve that nagging little question of those numbers. In other words, how much means what?

WHAT DOES THE AMOUNT OF MONEY YOU MAKE REALLY MEAN?

A second critical relationship between your life and money lies in the interpretation of the numbers on your paycheck.

People with True Wealth understand that *your income is simply that part of your generated value that you can readily exchange.*

The word *part* in the above sentence could be *the most crucial word in the creation of True Wealth.*

The money in your pocket represents that part of everything you do throughout the day on which the marketplace has placed a price tag. That's all. It doesn't begin to account for everything you do—and the full scope of the value you create in your life.

Imagine the following scenario: You go through the grocery checkout with a full cart, and when it's all tallied up and it's time to pay, you don't reach for your wallet.

Instead, you smile at the clerk and calmly say: "Today I exercised and steered clear of the office donut box."

When you get a puzzled look, you say: "Last night I made sure my son completed his homework—without his headphones on."

When the blank look continues, you say: "This morning I smiled at the temp receptionist and tried to make her feel comfortable as she struggled through the first hour."

When you don't get waved along, you offer: "I'm working at being a more confident public speaker."

Finally, when you hear the words "Store Security—Register Five" booming over the public-address system, you pay up and leave.

So what happened in this theoretical exercise? None of the actions you described to the clerk have been deemed valuable by the marketplace. But there's no doubt that each of the actions over time will create something of real value—something you can't just go out and buy. The little things—like your health, a brighter future for your son, the goodwill of your fellows, and your ability to communicate.

You certainly have created value—you've just cut out the middleman. And you knew that embracing value without a price didn't mean you were turning your back on value with a price tag. The fact is that each of the actions that directly created value in our experiment didn't preclude their being translated into actual dollars and cents down the road. For example, if you're in good health, you can save thousands of dollars over your lifetime.

This exercise contains the first key to living a life that money can't buy.

THE FIRST COMPONENT OF TRUE WEALTH: MAKE VALUE—NOT MONEY—THE BASIC CURRENCY OF YOUR LIFE

Generating value is the fundamental force in shaping our lives. More than anything else, the value we generate in our lives—at work, at home, and in the community, in our minds, our hearts, and our souls—shapes and gives meaning to our existence. To make decisions that are aligned with that force, *you have to see your life as a transaction of value with the world around you.*

Only if you think first and foremost in terms of creating value, *not* making money, will it be possible to have the things in life that money can't buy. By making value the currency of your life, money will be reduced to a means of exchange—not a scoreboard—and what you exchange it for will be determined by *your* needs.

When you make value the currency of your life, you are not turning your back on money. You aren't faced with a choice between money or value. *If money derives from creating value, it simply makes sense to think first and foremost of that which comes first.* If value encompasses both money and the things in life that money can't buy, it is fundamentally logical to adjust your sights to the bigger picture. Let's meet someone who has made value the primary currency of his life.

In his late forties, bassist Ray Drummond is one of the most in-demand jazz musicians in the world. Watching Ray perform with his characteristic unwavering intensity—eyes fixed, head bobbing—whether it's with the Kenny Barron Trio or leading his own group, Excursion, you can almost see the power of the sound emanating from the strings of his instrument as Ray pulls his fellow musicians into his propulsive groove.

Built like a defensive tackle, Ray would seem to embody his nickname, "Bulldog." I've got to admit, the first time I saw him play at Bradley's in New York City, he looked downright intimidating. But when Ray speaks, it's with a warmth and friendly intelligence that belie any notion of belligerence. Ray is the "Bulldog" for his tenacious commitment to his own vision.

In the early 1970s Ray was on a track that would have enabled him to write his own ticket in the business world—a fellowship in the prestigious Stanford University MBA program. But the lure of the bandstand proved too strong. Despite having had no formal musical training, Ray turned pro.

It would have been easy to conclude that Ray had lost his mind, turning down a blank check for the hustling and scuffling life of a jazz musician. But according to Ray, "You have to have the courage to trust your instincts, to stand your ground when people are telling you that you're crazy to even try something. Money is not the centerpiece of my life and never has been. Developing as an artist in a way that pleases me is my objective— and I hope the audience enjoys it too." In other words, Ray's main currency is value.

Quickly finding himself playing with established jazz veterans on the West Coast, it wasn't long before Ray had the confidence to move to the jazz capital of the world, New York City. Since then Ray has appeared on over 200 recordings and toured the world countless times. The sensitivity and open-mindedness with which he approaches his art have made him the bassist of choice for everyone from harmonica virtuoso Toots Thielemans to flame-throwing saxophonist David Murray.

Ray readily acknowledges that his family—wife, Susan, and daughter, Maya—are a team that makes his work possible. "We're like any other middle-class family paying the overhead. We're never going to be starving artists," he explains. "But I believe that enhancing your self-development however you choose to is more important than dollars." Ray admits to having "a million interests"—one of his recordings is entitled *Camera in a Bag,* in reference to his passion for photography—and tries to balance his desires to read "all the books waiting to be read" and develop "a more contemplative approach to my music."

If you ever have the experience of sitting in a small club while Ray follows his musical instincts, you'll feel that his pursuit of value has enriched everyone within earshot. I don't think that anyone ever listens to a musician of Ray's caliber and level of creativity without a twinge of longing: "I wish I could be in his shoes." You may never be able to play a note of Thelonious Monk, but you can use the same currency notes Ray used to get to where he is today.

Ray Drummond set out on an adventure early in his adult life, one whose rewards have muted the economic risks of being a jazz musician. Does Ray ever regret the path he's chosen? Only in that he doesn't like northeast winters and misses the people of San Francisco. But wherever you are in life, it's not too late for you to alter your path or *change the scenery along your path.*

REPHRASING THE PROBLEM
CAN BE PART OF THE SOLUTION

Think for a moment about whatever financial stress symptom is grinding you at the moment. Odds are you thought about it immediately in terms of dollars. But if you look at these problems in terms of generating value, you'll see them in a light that is less stressful right off the bat.

"I need a higher-paying job" becomes "I need to generate more value in my work" or "I need to do a better job polishing and marketing my value."

"I need to stop spending" becomes "I need to generate more value in my life without relying on money."

"We need to quit arguing about money" can become "We need to generate more value in our relationship that will overcome our differences" or "I need to handle money in a way that doesn't undermine the value of our relationship." (Face it, sometimes we create our own problems. It often *is* our fault.)

In each of these cases, *thinking in terms of value rather than money*

- Placed the emphasis on where the solution lies: with you
- Phrased the solution in positive terms
- Positioned you to explore the widest range of possible actions, both financial and nonfinancial
- Pointed you toward solutions over which you have control
- Didn't negate or deny the role of money in life or preclude the possibility of making more

Simply by changing your currency from money to value, you can break the logistical logjam that seemingly confines you to the exact life you're living. It is a shift in perspective that can dramatically change your circumstances without demanding an immediate and drastic decision. Here's someone who has made value the currency of her life without turning it upside down.

Nancy Jackson walked away from an abusive husband sixteen years ago with no money in her bank account and all of her belongings in a single trunk. Even for someone who is often described as "perky," the immediate future did not look like a walk in the park.

Having recently started a job in sales, Nancy threw herself headlong into her work. "At the start I really did need all the money I could make. But I just never let up, even for a second. I kept working fifteen hours a day long after I really had to."

After six years, Nancy "had it all": a home overlooking the ocean in Laguna Beach, California, and a vacation in a different part of the world every three months. With it came financial stress: "My whole life revolved around sales numbers. And I thought I needed things to show for it—I was continually agonizing over whether or not to sell my house and trade up to something bigger, even though it was more than big enough for an entire family, let alone just me.

"I began to hate my job and thought I needed to find something else to do. Then I realized the problem wasn't work—it was what I did when I wasn't working. My entire life was about money—I had no sense of fulfillment outside my checkbook. So I reconnected with some things that were important to me that I had ignored for too long."

An art major in college, Nancy hadn't picked up her brushes in years. She decided to rekindle her passion through community involvement—by volunteering as a tour guide at a nearby museum. "That really was pivotal," she explains. "I began to think a lot more in terms of giving rather than getting—expression rather than acquiring things."

When she was ready to express herself on paper, it wasn't with paint, but with words. "I started writing a murder mystery on weekends instead of shopping. I've always been an avid reader, and I just got to the point where I thought, 'Maybe I could do this,' and then I discovered I could. Joining a writers' group was really great because I met all kinds of interesting people. The feedback kept me psyched to write."

Over the months she experienced a gradual yet remarkable change. "Because there was more balance in my life, I could relax at work—everything wasn't all tied up in my production. I ended up working fewer hours and doing even better. Once my life became more about what I did inside my house rather than the house itself, I decided that moving was ridiculous. I decided to renovate several rooms and leave it at that."

Nancy's switch from money to value has an ending that might have been dreamed up a few miles to the north, in Hollywood: She married the contractor who worked on her house. Together they have a five-year-old son and, just as the story line ends, are living happily ever after. Her career as a writer is on hold, though: "A literary agent in New York agreed to take me on as a client. But then came a family, and I've only recently resumed my writing. In a way, though, it doesn't matter if I ever get published because it was the act of doing one thing I loved that got me to a life I love."

Nancy made value the currency of her life while staying right where she was. But there are cases where your life can be so jerry-built that the only sensible thing to do is to level it and start over. In other words, begin with a big decision.

Recently my wife and I watched a television news segment about the trials and tribulations of a two-career, two-child couple. From the moment the three-year-old started his day before dawn by watching a video to the end of the day, when the parents collapsed with less than thirty seconds of face-to-face conversation between them, the family appeared trapped in a modern nightmare. And one with no apparent escape, either. Had the house, had the kids, needed the jobs . . .

Several well-known family experts were asked for suggestions as to how the parents could make life more manageable, let alone bearable. But while the experts were offering helpful hints like fixing an entire week's meals on Sunday or going out on a date once a month, my wife and I were screaming at the television: "Get out. Sell the house. Quit the jobs. Move. Do something!" In other words, start over—using value rather than money as a primary currency.

We weren't giving advice of the "that's easy for you to say" variety, either. Some of the best things in our life can be traced to our single decision I discussed in the introduction: to move to Buffalo simply because we believed that we would be better able to generate value in our lives. (And, yes, there was also a time in my life when getting out of Buffalo was the right move to make.)

If you are under financial stress, even factors such as careers, kids, and a mortgage shouldn't hold you back from considering a radical change in your life. There is quite possibly no better step toward True Wealth than to restructure your life around the concept of generating value rather than making and spending money.

VALUE VS. MONEY: WHAT'S THE WINNER THROUGHOUT YOUR LIFE?

Now let's pause for a moment, sit back, and have a little fun—and watch value and money go head-to-head in an eight-round bout. The purpose? To demonstrate the hands-down superiority of generating value over spending money in making sure that what's really important to us is a part of our lives.

VALUE VS. MONEY: ROUND #1

What's important: Your health.
Value: You can exercise, eat a sensible diet, and get a grip on proven harmful habits.
Money: You can try to buy your health back somewhere down the line for a huge price—if you can buy it back at all.

Lost in the deafening debate over the rising costs of health care is the fact that as a nation we spend hundreds of billions of dollars doing our darndest to ensure that we'll need health care. We help create the demand for the care, demand that someone else pay for it, and then are surprised when the cost spirals. Yet we'd all have less financial stress—collectively and individually—if we did more about generating health on a daily basis rather than letting the bills add up and paying for it later.

VALUE VS. MONEY: ROUND #2

What's important: Your children.

Value: You can monitor your children's activities in order to steer them away from trouble.

Money: You can try to bail them out—one way or another—later.

What's the most effective way to keep a teenager out of trouble with drugs, alcohol, and crime? According to a study of 699 adolescents in the Buffalo area over a six-year period, the most effective means is monitoring your child's activities.

"Monitoring means knowing where your kids are, who their friends are, when they are coming in, and so on," said the conductor of the study. This proved to be true across racial and socioeconomic lines: Inner-city adolescents, in fact, had lower rates of drug and alcohol abuse.

So what's the lesson? That the time and energy it takes to set and enforce guidelines for your children—right through high school—in a supportive environment is more effective in keeping them out of trouble than where you send them to school or the possessions with which you surround them.

VALUE VS. MONEY: ROUND #3

What's important: Liking your job.

Value: You can find enjoyment and purpose in your current work.

Money: You can spend your earnings trying to fill the void of an unsatisfying job.

The choice to work may be out of your hands, but the choice to like your work is yours to a large degree. If we see work only as something we have to do for money, we can think, "Darn it, I spend all this time working for money. At least I'm going to get some enjoyment out of it." In that case, the only enjoyment derived from work is spending the money. This is a dangerous state of mind to say the least. The fallout from this perception can go far beyond an increasing spiral of debt. It potentially includes depression, divorce, alcoholism, drug addiction . . . nothing fun. And yet there's hardly a job in the world that doesn't contain the seeds of a great adventure if only they are watered with a sense of levity, enthusiasm, and curiosity.

VALUE VS. MONEY: ROUND #4

What's important: Having opportunities in life.

Value: You can continually broaden your expertise in and beyond your field—and expand your opportunities.

Money: You can deplete your savings while you go back to school full-time or look for a job just like the one you had.

"Career stuck in a ditch? Dial 1-800-BIZ-SKOOL." Why does it seem that this notice is stuck on the wall of every washroom in corporate America? Because it is a classic opportunity in a box, one that the bearer hopes will entitle her to hop a few rungs up the salary ladder or open closed doors. Yet despite the aura of certitude and precision surrounding executive education, studies of the concrete benefits to the participants are rare. And those benefits are never compared to the results of someone who tells herself, "When I walk through the door at work, I'm already walking into a classroom. Here's where I want to go, and here's what I need to learn to get there."

VALUE VS. MONEY: ROUND #5

What's important: Living in a good neighborhood.

Value: You can help to effect directly a positive change in your community.

Money: You can hand over your tax dollars to the government and expect it to solve the problems for you.

Is the fact that we can spend trillions on our social problems and not see any progress enough to convince you that money pales in efficiency next to people solving problems in their own communities? In many ways our entire national fiscal mess is the result of our collective belief that money is the great problem solver, and that more money can solve problems even better. It may take money to run a poorhouse—as the saying goes—but it takes people generating value for it to have a positive impact.

VALUE VS. MONEY: ROUND #6

What's important: Enjoying life to the fullest.

Value: You can develop an active and absorbing interest.

Money: You can amuse yourself with constant and sometimes costly fixes of superficial entertainment.

The analogy might seem extreme, but it is actually easy to find ready parallels between drugs and a lot of what gets pushed as entertainment today. Both require money. Both eat up time. The pleasurable effects of both wear off quickly, leaving the user anxious for more. Neither leaves the user with any long-term positive effect. Even sitting in your real living room watching television shows set in fake living rooms is not exactly, shall we say, living life to the fullest.

Our interests can't always be pursued completely free of cost. But a genuine interest should be able to be sustained by passion and creativity in the absence of cash. When you can entertain yourself through the generation of value and not just by spending money, you'll never have to utter two of the most senseless words in the world: "I'm bored."

VALUE VS. MONEY: ROUND #7

What's important: Having what you need to live comfortably.
Value: You can take care of what you own.
Money: You can pay to fix or replace it.

We've often been pegged as living in a disposable world. This has a ring of truth to it—a lot of things we spend money on have a useful life about as long as a gnat's. But many goods are built to last a long time—if we give them half a chance. A friend in the heating and cooling business tells me that the majority of his service calls—and major repairs—are the result of the owners failing to follow simple low-cost maintenance procedures. And my local shoe repairman says that you can double the life of a pair of shoes with proper care.

VALUE VS. MONEY: ROUND #8

What's important: A sense of meaning in life.
Value: You can cultivate a genuine spiritual presence in your life.
Money: You can try to go out and buy one.

Faith is founded on desire and devotion, not dollars. Any group or individual who predicates your spiritual gain on their financial gain—whether it's a fake-tech pseudoreligion or high-tech evangelist—probably does have a spot waiting in a dark, noisy, and overheated subterranean location.

And the winner is . . .

So there you have it: Value sweeps the series over money 8–0. And we've just looked at a few choice matchups. You could play the game all day long, and money would never wrest the title belt from value.

HOW DO WE GENERATE VALUE?

Value isn't just some cosmic catchall—a flabby word for something we really can't visualize or get a handle on. We generate value through a definable process:

$$Value = Time \times Energy \times Resources$$

In other words, using whatever resources we can muster, we apply energy over a period of time and generate value: something of importance. This same process applies whether you're mastering a lifelong skill like painting or doing a simple task like winterizing your car. The outcome might be a work in progress over a lifetime—a marriage or a business. Or it might be as temporal as making a turkey sandwich.

Back in the first chapter we noted that it's common to believe that money is the horse that pulls the cart of stress into our lives and that it's also going to carry it away. To use another beast of burden metaphor, that thinking is ass backward.

Time, energy, and resources are the horse before the cart of stress. It's how we use them, or, to be more precise, misuse them, that drags financial stress into our lives. Money simply tags along. And it's our time, energy, and resources that are going to haul our financial stress off to the dump. Let's look at each one individually:

TIME: EGALITARIAN AND ELASTIC

Time is, if nothing else, egalitarian. We're all born with twenty-four hours at our disposal for each and every day of our lives. No matter who you are, an hour is an hour. Unless, of course, you're sitting in the dentist's chair listening to Michael Bolton—then an hour seems like a long time.

Time is elastic and can be stretched by energy and resources—what we refer to as "using your time wisely." Mary might accomplish in eight hours what Gord does in twelve hours, despite Gord's self-nomination for martyrdom.

By itself, to put it bluntly, your time is worthless. When you give something an hour of your time, you're merely putting a frame around a blank canvas. Using your energy and resources, you can create a rich tableau that's priceless or halfheartedly draw a few scribbles and hope to get a gold star anyway.

It almost goes without saying that value of any type can't be created unless you give it some time. And giving something *any* time is just as important as how much time you give it. Fifteen minutes a day doing any one thing is enough space to generate a lot of value over time.

ENERGY: YOUR PERSONAL UTILITY COMPANY

Energy is the intensity or level of effort applied to an activity within a given time frame. I've put energy smack in the middle of the value equation to signify its pivotal role. We all have the same amount of time. As we'll see, each of us has far more resources than we might think. But without energy as a catalyst, time is going to pass and our resources will stay undeveloped or idle. If you downplay the role of energy in creating value, not only are you tying one hand behind your back but you're also tying your shoelaces together.

There are three aspects to energy:

1. *Physical energy.* Physical energy is the actual physical effort you put into whatever you're doing. In a sedentary world, we tend to think of physical activities as confined to sports, the outdoors, and blue-collar labor. But even in activities that don't require much outright exertion, physical energy plays a vital role. It takes physical energy to have an effective conversation or even to read a book.

2. *Mental energy.* Mental energy is concentration—the intensity of your mental engagement. Think of yourself as having a laserlike beam emanating from your mind that is directed by your thoughts throughout the day. The beam will just glance off the surface of whatever's on your mind unless you focus and "lock it" on something—an idea, an activity, an observation, a task—and turn up the intensity. The more we consciously direct our mental engagement, the greater our level of mental energy.

3. *Emotional energy.* Emotional energy has two major aspects—outlook and constancy. Your outlook is your attitude—from positive to negative. Your attitude can be fairly consistent to wildly fluctuating. Everyone goes through moods, and I imagine that there were times when even Pollyanna felt like running over a bunny with her bicycle. But there is no doubt that (1) positive emotional energy creates positive results, and (2) the more consistently positive you are, the more consistently the results of whatever you undertake will end up being positive.

YOUR HAND IS ON THE SWITCH

How powerful is energy in creating True Wealth? Remember that True Wealth is action-created. Energy is what makes the difference between wishful thinking and results. It is what makes it possible for those from humble backgrounds to create True Wealth and—quite often—tremendous financial wealth right along with it. Energy can overcome a huge deficit in resources and trump the mediocre effort of someone who seemingly has everything it takes.

There are two important things that further underline energy's pivotal role:

1. *Your energy is at your disposal.* Throw out all of the excuses and accept the truth: Your hand is on the control switch. We've noted that one of the general symptoms of stress is the feeling that you are not in control of your life. You can begin to turn that perception around right now by telling yourself: "I've got a tremendous reserve of potential energy, and only I can tap into it, harness it, and make it work for me."

Everyone I've encountered with True Wealth is a self-starter. If it were not for their ability to kick their energy into gear, Muzaffar Afzal would still be in Pakistan and Jonas Gadson would be numb from his third decade of repetition on the job.

2. *Your energy is free.* You are not going to get a bill at the end of the month because you tackled a long-delayed project. It doesn't cost money to think or pay attention in a class or meeting, speed up your pace a step when you need to get out of a rut, or concentrate on a task that has to get done.

Energy should not be confused with merely whatever you have to do just to get through a time frame without sliding backward or remaining unscathed by criticism. In other words, it's above whatever you do just to make it through the day. When you were a kid and your parents dragged you to visit Aunt Edna on a Sunday afternoon, you probably put just enough effort into the occasion to escape the threat of a backhanded swat. Energy is your effort above and beyond the "swat line."

One big stress-creating notion is that energy is equivalent to "time spent"—that hours are the same as effort. *But time spent has nothing to do with energy expended and even less to do with value created.* The idea that, because you've put the time in and are a good employee, you're deserving of a certain result is foolhardy at the least in today's business environment.

By itself, time is raw, untilled land. With energy, it can become a fertile plot that nurtures and enriches. When you equate employment with wasting time and energy, you're turning a pretty considerable amount of fallow ground into a toxic dump.

Remember, you don't have to choose between generating value and making money. You just have to choose between taking command of your energy and relying on a combination of shortcuts, osmosis, blind luck, and everyone else to create a life beyond financial stress. If you stick with the latter route, your odds of achieving True Wealth are slim indeed. If you take command of your energy, the odds are over-whelmingly in your favor.

THE SEVEN RESOURCES: THE GOLD MINE YOU'RE SITTING ON

Resources are the third factor in the generation of value. They are the tools and materials you have to work with. When you make value the primary currency of your life, you immediately open your mind to the full range of resources you have at your disposal: ability, infor-mation, organizations and institutions, what you already own or have access to, opportunity, and money. Let's look at each resource individually:

1. *Ability.* Ability is the combination of knowledge, experience, and practice that adds up to "can-do." Ability is activated potential—un-tapped aptitude and raw talent—that, through time and effort, be-comes an integral and permanent part of who we are and what we do. In fighting financial stress, it is the most potent of all resources. If our quest for greater ability were anywhere near as constant as our belief in the miracle power of more money, our financial stress would be diminished greatly.

2. *Information.* Never in history has there been readier access to in-formation on any topic imaginable. If you want to know how to do something, you can find out how to do it.

3. *People.* Not just the people you know who you think have the power to "do something for you"—it's everyone who might have in-sight into how to achieve a desired result.

4. *Organizations and institutions.* Institutions of learning, non-profit and service groups, government agencies, clubs, businesses, and churches are all potential resources.

5. *What you already own.* The oft-overlooked half-full glass. What-ever your endeavor, it's highly likely that you have things sitting around your house that need only your energy to help you generate value.

6. *Opportunity.* An opportunity is an existing arena or platform for action—to show what you can do. A job, a college course, a volunteer position, a personal relationship—all of these are opportunities that we can either squander or capitalize upon to create value.

7. *Money.* We're certainly not going to overlook money as a resource—but you'll need and use far less of it if you think in terms of time, energy, and the other six resources first.

More often than not, you don't need all—or even half—of these resources to generate desired value. And you already have enough of the necessary resources to at least get started.

All too often a lack of energy—to identify the full range of our resources and then to avail ourselves of them—is confused with an actual lack of resources. We've all seen people with seemingly every resource imaginable fail to accomplish a single thing.

The fact is, most great adventures in life aren't completely outfitted at the beginning. The key to generating value is to use all the resources you have—not to wait until you have all of the resources you imagine you need.

CHANGING CURRENCIES DOESN'T
MEAN TAKING A VOW OF POVERTY

Expanding your focus beyond just "making money" doesn't mean taking a vow of poverty or committing financial hara-kiri. In fact, many fortune-creating enterprises are the result of value generated beyond workaday boundaries.

Entrepreneur Richard Branson—the founder of Virgin Atlantic Airways and Virgin Records—began his career publishing an upstart literary newspaper. When he surmised, through reading the ads in his own paper, that fans of underground rock bands had difficulty finding their favorite groups' recordings, Branson started a mail-order business and opened a store selling records at cut-rate prices. His spirit of adventure led to close relationships with progressive rock artists (his first big hit was Mike Oldfield's *Tubular Bells,* but don't hold it against him) and, ultimately, a major international record company. Ignoring a legion of naysayers, he turned around and made a successful entry into the high-risk airline business. None of this might have happened if Branson had merely focused on meeting his next deadline rather than recognizing an opportunity hidden in his back pages.

Like millions of other people, Eugene Hughes suffered from a stomach ulcer. Because of that ulcer, he and his family are worth tens of millions of dollars. And no, they didn't get it from suing someone and getting a big settlement.

Desperate for relief, Hughes decided to try a home remedy for ulcers that was passed along by a neighbor: cayenne pepper. Bizarre as it seemed, it worked. And rather than just treat it as Eugene's weird medicine, the Hughes family saw an adventure. Before long the entire family was filling gel caps with the fiery powder to sell at local health food stores. Other herbal remedies were added to their line. Today, what began as a family activity around a kitchen table is now Nature's Sunshine Products—an international leader in herbal medicine with sales of over $200 million. All beginning with an idea that had long been in the public domain.

Now you may be thinking, "Okay, record companies, health care, airlines—this is big stuff. What is there possibly in my life that has the potential to generate True Wealth that leads to financial wealth?" It may lie in an idea that thousands of people have overlooked or in an activity that millions of people participate in. This was the case for Dick Kirby, who by generating value has made himself wealthy by any definition.

When I called on Dick Kirby for an interview at his place of business, some things hadn't changed in the twenty years since my last visit. He was an avid outdoorsman, and the walls were covered with hunting trophies. In his early fifties, Dick still had the same look of the star of a television detective series that he had had when he opened shop in the town of Orchard Park, New York, in the late 1960s. As I sat down in the chair, the head of an enormous white-tailed deer looked me over.

But other things had changed. Twenty years ago, Dick Kirby was the proprietor of the Quaker Boy Barber Shop. Today he is the president of Quaker Boy Inc., a multimillion-dollar company. How this came to be is an inspirational adventure that began when he was five years old.

"My dad took me hunting at a young age, and I fell in love with the outdoors, being surrounded by nature." In 1971 a friend introduced Dick to wild turkey hunting. "From the first day, I was hooked. I practiced turkey calling around the house until my family threatened to lock me out." The practice paid off; within several years Dick won the New York State turkey-calling championship, soon followed by the U.S. Open and the Grand National Championship. But a problem developed along the way: Like a virtuoso playing a student fiddle, Dick felt limited by the existing turkey calls on the market. He began to experiment with making his own calls. By letting his curiosity and enthusiasm lead the way, Dick soon found a path overlooked by millions of others.

"I started off fooling around in my shop in my spare time," he explains. "One day a customer in the aluminum siding business brought in a few scraps. I made a turkey call from the scraps, strips from surgical gloves, and duct tape." Through trial and error, Dick fashioned his personal Stradivarius and, soon after, began turning them out by hand: "I was winning championships with my call, and other people were interested in trying it out." Rather than keep his championship turkey call under lock and key—and out of the hands of the competition—Dick was happy to make up a few for his fellow enthusiasts. Interestingly, his willingness to share his technology was the exact opposite of the fateful decision that has crippled Apple Computer.

Several of Dick's barbershop customers (obviously they liked him as a person) offered to help him make the transition into mass production, and then "It just mushroomed." Dick gradually phased out of barbering and in 1981, Quaker Boy Turkey Calls became a full-time enterprise. Dick knew he needed help—his first employee, Dave Strab, was a hunting companion who left behind the security of being a postmaster to become head of sales. Beverly Kirby, Dick's wife, gave up her beauty shop to become the financial officer. Without a willingness to accept prudent risk, the adventure would never have gone past barbershop banter.

Today, Quaker Boy Inc. employs over sixty people in two locations: a modern building in Orchard Park that includes the offices, showroom, and distribution center, and a woodworking plant in Bradford, Pennsylvania. With worldwide sales well into the millions, the company now offers a diversified line of game calls and videos, many of which are filmed on location featuring Dick Kirby in action. "Our success makes the statement that the opportunity is there if you work hard, are sensible and sincere, and have good help." And although he enjoys his lifestyle, Dick has never been driven by personal gain. "One day Beverly came back to the office with a surprising bit of news. The accountant had told her that by standard business valuations, we were millionaires. The possibility had never entered my mind."

When talking to Dick about his adventure, one gets the immediate impression that his True Wealth is the result of his generating value throughout his life. He sees his business as an extension of his family: "I wouldn't be able to do it without tremendous support from my family." In addition to his wife, his sons work in the business. Chris has captured the World Turkey Calling Championship. Scott produces the company's videos.

"Many of our employees are friends of our kids. As they've gotten married and started families of their own, I feel that the business takes on an added responsibility to make sure that our decisions are sound. I want to be able to do the things that are important, but I'm careful not to cut our employees short. You've got to be loyal to the people who you depend on because they depend on you."

A religious man, Dick sees the business as a blessing. "It wasn't me that brought this about. It was an opportunity that was just out there that I took hold of. God chose to bless our commitment—it has to be treated with care." He loves his community and serves as an informal ambassador of goodwill: "I travel a hundred thousand miles a year in fifteen to twenty states. I've made friends all over the country. And I'm always talking about Orchard Park as a great place to live and work."

Dick is also a driving force in several conservation groups, including the Rocky Mountain Elk Foundation. "My father always impressed upon me the responsibility to put back anything you take from nature and to maintain it." And what about the twin bogies of investing and retirement? "I don't plan on retiring—I retired in 1981. And all my investments are in the business."

After listening to Dick, I came away with the strong feeling that no matter what he was doing, he'd have a life that money can't buy. And only by generating value across the entire range of possibilities did he develop a business that all of the consultants in the world couldn't have dreamed up.

Is there a True Wealth adventure like Dick Kirby's in your future, or even right under your nose? You might be thinking, "Well, if I knew what it was, I'd be doing it." If money remains the basic currency of your life, you may never see the opportunities that surround you. After all, how many business consultants were touting the tremendous potential in turkey calls? But if you make value your basic currency, you'll see the world in a whole new light.

CHANGING YOUR CURRENCY
FROM MONEY TO VALUE

Changing the basic currency of your life isn't an overnight task. After all, you've probably been thinking in terms of money your entire life. But it also doesn't require a Herculean effort over a forty-eight-hour day. You simply have to be persistent and consistent. Here are some ways you can make the switch from money to value:

CHANGE YOUR LANGUAGE

The language we use to describe an activity has a strong relationship with how we perceive that activity. (If you don't believe me, consider the various ways that sex is referred to.) So if you want to make value the currency of your life, you have to think in terms of value, talk to yourself in terms of value, and use the concept of value whenever and wherever appropriate in your conversation with others.

The best place to begin is by using these three verbs: generate, exchange, and preserve.

Use *generate value* instead of: work, put in time, do something, hustle, slave, sweat, grind, knuckle down, get going, set about, tackle, get around to, fix, labor, earn, make, get paid, donate time, or spend some time.

When the alarm clock goes off, think, "It's time to go generate some value." Don't think, "I have to go to work."

When you think about that oft-delayed project, tell yourself that it's time to generate some value. Don't tell yourself that someday you'll get around to tackling it.

Look at the time you spend with your young children as an opportunity to generate value. Don't think that you "have to watch the kids."

Whatever you do, however mundane, try to phrase it in terms of generating value. Even doing the laundry generates value, as you might remind yourself when you're out of clean underwear.

Think *exchange value* instead of: spend, pay, fork over, cost, shell out, squander, splurge, sink money in, blow money on, go through, or charge.

Every financial transaction is an exchange of value. Whenever and however you spend money, describe the transaction to yourself. "I'm going to exchange some value for . . ." We're going to look at spending in detail in Chapter Eight, but just in thinking of exchanging value rather than spending money, you're putting yourself in a frame of mind that encourages a second thought and a rational assessment about what you're doing.

Think *preserve value* instead of: save, economize, scrimp, skimp, budget, manage, put something aside, curtail, cut back, retrench, sock away, save for a rainy day, build a nest egg, invest, do something with, take a flier on, get into or involved with, or put your money in.

Aren't saving and investing good things? They sure are. But *preserve* most accurately describes what we are trying to accomplish by setting value aside—usually in the convenient form of money—for the future. Many people see saving and investing as discrete events: "I've saved some money, and now I've got to find something to do with it." That "something" often turns out to be an ill-fated gamble that would never have been made if the word "preserve" had driven the decision.

Preserve encompasses the entire process of setting aside a dollar and doing something with it that ensures that its value will be intact and accessible when you need it in the future. If you were going on a twenty-mile hike, you'd not only need to set aside some water for the journey, you'd want to carry it in a solid vessel, not a leaky bucket. And you'd want to be able to get at it when you were thirsty. What good would the water be if it was "all tied up"?

Preserve also puts a positive slant on saving. We save a lot of things, including a lot of junk. Go look in your garage or attic. We preserve those things that are important, that we want to ensure will be a continuing and intact part of our lives: food, nature, and our heritage, for example. Preserve connotes positive desire—we preserve value for the future because we want to, not because we have to.

We'll continue to refer to saving and investing to describe respectively the specific acts of setting aside money and selecting a proper vehicle. But as they fall under the larger umbrella of preserving value, the more we think in terms of preserving, the easier it will be to preserve.

How do you put *generate, exchange,* and *preserve* at the top of your vocabulary list, so you don't have to dig for them? Through practice, through getting into the habit.

GET IN THE TRUE WEALTH STATE OF MIND

○ Repeat "generate, exchange, and preserve value" over and over a few times a day. Think of it as the True Wealth mantra. Whenever you have a few minutes to yourself, whether you're taking a shower, walking a few blocks, waiting for an elevator, or driving to work, use the time to remind yourself of the three verbs that can change your entire outlook on life. I've found it especially effective to repeat the words before I get out of bed.
○ Write "generate, exchange, and preserve" where you'll see them throughout the day. A few discreet Post-its on your bathroom mirror, desk, computer terminal, or refrigerator door will help jog

your memory. (But don't do this quite yet. In the next section, you'll learn how to make this even more effective.)

○ Tape a piece of paper with the word "exchange" inside your wallet near your credit cards and on the cover of your checkbook.

○ When you're faced with a financial challenge, problem, or stress symptom, frame the question in terms of value. Take another look at the examples starting on page 75. Here are a few more:

How can you generate more value in your work?

How can you provide for your children in terms of value?

How can your marriage best generate value for all?

How can you exchange money in a way that adds to rather than drains value from your life?

How can you preserve value in the way that is best for your future (not someone else's)?

How can you generate value to reduce the frenzy quotient in your life?

Now, admittedly some of these questions are "big" questions. But by asking them using terms of value, you're facing them with the full deck of solutions. And you can use the same approach for even the most specific and practical of matters, like lowering your utility bills.

Generate, exchange, preserve, generate, exchange, preserve . . . now it's your turn.

CHANGE YOUR MENTAL LENS TO THE VALUE CYCLE

The next step to making value your currency is to change the way you envision your life.

Most people visualize their lives in a linear framework—a string of days stretching from earliest memory into the unforeseeable future.

Using money as the basic currency of your life reinforces your conceptualization of life as a straight cruise through the calendar. How often do you think of your life in terms of pay periods? Yesterday you worked. Today you got paid. Now you can pay some bills, buy what you need, and then get to the fun part of money—spending the rest on what you want. If there's nothing left over, well, there's always next time. (With our low national savings rate, we seem to feel that while we don't have enough *time,* we've still got plenty of *next* time.) And tomorrow you go back to work.

When you see your life like the bouncing ball in a sing-along cartoon, hopping from one thing to the next, change is always on the next reel. The result: You stay on autopilot, making the same stress-perpetuating decisions over and over.

The true visual framework for making decisions that create True Wealth is circular:

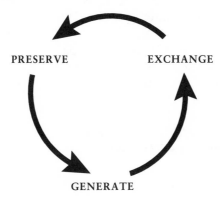

PRESERVE   EXCHANGE

GENERATE

This is the Value Cycle. You generate value. A part of that value you are able to exchange—in the form of money—for value in a different form. You set aside the value you don't immediately exchange for a future use. The value you preserve then adds to your actively generated value. (Retirement is simply having enough value preserved so you can cut back on your active generation.)

Each aspect of the Value Cycle is vital to your True Wealth. You cannot ignore, overemphasize, or misjudge one aspect without the risk of throwing the entire cycle out of equilibrium and creating financial stress. For example, if you make stress-creating decisions about generating value, it will be difficult to exchange your way out of your quandary.

Just as in the case of the water cycle, value is continually flowing throughout your life. Water doesn't fall to the Earth on Friday, run through a river on Saturday, and get back into the clouds on Sunday in time to rain on Monday. And your financial decisions are not sequential—you don't hop along from one area of your life to the next.

You are making decisions simultaneously throughout the Value Cycle. Each minute involves a value-generating decision. You may write a check for your rent or mortgage once a month, but that's strictly for convenience—you're exchanging money for shelter every day. Your investments are in place around the clock, seven days a week. There are no clearly defined points where one activity ends and the next one begins.

Because each aspect of your financial life is continually in motion, there is no difference between today and tomorrow. What you do today *is* the reality of your tomorrow. This is a critical concept, because if you see your life in a straight line, the effects of change are always somewhere down the road.

But if you understand that whatever decisions you make today immediately change the context for the decisions that follow, then the motivation increases to make what may seem to be the "harder" decisions—decisions that will ultimately make your life easier.

The Value Cycle should be the lens through which you view your financial life. And just as with a contact lens, all you have to do is get used to "wearing" it.

IDENTIFY YOUR VALUE-GENERATED ACCOMPLISHMENTS TO DATE

Generating value isn't new for you—you're not going to be starting from scratch. If you look at generating value as if it were painting, you already have many of the basic techniques. All you'll need to do is enhance the picture on your canvas. So before you go any further, it will be helpful to look at your life to date in terms of value.

Write down the accomplishments in your life that have given you great satisfaction. Don't limit yourself to what you might put on a résumé. Don't confine yourself to awards, titles, or anything else that is commonly used as a marker of success. Forget what anyone else might think or how it may or may not impress anyone.

Include anything on the list that you think belongs there, whether it's your equivalent of a turkey call or Civil War map, your marriage or your children, or the fact that you've never missed a day of work. All that counts is that the list includes those things that you'd give yourself an A for. When you've compiled your list, narrow it down one by one until you're left with your top five. Don't fret over this too much—it's an exercise, not an epitaph.

For each accomplishment, trace to the best of your ability how it came to be, taking into account the time and energy spent and the resources used. In the case of an accomplishment that developed over years, focus on the key or pivotal actions that kept your value generation on track. For example, let's say that you led the effort to turn a vacant corner lot into a neighborhood playground. It's unlikely that you bought the land and the equipment. So what was the process from weed patch to jungle gym?

After you've reflected on your life to date, you're not going to have to tell yourself, "I think I can." You *know* you can generate value. Now let's look at *how*.

4

What You Really Want Is What You Really Need

AS COMEDIAN Steven Wright has observed, "You can't have everything. Where would you put it?" But that hasn't stopped many of us from wanting to have a good-sized chunk of everything—or at least creating the impression that we do.

The truth is that just about no matter who you are, if you're alive today, you've probably gotta lotta wants. Your wants can:

Involve the biggest issues in life—I want my children to be safe. Or be downright inconsequential—I want the zit on my nose to disappear before my presentation on Friday.

Be constant—I want a house; or fleeting—I want ranch dressing with my salad.

Be impulsive—I want to have this cool computer gadget right now; or foot-dragging—I know I really should want a carbon monoxide detector enough to actually get one.

Where do all of these wants come from? Start with the fact that on an average day you're bombarded with no fewer than 16,000 advertising images. (Just think how a squirrel might react if he saw that many nuts on a given day.) The door to every store, the cover of every catalog or magazine, and every click to a new channel or Web site is like the lid to a Pandora's box of wants.

Now add access. Just about everything you see or hear about can be shipped right to your doorstep—often within twenty-four hours. The only item you can't get when you want it is a hot toy at Christmastime. Top it all off with ready credit—anything you want is just a plastic slap away.

When you gather all of your wants together, they form a massive, shifting, almost incomprehensible 3-D jigsaw puzzle in which you struggle to assemble order and meaning. If only you had the ideal combination of wants and could fulfill them, boy, then life would be perfect. But when you start working on the puzzle there are far more pieces than could ever fit in any sensible picture. Just cataloging your wants could be a full-time job, let alone sorting them out and acting on them.

We want to do things—often three things when there's room for only one: play golf, play with the kids, travel the world, vibrate in a recliner, be a concerned citizen, wall out the bums, open a restaurant, have a lifetime job, live like the rich, live in a monastery, work out, eat a bag of Oreos, learn a second language, learn to program the VCR to record one show while we're watching another.

We want to be things—a different person for different situations. One result of media overload is that individuals who are at the top of their field become so familiar that we start to believe that with a few of the right steps, we can be right in their shoes. We don't just want to have a few friends over; we want to entertain like Martha Stewart. We don't just want to be sports fans; we want to be surrogate assistant coaches while we pace the family room sidelines barking out the plays. We don't just want to be adults making responsible common-sense decisions; we want to synthesize everything from the wisdom of kindergartners to the vision of angels. And when the lights are low, we don't just want to be ourselves; we want to be some mutation (hopefully not a combination) of Fabio or Cindy Crawford.

We want to have things. To get a feel for just how many wants you have, let's take a look at just one small corner of your life: your sock drawer. Socks would seem to be a mundane and utilitarian part of life—something that keeps your feet warm and comfy and your sneakers from turning into swamps. You might even think, "I don't want socks. I don't even think about socks. I've got the sock situation under control."

But open your drawer and what do you find: dress socks, athletic socks, summer socks, winter socks, white socks, match-an-outfit socks, wacky socks, cashmere socks, and tube socks. Even when you factor out the socks Aunt Edna sends you for your birthday, your sock wants are actually pretty substantial. And we're just talking about socks.

Combine all of your current wants and you might find that they stretch far beyond what you'll be able to fulfill in your lifetime.

WHY DON'T OUR WANTS ADD UP TO THE LIFE WE WANT?

As someone who has wants just like everyone else, I've found that putting a rein on your wants in a way that doesn't make you completely uptight—to walk out of a store empty-handed, for example, and not feel as if you've won a do-or-die struggle—is a real key to conquering financial stress.

But how do you organize and prioritize all of your wants? You probably just scoop them all up and dump them into your Buck-O-Matic. It grinds away, sifting through all of your wants and then—kerblunk!—out they come! You're making decisions and taking action. What could work better? After all, the wants we act on must be the most important ones. Right? We must really think that a new set of pit furniture is a higher priority than money in the bank. So what's the problem?

The problem is that the wants you act on don't quite add up to the life you really want. You make some good decisions that generate value. You've got the paycheck to prove it. You make some seemingly minor decisions that over time can turn into a wall of stress. And you make some pretty stupid decisions. Sooner or later, almost everyone has a boat for sale on their front lawn, figuratively speaking.

When it comes to prioritizing and acting on our wants, we're pretty much on our own most of the time. We've got to get very close to the edge, if not a few yards past it, for someone to take us aside and tell us to "shape up"—the vernacular for "you'd better get your priorities straight." Even then there are way too many people who will write us up a ready excuse for anything from being late for work to first-degree murder.

But even when by all accounts you're doing all the right things—got the job, got the house, got the cars, got the kids, got the CD-ROM for the kids—you still might feel that there's not enough value in your life. More to the point, there's not enough value that *you* value. You may be generating enough value to take care of some of your wants, but all of the time you're chasing after your wants, you're overlooking something far more important: your needs.

IF YOU WANT IT, DO YOU NEED IT?

What is a need? According to *Webster's,* a need is a lack of something requisite. It is something we cannot do without.

What we need is often confused with what we want or is used interchangeably. And the dictionary even lists "need" and "want" as synonyms. But there is a subtle and important distinction between wants and needs.

Needs are internal in origin—they emanate from the core of your being to meet the demands of existence. They are a basic requirement for your well-being. You don't have to think about needs too hard—if at all. They're simply there. Which may be why they sometimes can be ignored, overlooked, or taken for granted.

Wants are external in origin—a response to an image or an idea. If you didn't know that whatever it is you want existed in the first place, you'd have no way of wanting it. Or thinking that you need it.

Let's take a look at the difference between needs and wants by looking at some of the basics of life:

You *need* food. You *want* a Mexican combo platter.
You *need* clothing. You *want* a DKNY suit.
You *need* shelter. You *want* bedrooms and bathrooms for all.
You *need* transportation. You *want* a little red wedge of a sports car.

Admittedly, the precise dividing line between needs and wants isn't always clear. But the broader difference between the two is clear.

A need is something that has to be fulfilled or you're up the creek, hurtin' for certain. As for a want? It's something that would be kind of nice to have, but even without it, life could go on pretty smoothly. Your body, for example, has a real physical need for water. It doesn't care if your drink has a natural loganberry flavor or not. But if you don't drink enough water—H_2O—before long you'll have serious physical stress and your very own expiration date.

Just as we have physical needs, we also have financial needs—needs that must be fulfilled if we are to avoid financial stress. If we don't make fulfilling our needs a part of our day-to-day lives, we will have financial stress. The trick, of course, is to know what our financial needs are.

Just as the financialization of stress has narrowed our perception of possible solutions to a single one—money—so has it limited our perception of our real needs. We've reduced them to neat little targets. So what do we perceive as our major financial needs? The answer lies in what people think they need money for.

When working adults are surveyed for their goals in life, the top three responses are inevitably "to have a nest egg for retirement," "to send my kids to good colleges," and "to buy a bigger house." Each of these goals is, at its core, financial—denominated in dollars and cents. But even if you reach each of the big three goals, things can go awry.

I'd like to illustrate just what I mean by looking at one of the biggest stress-boosting words today: retirement.

Indisputably it is desirable to have enough savings to cover your basic needs when you're no longer able to work. Let's say you want to retire at age sixty-two with 80 percent of your current income. So you sweat and slave for decades, scrimping and saving along the way, making all the right investments, maybe hanging on to an unsatisfying job just to get all of the benefits. But it's all going to be worth it when you get to the theme park called Retirement World at the end of the long gray road through the prime of life.

Finally the big day comes: the Monday morning when you have no alarm, no boss, no customers, no job, no nothing except the day stretching ahead of you. So once you've rolled out of bed and checked all of your financial statements, then what happens? What good is a hefty retirement account if you're going to spend your golden years grumping at your spouse and watching *The Newlywed Game* in between trips to the medicine cabinet and the Chomp Elysses Super Buffet in a nearby strip mall? The day-to-day reality of a comfortable retirement certainly includes money—but it also includes health, satisfying relationships with family and friends, and activities you just can't wait to get to.

Now you might think, "Yeah, yeah, yeah. Give me the money and I'll worry about the rest later." I'm willing to wager that someone out there worrying about retirement is on his thirty-first cigarette of the day, talks to his kids only on the car phone, and thinks that he's going to be satisfied lying in the sun all day. But reality is stronger than any presumption. Let's look at the retirement years of Harvey and Bud—real-life men of similar means whose final years were as different as can be.

Harvey worked for the railroad. When he wasn't at work, he was stockpiling every cent he could get his hands on—going to extraordinary effort to get a refund for a quarter lost in a vending machine, applying every bit of available leverage to the tenants in his rental property, filing marginal claims for workmen's compensation. As the years went by, Harvey's net worth soared well into six figures—and his circle of friends and family dwindled. Six months into an empty retirement, he was diagnosed with cancer. Living alone, Harvey found that his biggest concern was that he had no one in his life he wanted to leave his money to. From his deathbed he had to beg his ex-wife and children to visit him one last time.

By contrast, Bud worked in a printing plant. When he wasn't at work, he was busy with an ever-increasing circle of friends: dogs and their owners. Known as "the Dog Man," he had the rare gift of communicating with both man and canine—whether a neighborhood pet or a championship pedigree—with equal skill. In retirement his dogs and his grandchildren kept him busy. His modest means were of little concern. His son had to "trick" him into a car deal in order to replace his worn-out station wagon. He passed away surrounded by his wife, children, and grandchildren. Next to his obituary there was a photograph that captured his essence: a man with a big smile, wearing a hat covered with commemorative pins from dog shows around the country.

As dramatic as the contrast between the two might be, there is hardly any adult who can't identify a Harvey and a Bud in her own life. What is the crucial difference between the two? In retirement, Bud's life was the fruit of all the value he had generated throughout the years to fulfill his needs. Harvey's harvest was a pile of cold, disinterested cash.

Bud knew what had to occur in his daily life to have True Wealth.

THE SECOND COMPONENT OF TRUE WEALTH: HAVE A CLEAR PICTURE OF YOUR H2OS

Your H2Os are those things that Have "2" Occur in your everyday life if you are going to live free from financial stress.

In order to live today, right now, in the moment, without financial stress, you first have to know what *you* need to be a part of your daily experience—from adequate shelter to the joy of work, from close family ties to the freedom to explore an intriguing aspect of the world—in order to have a life that money can't buy. Because unless you understand what has to occur in your life, your odds of generating True Wealth will be entirely random, approaching nil.

People with True Wealth not only have a clear picture of their H2Os, but are able to see them within the context of day-to-day reality, not fantasy or presumption. In a sense, life is like a Georges Seurat painting. (If you slept through art history, he's the French painter who used little dots of color to depict *Summer Sunday on the Grande Jatte*.) It's the hours and minutes—not the broad stroke of a single event—that create the big picture.

Your H2Os are your true, essential needs. You must determine just what it is you really need to *experience* on an ongoing basis. And if each day or week, you aren't putting enough dots—value-generating action—on your canvas that are a direct reflection of your H2Os—your real financial needs—the picture is going to include a lot of financial stress.

In the last chapter, we set forth how value is generated:

$$\text{Value} = \text{Time} \times \text{Energy} \times \text{Resources}$$

But even though we may be taking lots of action and even generating loads of value—in the form of anything from a six-figure salary to a perfect tan—there's still no guarantee that the value we generate is of real solid worth to us unless it matches our H2Os.

How much of the value that you generate is a direct response to your real needs of value? That's a critical question because you might be running around like an espresso-guzzling chicken yet be steering clear of generating value that fulfills your financial needs—your H2Os.

So now we're going to add another part to the value-generating equation that gives us more control over the outcome, that will help to ensure that the value we generate is of value to us:

$$\text{True Wealth} = [\text{Time} \times \text{Energy} \times \text{Resources}] \rightarrow \text{H2Os}$$

True Wealth is generated by converting your time, energy, and resources into those things that have to occur in your life if you are to live free from financial stress. In other words, by weaving that which you hold dearest in your heart and mind into the fabric of your everyday life.

Where do we begin to look for our H2Os? In this simple line of reasoning: If money is the basic currency of your life, then it only makes sense that you see your financial needs as being strictly a money matter. You either need more money or, if you're a New Frugalist, you need to need less. But, *if value is the basic currency of your life, your real "financial" needs are needs of value.*

Let's then investigate the concept of value—and how it can address our H2Os across the board.

THE EIGHT TYPES OF VALUE

So far we've looked at value as a homogeneous concept. But just as with a stream of light—if we were able to look at value with a special spectrograph—we'd see eight distinct bands, or types, of value. When viewed by the naked eye, these bands blend to form the content and character of your life.

Your life begins in a universe beyond your singular and immediate comprehension. *Spiritual value* is the value you generate in your quest for an understanding of life beyond your immediate plane of existence in seeking divine guidance for living on earth.

You are handed the ultimate responsibility as the developer and caretaker of a living entity: yourself. *Personal value* is your value as an individual to both yourself and others. You carry your personal value with you throughout the day, no matter where you are, no matter what the situation.

The core unit of our civilization is the family: parents, siblings, spouses, children, and those whom we adopt as family. *Family value* is the value you generate within your primary relationships—most notably through marriage and the raising of children, the next generation.

You live your daily life and raise your family in a community. *Community value* is generated by your participation in the weaving, reinforcing, and even repairing of the fabric of society—whether it's on the street where you live or on the other side of the globe.

You live in an astonishing world, which offers an infinite array of opportunities to engage your intellect, raise your passion, and inspire you to action: science and technology, the arts and literature, the study of history or the shaping of the future, being of service to others or competing in athletics, the solitary pursuit of a craft or the interactions of commerce. *Horizon value* is the value you generate in your life by absorbing various aspects of our world through learning and experience. Through expanding your own horizons, you increase your ability.

You use at least some portion of your ability to provide for yourself and your family. *Work value* is the value you generate through your means of paid employment, whatever activity you pursue that connects you to the economy.

Two more types of value complete the spectrum: practical value and preserved value.

You use the money you earn as a means to assist you in meeting the practical needs of everyday living: food, clothing, shelter, transportation, and so on. *Practical value* is the value you generate by exchanging your money in a way that both fulfills these needs and provides the tools to generate additional value.

Not all of our living needs are immediate or even known to us at present. *Preserved value* is the value you generate by saving a portion of your income and investing it in such a way that, when you need it, you'll have it.

We've noted that one of the causes of stress is a loss of equilibrium—when one area of your life is so off-kilter that your entire life is out of whack. These eight bands of value are the areas among which we want to create relative balance. Now that they have been introduced, we're going to set aside the concepts of exchanging and preserving value for a few chapters to concentrate on generating value. How you generate value plays a defining role in how you deal with money once it reaches your hands.

HOW DOES GENERATING VALUE RELATE TO OUR H2Os?

Why do the different types of value exist? Because each type of value addresses at least several basic H2Os—things we need to occur in our lives. Identifying these potential H2Os not only helps us grasp what might encompass the big picture of our lives, but also points the way toward the specific actions and experiences that will best reflect our individual needs.

So let's take a closer look at the six types of value that we can generate, the specific H2Os they can address, and their relationship to True Wealth.

SPIRITUAL VALUE

As I've interviewed people with True Wealth, the overwhelming majority have identified—without prompting—their strong faith as the most important reason for their lack of financial stress. "It all begins with the Creator" summarizes the beliefs of many. Jonas Gadson adds, "If you put God first in your life, you'll never come in second."

I think there's a simple explanation for this. A strong spiritual presence in your daily life makes possible the following:

H2O #1: *Having an understanding of life that extends beyond the immediate here-and-now material world.* The less your existence is pinned to what you can wrap your hands around—what you *own*—the less your potential for financial stress. That is only logical.

H2O #2: *Having a code of moral conduct that serves you well in life.* We're generally smart enough to realize that by the time we could invent a code of moral conduct via our own experience, we might not have a whole lot of time left on the shot clock. So we look to principles that have been handed down through the ages and that have been tested by generations. Simply following the Ten Commandments or the Golden Rule, for example, will steer you clear of a whole lot of potential financial stress.

Spiritual faith was not a part of my life until recent years. Quite frankly, I've always been turned off by the entire idea of converting to anything—even more so by the in-your-face zealotry of some of those who've made the switch to a new and improved, zestier brand of enlightenment.

I'm more comfortable with the process of "becoming" something: discovering your own private path over time, even if it turns out to be right down the middle of a well-traveled highway. For me to say "Here's the way" would be presumptuous from my vantage point and useless from yours. The wealth of printed words hardly needs my two cents.

I know Jews, Muslims, Catholics, Protestants, Mormons, Buddhists, and Hindus, all of whom have a strong belief in their respective faiths. I also know people of no formal faith who consciously cultivate a spiritual presence in their lives to great effect. To say that only one group has it right and the rest are barking up the wrong tree is to deny the validity of something really powerful in the lives of others. While some people have no problem making that call, it isn't going to be me.

I once worked with an earnest young fellow who carried his Bible wherever he went. A purported Christian, he had written in the inside cover all the reasons why his particular denomination had an exclusive pass to the hereafter. All other denominations were barred by a logic that went along the lines of: "We believe this is what the Bible says. They believe something else. They're going to Hell. We're not." This kind of spiritual one-upmanship helps give religion a bad rap.

I'm not advocating that moral standards are all relative or that there is no dividing line between right and wrong. As a society, we've done a good job of proving the perils of believing such. But we'd all be better off if religious groups quit jockeying for position with each other and focused more on advancing the value of the common principles of faith toward public discourse.

I recognize that some readers may bristle at the notion that spiritual value has anything to do with fighting financial stress. But consider this: A six-cylinder engine may still chug along if one piston is out. But the remaining five cylinders will have to be well maintained or the whole generator might blow out when it has to climb a mountain. Spiritual faith can sustain you through the most difficult of times in ways that a big bank account or a case of pop philosophy never can.

In his book *Growing in Faith,* David Yount answers in part the question "Why believe?": "We all want to be faithful—to ourselves and to others. . . . Faith also offers us perspective, a place to stand and view with calm purpose and some understanding of what appears to be a bewildering and often tragic universe."

That "place to stand" is the most valuable spot of real estate on Earth. It's also yours to occupy—no money down.

PERSONAL VALUE

If you take into account the value of all the minerals and compounds that make up your body, you're worth less than a buck. If you add whatever you have in your wallet, hopefully it's a little more than that. Yet there's no doubt that we carry with us wherever we go, into any and every situation, a value as individuals that is important not only to ourselves, but to others as well. Personal value can generate the following:

H2O #3: *Being of sound character—having the judgment to know right from wrong and the resolve to make decisions accordingly.* Each of us has our own ethical compass to guide us through daily life. Some of us have compasses that are unfailingly clear and accurate. Others have compasses that can be manipulated to suit the moment.

While words like honesty and integrity are bandied about in the business world—right along with "total customer satisfaction" and "lowest prices in town"—to the point where they have little impact, the failure to make ethically sound decisions can lead you right to financial stress. And not just through premeditated scams.

A study published in the February 1996 *Journal of Business Ethics* found that nearly half of top executives and over three quarters of graduate-level business students were willing to use fraudulent numbers to overstate their company's profits—a criminal offense. Remember Stress Symptom #5: You're leaving the back door open to financial disaster, and deep down you know it? Try carrying the phrase "possible felony indictment" around in the back of your mind and see how relaxed you are. And we haven't even mentioned "attorney fees."

H2O #4: *Being in good health.* Your physical well-being—your health—is with you around the clock. You cannot be in two different states of health at once except on a day when you call in sick with a raging sore throat that mysteriously disappears at 9:05 A.M. (ah, but you've never done that).

That ongoing good health is valuable should go without saying. If you lose your health, it can cost you every last cent. And you have the opportunity to generate health every day.

H2O #5: *Maintaining a good appearance.* Physical appearance is a form of value that plays a significant role in our interaction with others in all areas of life—not just the mating game. We're often judged by our appearance—the proverbial first impression—long before we get a chance to demonstrate any other type of value, if we get a chance at all. You can go way overboard dressing for success, but try walking into a job interview in an old pair of sweats and unwashed hair and see if you get asked to stick around for the aptitude test.

Some people devote almost their entire time, energy, and resources toward this one aspect of value—whether it be abs of steel or suburban couture. Others choose to ignore it totally and force the world to try to look past their ill grooming. Either stance is counterproductive.

As much as some of the P.C. thought police protest the notion of "lookism," there are two truths: (1) It is human nature to react to someone else's appearance, and (2) a pretty wide "neutral zone" of acceptable appearance exists that won't cover up and hide the rest of your value.

H2O #6: *Interacting positively with the people around us—conducting ourselves in such a way that we can be net contributors in any and every situation.* We have the chance to generate value in our interaction with others wherever we go, in whatever situation we face. Some individuals are best described as loads—they can suck the collective goodwill out of any gathering of two or more people. And there are others who by their interpersonal skills are able to elevate themselves and those around them.

When I began work on this book, the concept of "emotional intelligence," as advanced by Daniel Goleman in his book of the same title, hadn't yet entered our collective vocabulary. But all the while I thought that there had to be a way to describe people who enhance almost any situation—from a business meeting to a block party.

Goleman includes in his definition of emotional intelligence such traits as rapport, empathy, cooperation, persuasion, self-control, self-motivation, self-resolve, personal responsibility, and the ability to build consensus and express one's thoughts and feelings in a clear and appropriate manner. I'd throw having good manners in there too. Combined, these traits enable us to generate a personal value to ourselves and to the people with whom we come into contact.

A few words about the current worship of self-esteem as it relates to personal value. It is certainly of value to you to feel good about yourself and your life. It is through our decisions and actions that we generate value and ultimately determine how we feel about ourselves—not through fraudulent or delusional self-congratulation.

I have yet to meet someone with True Wealth who didn't possess a healthy amount of the coveted self-esteem—without ever having thought about it.

FAMILY VALUE

Family value represents the things in life that can best—or only—be generated by a family—not a government, school, church, or village. The word "value" is singular and an altogether different item than the "family values" grab bag that every other political, social, and religious group is trying to stuff full of its own agenda.

It could be reasonably argued that all value while we're on Earth begins and ends within the family. The nature of a person's upbringing in her formative years can smooth her transition into independent and responsible adulthood or lay down a rocky road. When we're raising our children, the value we generate will enrich our lives and the lives of others in a way that all of the money in the world cannot. And when we're lying on our deathbeds, we're not going to be wondering why our boss hasn't come by to visit us.

Family value addresses the following:

H2O #7: *Being an integral part of a close-knit circle of family and friends.* How valuable is it that we have people in our lives who will encourage us when we need to be encouraged, caution or restrain us when caution or restraint are warranted, care for us when we need to be cared for, and keep company with us when companionship is desired? Ideally, family and friends not only fill all of these roles in our lives, but also provide the enjoyment of shared experience over decades—keeping our past a part of the present.

Included within family value is the value generated by close friendships and partnerships that have the depth and strength to last a lifetime. Beyond our circle of social and business friends—the people we like to hang out with—there are those individuals with whom we form a bond that has the character of a family tie. Whether or not we live under the same roof, it takes a cold and stubborn heart to deny that these friends and lifelong partners are indeed family.

How does a close family keep financial stress at bay? Family crises often come with a significant financial burden, which can be all the more exacerbated by strained, withered, superficial, or dishonest family relationships. Not only do the ties have to be suddenly and forcibly rebuilt, but they are immediately subjected to a game of financial hot potato, i.e., who should shoulder the load. It's bad enough if you haven't talked to your brother or sister in a year. It's going to be much worse if you're suddenly thrust into making decisions on how to deal with aging parents.

H2O #8: *Having a strong and lasting marriage.* Divorce and single parenthood are among the greatest causes of serious long-term financial stress today. The fundamental reasons: It takes more money to run two households than one, and it is less costly for a couple to run a household than for a single person to do so. Then add the cost of the pathologies that are the frequent result of a broken home.

Divorce and single parenthood virtually guarantee financial stress—along with a whole lot of other misfortune. Yet our divorce and illegitimacy rates indicate that too many people would rather pay the price than generate the necessary value to maintain a strong and lasting marriage. That might be fine, if those directly involved never asked for help in bailing themselves out of their financial fix and if there were not kids involved. But they do and there are. Which is why the value generated within marriage will be increasingly emphasized in public debate as a primary long-term solution to our societal ills.

H2O #9: *Raising your children to become self-sufficient and happy adults.*

When I talk with other parents about financial stress, inevitably the topic of college education comes up. Often there's an underlying tone implying that all of childhood is a dress rehearsal for the big show. If the parents can't buy a ticket, the misfortunate child will be stuck sweeping up after others for the rest of his or her life. So I ask this question: What traits do you want your child to have upon reaching adulthood?

I begin with John Rosemond's "3R"s: resourceful, respectful, and responsible. Parents quickly add to these qualities at least some of the following: joyful, independent, thankful, well-mannered, happy, adventurous, optimistic, healthy, honest, a good citizen, moral, competent, confident, well-adjusted, tolerant, enthusiastic, open-minded, compassionate, sociable, even-tempered, persistent, consistent, inquisitive, cultured, well-rounded, reaching full potential, and having developed strong skills.

So here's the question: Given that children will have spent only 10 percent of their lives in school by the time they reach the age of eighteen, who has the greatest opportunity to instill in them the qualities we most desire? *Parents.* Even when you get down to the last few qualities in the previous paragraph, those usually associated with education, the ultimate responsibility rests with the parents, not the school.

While we're driven to distraction over the costs of sending Jason and Jennifer to college, we're ignoring a fundamental reality: By the time we box them up and send them off to college, their cake (i.e., the kind of person they are) has already been baked. College is merely a little frosting. No matter what his grades or test scores, if you raise a self-absorbed chameleon who's willing to cheat to get ahead or is distrustful of personal relationships because his parents have failed miserably at theirs, there's not a college in the world that will open the doors that really need to be opened for him to be a happy adult.

Children learn from their parents in two ways: (1) through positive experience and example, and (2) through negative experience and example, i.e., parents do things so poorly that their children vow never to make the same mistake(s). The second way, of course, is miserable and heartbreaking. But you do have over 6,500 days until your child turns eighteen to generate value in such a way that he or she enters adulthood fully prepared.

COMMUNITY VALUE

Community value is your contribution—in whatever way you choose—toward making the world a better place to live.

Community value has its roots in your own backyard or hallway: being a good neighbor. It can range from patrolling your neighborhood to serving as mentor for a disadvantaged child, from picking up rubbish along a highway to collecting clothing for the needy.

Your community extends beyond your town or city. Whether inside the Beltway or on the other side of the equator, events around the world play a huge role in our lives and are certainly worthy of our time and energy beyond pulling the occasional voting lever after digesting a few spoon-fed sound bites. Think of the value that would be generated if every person who was concerned about the future of Social Security—the congressional "third rail"—spoke out against the fear-mongering tactics of pandering politicians.

Generating community value addresses the following:

H2O #10: *Living in a community that maintains and enhances rather than impedes or destroys the overall quality of the lives of its citizens.*

This is a need our society has tried to address more and more with money, government, and laws—to lesser and lesser effect. And what kind of financial stress have we suffered in return? Declining neighborhoods with plummeting real estate values. Public schools that in many cities almost necessitate the cost of a private education. Unsafe streets that push families to higher-cost suburban housing. A welfare system that has multiplied rather than reduced the underclass.

For a while our combined response was to write a bigger check and move further away from the problems—if they didn't go away, at least they'd be out of sight. But as we're running out of money and room to move, generating community value stands as one of our foremost challenges heading into the next century.

The ideal community is one that doesn't try to ensure that everyone is equally (or unequally) happy, but rather tries to ensure that each individual has the basic tools and the freedom to make herself happy. We all can generate value toward that end.

Caveat: All too often people confuse generating community value with generating social status or connections. Their biggest time commitment might be shopping for the right outfit to wear to a fund-raiser, or their grandest effort might be reserved for distribution of their business card. These "networkers" might be better described as *nyet*workers. Generating community value is certainly a great way to meet other people. But it's getting the job done that generates the value.

HORIZON VALUE

From the moment our parents tried to teach us how to hold a rattle and point to the doggie in the picture book, we've been adding to our abilities. Our challenge is to increase and manage our abilities in a way that generates optimal value in our lives in and out of the workplace.

What aspects of the great big world do we want to make our own, to become a part of us? Early on in life, the answers are easy: We need to be able to read, write, count, play soccer, dress Barbie, and make a water balloon.

The older we get, the more choices we face. And the more there seems to be a distinct fork in the road between the abilities that enable us to make a living and the abilities that we develop to enjoy life.

Do we add to our ability to mountain bike or devise a marketing plan? Do we learn how to make a wreath out of macaroni and seashells or drive a big rig? The answer is: Why not both?

We take some portion and combination of our abilities and in some way use them to provide for ourselves and our family. But as the boxer Leon Spinks noted in one of his more philosophical moments, "Life's a funny thing."

You cannot identify with any certainty exactly what abilities will be moneymakers and which ones won't. The best-laid career plans can go for naught. Something done on a whim can become a lifelong vocation. Someone somewhere is making a living from making wreaths.

The key point is this: You never know in what ways you'll be able to make use of what you know or what experiences you'll be glad you can draw on in the future. *Anything you can think of is someone's livelihood.*

Beyond the general unpredictability of life, there's something wrong about separating ability into two boxes: that which we can use to make a living and that which we can't. It has created the widespread belief that the only reason to increase our ability is to better navigate the job market. Although that is certainly important, the overriding reason to increase your ability is that it enables you to live life to the fullest—to create your own collage from everything the world has to offer.

Ability is your most valuable resource, far more so than money. And as such, it makes immanent sense that you be continually increasing your ability however you can in whatever way you can, in and out of work, even without the prospect of imminent financial payoff. People with True Wealth are invariably continual learners, seeing each day as a classroom, each situation and person they encounter as a potential teacher. To them, learning is an approach to life.

In generating horizon value, we can fulfill the following:

H2O #11: *Using our innate talents.* We're all born with certain talents that give us a jump start and supply an unlimited reserve of energy whenever these talents are applied.

It is one of life's greatest gifts to discover our talents and use them on a daily basis. And the failure to open this gift and use it can create lifelong stress—you know there's something missing in your life, and it's right under your nose. I believe that far more envy and jealousy—often well-camouflaged—is directed toward people who have tapped into their innate talents than is supposedly directed toward those with monetary wealth.

H2O #12: *Developing a breadth of ability: to have a broad range of knowledge, skills, and experience.* Consider the term "well-rounded." If we think of the big wide world in relation to ourselves, being well-rounded can imply that we have absorbed enough of all the various aspects of the world to be able to roll through life unimpeded by basic ignorance.

"To be culturally literate," explained E. D. Hirsch, Jr., in the book *Cultural Literacy: What Every American Needs to Know,* "is to possess the basic information needed to thrive in the modern world." In addition to knowledge, we need to have a range of skills, whether balancing a checkbook, changing a diaper, or sending a fax. And we need to have a range of experience, whether it be traveling alone to an unfamiliar city, sampling a foreign cuisine, or hearing Beethoven's Ninth.

A broad mix of knowledge, skills, and experience gives us the flexibility not only to deal with the demands of day-to-day life, but also to access opportunity and discover those adventures that await us. And the more we know, the more we've experienced, and the more developed our skills, the greater the chance that we will discover our innate talents.

H2O #13: *Developing a depth of ability: to have the knowledge, skills, and experience needed to excel in a specific area or areas.* We need to be really good at something—and hopefully at more than one thing. And we need to be way better than average for more than economic reasons.

There is a rich quality of experience when you are really good at something that cannot be had in any other way. You get closer to the essence of endeavor, appreciate the nuances, and are able to revel in the intensity in ways that others can't. And, as you illuminate yourself, others will be drawn toward your light.

H2O #14: *Participating in an activity that we love.* There are some activities we just love to do. We're happy when we're doing them, and nuts to all who dare to criticize. It doesn't even matter if we might flat-out stink at them. So what if you've never shot below one hundred, your poetry is leaden, or your home inventions never work? More likely, though, you'll get pretty good at something you love to do, even to the point of marketability, if you do it long enough.

Nor does it matter that your passionate pursuit seems obscure or even trivial to some. There are countless people who have focused on one itty-bitty aspect of the big wide world and turned it into something significant in their lives and the lives of others. To put it another way: There's an unlimited number of turkey calls out there.

As singer Billy Joel has remarked: "If you aren't doing what you love, you're wasting your time." If you aren't doing something that you love, you risk ending up feeling that your life is being wasted.

H2O #15: *Developing options in life.* This need is a synthesis of how we address the preceding four needs. But having options in life is crucial to believing that you are in control of your life. So it cannot be overemphasized: The more you use your innate talent, the broader you develop your abilities, the more areas in which you excel, the more you do the things you love, the more options you will have in life.

WORK VALUE

Work is the most direct and visible means of income—you work, you get paid: sometimes according to a straight mathematical formula (hours × wage); other times only after a long and winding route through the marketplace, as in the case of an entrepreneur.

Work plays the primary role in enabling us to provide for ourselves and our loved ones and to live a comfortable life. In and of itself, that is a tremendous amount of value. But work is more than that. In addition to putting food on the table and a roof over our heads, work provides one of our most powerful means of development, self-expression, and gratification. And it's not just *what* we do that generates value, but *how* we do it.

What's often lost in today's economy is the entire notion of craftsmanship: performing a task—any task—with care, skill, and ingenuity. We admire—even envy—an artisan like a glassblower or silversmith without ever realizing that we can approach our work with the same spirit to great ends.

The spirit of craftsmanship is lost in the shuffle of making it through the day with your butt covered and finding the right vehicle to hitch your star to. We must work to get paid. But if we work with the spirit of a craftsman, we will be paid well beyond the numbers on the check—and meet a greater number of our needs.

In generating work value, we can fulfill the following:

H2O #16: *Providing ourselves and our family with the basic necessities of life and a reasonable level of comfort.* If your roof leaks buckets, the heat is shut off for nonpayment, the refrigerator is empty, your children's clothes are ragged, or your car breaks down every tenth mile, your financial stress will be a tight perimeter around your life.

H2O #17: *Enjoying our work.* Given that we have to work and that work demands a fair portion of our waking hours, it's almost implicit that we have a need to enjoy what we do. After all, it is difficult at the least to build a stress-free life around eight or more hours of being miserable.

To deny or ignore this need, as all too many do, is to cast yourself adrift in a Bermuda Triangle of financial stress: Gotta work, wouldn't do this job if I didn't have to, hate my job because I have to. To fulfill the need of enjoying your work is to have taken a huge step toward a financially stress-free life. Why write off such a big chunk of time without even a solid fight—looking for ways to enjoy work rather than counting the reasons to despair of it?

Here's added incentive to finding ways to enjoy our work. If you don't consciously try to enjoy your work, you'll never be able to love your work. And loving your work—what you do day-in, day-out to provide for yourself—is one of life's greatest joys.

H2O #18: *Being of increasing value to all of your customers.* Who are your customers? Anyone with whom you interact in your work, you are doing business with. They are all customers: your employer, employees, managers, coworkers and support staff, and the people who plunk down the green that keeps your enterprise afloat— whether they be car buyers or taxpayers.

When you start a new job, you aim to be of increasing value to your customers in order to move up and stay employed. If you start a business, you aim to be of increasing value to your customers in order to keep your business growing and fend off any competition. But if your company is losing its shirt, it may not matter how much your manager likes you. And if your staff walks out on you because of the way you treat them, it may not matter how good a product you have. In either case, you could be headed for financial stress.

By being of increasing value to *all* of your customers, you not only generate value to your full potential, you also increase your chances of always having an arena in which to generate value.

H2O #19: *Having readily transferable skills within your field.* The longer you work in one place, the more your skills are developed and honed to meet the exact needs and demands of that organization. And with the passage of time come increased earnings. A raise here and a raise there and you're thinking, "Who would have ever thought I'd be making this kind of money?" But then comes the specter of lay-offs. Or maybe you just want to move or get a different job. The often agonizing question has to be raised: "How much of what I can do here is in current demand anywhere else?" You may find that a lot of your work value is situation-specific—you can't take your act on the road because there are no other takers, at least at your current asking price.

With the probability of ever finding a magic "job for life" rapidly diminishing, the need for transferable skills within your field becomes ever more crucial. And the only way to be certain to have them is to be consciously generating them on an ongoing basis.

H2O #20: *Generating options through your work beyond your immediate field.* Our work often puts us in contact with an extraordinary range of people and situations—one that we don't often recognize. These contacts can turn out to be an entrance into a different field of work, no matter how illogical it might look on paper.

If I were ever to open a service-based business, the first potential employee I would contact would be Bob, the UPS deliveryman for my Buffalo neighborhood. Bob's personal value—he's just plain energizing to be around—and the quality of his service are so great, I'm absolutely convinced that he would be a dynamic asset to any firm. Now, how many businesses does Bob come into contact with? Hundreds. Am I the only person who's taken notice of Bob's value? No. He often gets feelers for work in areas that don't have anything to do with parcel delivery. By generating value in his work, he has generated work options beyond his field.

Options beyond your field can also be generated through developing skills that can be carried from one field to another. With a degree in horticulture, Mary went to work for a large wholesale plant nursery. But as her company expanded into retail sales, Mary found herself increasingly active in the service side of the business: starting a newsletter for customers, setting up gardening seminars for novices, coming up with new ways to attract and assist do-it-yourselfers. Before long, Mary was manager of the retail store and had clean fingernails. With the experience and confidence gained from running a large operation, she is now managing a retail operation totally unrelated to petunias.

By generating options beyond your field, you are inoculating yourself from potential financial stress in several significant ways. First of all, the fortunes of your entire industry might be hurting across the board—if your company is laying off workers or having a tough time, there's a good chance that so are your competitors. It may not matter how good you are in your field—if the tide's going against you, you might want to find another ocean altogether. Second of all, generating options outside your field is one way to avoid the nagging feeling that you're stuck doing the same thing for the rest of your life. And lastly, it is one of the prime ways of adding adventure to your life. One day you're doing one thing and the next thing you know . . . you've left it far behind.

H2O #21: *Running your own business.* Owning a business isn't for everyone—including some actual business owners. But for many people, entrepreneurship is a driving need.

To be ultimately responsible for your business's destiny, experience the thrill of building something from the ground up, learn all of the things that are required of a person in charge, take on whatever challenges are necessary to keep a business thriving, chart your own course through the marketplace: These are all experiences that draw millions toward the dream of owning a business. For some it is a way out of the necessary constrictions of corporate life, for others it is a route out of poverty or the best way to capitalize upon their innate talents.

One thing should be clear: Those who do not hear the calling of entrepreneurship should in no way feel as though they've been relegated to also-ran status in the workplace. The best coach in the world can't win with a lousy team. The right employees are as critical to the growth of a business as any other factor—all the capital in the world can't compensate for an incompetent staff. And an individual with in-demand skills is in a sense a de facto entrepreneur, able to "hire" the employer of his choice.

On the other hand, if you're an entrepreneur at heart, that need has to be fulfilled in some way—even on a part-time basis—or every workday you're going to ask the question "What if . . . ?"

TARGETING AN IMPACT H2O

Change isn't easily translated from wishful thought to purposeful deed. There's no purpose in pretending otherwise. It's difficult to effect meaningful change in one area of our life, let alone a major overhaul. So here's what I recommend that you do:

Pick *one* H2O—just one—and consciously fulfill that H2O by generating value.

When you accomplish this, two great things will happen. You'll have reduced your financial stress. And the effect will be contagious:

You'll automatically begin to use value throughout your life to create a life that money can't buy.

What we're going to do now is identify *a single impact H2O—a need where the gap between where you are and where you want to be is so huge that it's creating stress throughout your life.*

For example, if one of your H2Os is being of increasing value to others in your work, but you're spending your days trying to hawk overpriced magazine subscriptions over the phone, not only do you need a new job yesterday (Stress Symptom #1), but this single value gap may also be kicking off as many as five or six of the other stress symptoms.

Step One: Identify Your Unfulfilled H2Os

So what are your H2Os and—most important—what H2Os are not being fulfilled? Below is a compendium of the H2Os we've just identified. Don't rush through it—take your time and consider each potential need carefully. Say them aloud. Try each one on for size—see how it fits you.

As you work through the list, *cross off any H2O that:*

a. *Doesn't apply to you.* If you don't need to have your own business, for example, scratch it off. These are *your* needs, not your interpretation of what others think your needs should be. If it's not important or not applicable, out it goes.

b. *You've already got covered.* If you're already satisfied with how you're fulfilling a need, set it aside for now. Our intent is not to fine-tune positives, but rather to search out and turn around those areas of our lives that are having a substantial negative impact.

Be candid with yourself. If saying an H2O makes you uneasy—if you want to rush through it to get it over with—then don't cross it off. Keep in mind that if everything were so hunky-dory, you wouldn't have financial stress. Have the courage to say, "This is a need that I've been ignoring."

Don't run and hide. Look at it this way: I could have made you take a test, but I've never taken a test where it wasn't obvious how to jigger the outcome. So I'm counting on you to look at yourself in the mirror and 'fess up. If you keep kidding yourself, you can only alter a falsehood. If you're truthful, you can effect honest change.

What you will now have is a handful of H2Os where your value generation is short of what you'd like it to be or misses the mark by a wide margin.

Copy any H2Os that you haven't crossed off the list on a blank sheet of paper.

WHICH OF THE FOLLOWING H2Os HAS TO BE A PART OF YOUR DAY-TO-DAY EXPERIENCE?

1. Having an understanding of life that extends beyond the immediate here-and-now material world.
2. Having a code of moral conduct that will serve me well in life.
3. Being of sound character—having the judgment to know right from wrong and the resolve to make decisions accordingly.
4. Being in good health.
5. Maintaining a good appearance.
6. Interacting positively with the people around me—conducting myself in such a way that I can be a net contributor in any and every situation.
7. Being an integral part of a close-knit circle of family and friends.
8. Having a strong and lasting marriage.
9. Raising my children to become self-sufficient and happy adults.
10. Living in a community that maintains and enhances rather than impedes or destroys the overall quality of the lives of its citizens.
11. Using my innate talents.
12. Developing a breadth of ability: to have a broad range of knowledge, skills, and experience.
13. Developing a depth of ability: to have the knowledge, skills, and experience needed to excel in a specific area or areas.
14. Participating in an activity that I love.
15. Developing options in my life.
16. Providing myself and my family with the basic necessities of life and a reasonable level of comfort.
17. Enjoying my work.
18. Being of increasing value to all of my customers.
19. Having readily transferable skills within my field.
20. Generating options through my work beyond my immediate field.
21. Running my own business.

Step Two: Identify Your Financial Stress Symptoms

We left the symptoms of financial stress behind in Chapter One. Now it's time to revisit them—and to identify the symptoms you are experiencing on a regular basis.

The pivotal phrase is "regular basis." Everyone experiences some form of financial stress at one time or another. Even if you love your job, there's still going to be the occasion when you feel like walking away from it. Mr. and Mrs. Happy Couple will still have a tiff over money from time to time. And there's not a person alive who has protected himself against every possible untoward event.

As you did with the list of H2Os, read carefully through the list of stress symptoms. Say each aloud. Which one(s) give you an "errrrhhhh" feeling? What's really grinding you? Envision your personal wall of financial stress. Try to identify the individual blocks of stress that make it up.

As you work through the symptoms, *cross off any symptom that you don't have:*

I, [YOUR NAME HERE] . . .
1. . . . need a new job . . . yesterday.
2. . . . don't have enough money to pay my bills.
3. . . . can't control my spending.
4. . . . am constantly fighting with my spouse or partner about money.
5. . . . am leaving the back door open to financial disaster, and deep down I know it.
6. . . . can't part with money, even if it's for my own darn good.
7. . . . can't hear the words "future" and "savings" without my stomach knotting up and my brain shutting down.
8. . . . am overwhelmed and intimidated by the prospect of making an investment decision.
9. . . . am losing money on the investments I've already made.

Now *copy your financial stress symptoms onto a separate sheet of paper.*

Step Three: Trace Your Financial Stress
Symptoms to a Specific Impact Need

You now have two lists on separate sheets of paper: H2Os and financial stress symptoms. Put them side by side.

Consider the H2Os on your list one by one, asking this question: "Which of these stress symptoms can I attribute to this unfulfilled need?"

In other words, if an H2O became part of your daily reality, how many of your stress symptoms might disappear or at least be greatly diminished?

Again, take your time. If you ask yourself how a particular stress symptom might be related to a particular need, you'll be surprised at the connections that will become readily apparent. You can even keep score of how many symptoms you can trace to each potential impact need.

I know that you might want me to spell out all of the possible connections between each H2O and each stress symptom, but I'm not going to. Because by making the connection between your needs and your stress symptoms on your own, the impact of that self-realization will be much greater than if you were to depend on my suggestions.

This is where "self-help" truly *means* self-help. You're smart, and if you're willing to be honest with and about yourself, you have the common sense and instincts to know what's missing in your life. The extra time and effort required on your part will pay off.

When you reach that moment of self-generated "Aha! This is an area where generating value will really make a big difference in my life," it will mean something far beyond "Hmm, that's interesting." I can tell you from experience that when you figure an impact need out on your own, you "own it."

If you have a handful of H2Os on your list, identify your top three—those that, if fulfilled, would have the greatest positive impact on your daily life and those who share that life with you.

Mull these needs over for a day or two (no longer, though—this isn't a theoretical exercise or protracted analysis). Discuss them with your spouse if you care to. When you get up in the morning, spend a few minutes contemplating how the day ahead of you might be less stressful if addressing a particular H2O were part of your day-to-day reality.

Remember, no matter which H2O you choose to concentrate on, as you reduce your financial stress through meeting this need, it will become that much easier—and in some cases unnecessary—to work on other H2Os as the positive force of cause and effect takes hold and grows.

Now *select your impact H2O*—the single H2O you believe is the best one to start with. Generating value toward this need is going to be your first big step toward True Wealth. Record it in the space below.

My impact H2O: _____

_____ .

Objectives:
The Generators
of True Wealth

L EST YOU'VE lost sight, True Wealth is the *action*-created absence of stress related to money, regardless of your income or assets.

Whose action? Your action. This is the point of no excuses: The dog can't eat your homework, and a note from your mother won't get you off the hook. And, it should be emphasized, *talking* about what you value *means nothing*.

Too often the concept of value floats around on the hot air of hypocrisy.

All too often we pay lip service to values in our personal lives and then continue on our merry ways. As examples:

How many parents who profess to value their children are going to have to tell them, "Sorry you don't have any money for college, but at least you rode to day care in a Grand Cherokee"?

How many people who profess to value their retirement have monthly charge statements that prove otherwise?

How many people who profess to value their careers haven't taken the first step toward learning anything on their own that might sustain a career?

How many people who profess to value their health act as if a ten-dollar copayment is an unbearable tariff but an extra order of french fries isn't?

How many women who profess to value their marriage use the word "decorate" on a regular basis?

How many men who profess to value their marriage still insist that every televised sporting event is the Big One?

Whatever your needs, you can adjust your outer appearances all you want, and, just like a persistent wedgie, your need will be pinching you where it counts for the rest of your life. And the only slack you'll get is what you generate for yourself. Action produces results—not talking, imagining, or reinterpreting events in a way that pretends to create a desired result. In the end, either you did or you didn't get results.

Whatever the exact composition of your wall of financial stress, there is a reinforcement running right through the center. This barrier is the dividing line between *doing* and *not doing*—between action and inaction. It is thin enough that it can be envisioned only in the imagination. At the same time, the barrier can be as thick and forboding as the Great Wall of China—you could try to run a tank through it and end up with a jumble of scrap metal.

If you are able to break through the barrier between doing and not doing, your financial stress will crumble. But how can you get through the barrier? Should you try to design your equivalent of a high-tech laser: the narrow and absolutely perfect stream of decisions that can penetrate it? You could spend the rest of your life at the drawing board. Should you grab an opportunity in the box and hope that it's big enough to allow you to climb right over? If the box is empty—or if you aren't willing to put something in it—it won't hold your weight. Should you hang around and wait for someone to give you a boost? You could still be in the same place a decade hence.

At the risk of stating the obvious, the only way to break through the doing/not doing barrier is to *do something*. There is no other choice. But that leaves a key question unanswered: Do what? Let's get the answer . . .

THE THIRD COMPONENT OF TRUE WEALTH: GENERATE VALUE THAT MAKES YOUR H2OS YOUR DAY-TO-DAY REALITY

Right now, you have an unfulfilled need—something that *has to occur* in your life and, at the moment, isn't. Think of that H2O as a blank canvas that, in order to bring it to life, you must fill with value, rather than paint. *To live free from financial stress, you must fulfill your H2O with value.*

Whatever your H2O, there are countless potential ways to fulfill it. What matters most is that they reflect your personal interpretation of what it will take for you to feel—day in, day out—that what has to occur in your life is, in reality, *actually occurring.*

In order to determine what action(s) will reasonably and effectively bring your H2O to life on an ongoing and increasing basis, you must look beyond the broad strokes of single and often distant events, to the hours and minutes that create the big picture.

ANATOMIZING YOUR H2O

Let's now anatomize the impact need you targeted at the end of Chapter Four—to tune your blurry vision of what's missing into a sharp picture of the day-to-day experience of your H2O.

Imagine that tomorrow you wake up and the world has magically conformed to your longing—the need that's causing you financial stress supreme has been fulfilled. What is your day going to be like? You ready to hop out of bed? Not so fast . . . take a moment to reflect on the day ahead of you.

What would be occurring that isn't occurring now?
What are you going to be doing that you aren't doing right now?
What will you be thinking? Feeling?
What would you know that you don't know now?
What experience would you be having that you don't have now?
  What ability?
What is your day going to be like if you are actively fulfilling this
  H2O?
How is it going to be different from today?

Reflect for a few minutes. Write down your answers to the questions posed above, and force yourself to be as concrete and specific as possible. Pretend that you're trying to keep the ball up in the air by asking as many additional questions as possible: What? When? Where? How? With whom?

Concentrate on the *experience,* not the end result, of your actions. For example, if you were developing employment options through your work, what might be happening? Would you be periodically approached "out of the blue" with unsolicited job offers? Would you always have several options at hand if your job vaporized tomorrow? Could you identify a customer or client who, based on your relationship, would be thrilled to hire you in a minute? Would you never feel as if you'd been checkmated in your career—instead, always seeing available moves ahead of you?

Walk yourself through your day and describe as clearly as you can the day-to-day experience of your need, *without regard to titles, positions, awards, salary, physical possessions,* or *one-shot events.* These are merely symbols of validation—often heavily dependent on the interpretation of others.

Consider the Academy Awards. When the Oscar nominations are announced, immediately there's a hubbub centered on those who were far more deserving and yet were left out of the running. And when a winner is announced, you can sometimes feel everyone thinking, "You've got to be kidding."

There is one way that Hollywood actually does mirror real life: The best isn't always first or even recognized. So, for example, you can say you want to be district supervisor and gear your entire performance to a "yea or nay" referendum, setting yourself up for huge disappointment and devastating stress if things don't go your way. Or you can think about the skills and the ongoing performance that would guarantee your success at your work—and that you could take with you anywhere.

If you really concentrate on generating value at a level that would merit promotion, guess what?—you might very well end up being district supervisor (or winning an Oscar). In fact, it might be your ticket. But even if you don't get the nod, your consolation prize is just as, if not more, valuable: You know what you can really do and can take your act(ion) down the road. Remember, Richard Burton never won an Academy Award.

There are two likely outcomes to this exercise:

1. *You have a clear-cut idea of the day-to-day reality of your H2O.* "I need to strengthen my community," by working in my church's youth program. "I need to increase my ability" to speak fluent Spanish so that I can make greater use of my existing abilities in developing the international market for our product. "I need to run my own business," consulting with corporations on how to maximize the profitability of their employees in order to minimize layoffs.

From these concise nuggets of reality, it is possible to select any number of actions that will create your personal experience. The challenge then becomes one of energy—getting going.

2. *You don't have a clue.* "I need to enjoy my work more." How would that be? "Doing something more enjoyable than what I'm

doing now." Like what? "I dunno, something more exciting or less stressful or somewhere where I'm not working with jerks or where there's more opportunity or . . ." You could take any financial need and re-create dead-end dialogue—hopefully not too much of it from your personal recitation.

When we draw a blank on our needs, we do any combination of things that reinforce our stress. We pin our hopes on totally unrealistic events. We get angry because no one will spell out exactly what we should do and hand it to us on a silver platter. We make the same decisions over and over, expecting different results. We do nothing.

How is it that some people seem to know how they can fulfill their needs and other people don't? I believe that the defining factor is a *proactive life.* The more you've done—the greater your combination of experience and learning—the more connected you are to the world you live in. And, therefore, the greater the chance that you've made connections that are meaningful—that grab your attention and intuitively say, "Do this and you'll move a step ahead."

So as we begin to zero in on what to do, there are two principles worth emphasizing:

1. *It is better to do something—as imperfect as it may be—than to do nothing.* You can accomplish far more through trial and error than through overanalysis or inertia. Thomas Edison would certainly have attested to this: His inventions began with innovative ideas, but many were brought to life through hours of trying everything and anything that came to mind until something worked.

2. *It is better to have a plan—as imperfect as it may be—than just to wing it.* Before you can start flying by the seat of your pants, you at least have to have some pants on.

"Plan." Uh-oh, you may be thinking, here comes the section on setting goals. I'm going to have to write down some goals, chart out all of the theoretical steps, and then hope the piece of paper disappears so it's not around to remind me how fast and far I got off the track, if I ever got on it in the first place.

Well, you can relax because . . .

WE'RE NOT GOING TO SET ANY GOALS

The world can be divided into two camps about a zillion different ways. One of these ways is how we deal with goals. Some people can set a distant goal and stick with it. And then there are the rest of us. We can set long-term goals until we're blue in the face and it's not going to change our lives one bit. The canon of self-improvement would lead us to believe that if we can't set big goals and stick to them, we're spineless slugs, condemned to be also-rans.

We're constantly reminded of all the amazing things accomplished by people who've set seemingly impossible goals. The athlete who overcame crippling illness to win an Olympic gold medal. The convict who took ten years to chisel through his cell bars with a nail file.

In fact, much of the corporate training culture is geared toward goal setting: "I'm going to be a division manager in five years" or "We're going to double our market share by the end of next year."

The corporate goal culture is heavily influenced by the culture of big-time sports (you don't need to be a radical feminist to guess why). One result is that any coach who directs his team to a wild-card berth has a ready audience for his management secrets.

Lost in this jock worship is a simple fact: Coaches and athletes have an ultimate singular goal because that goal is spelled out for them in twenty-foot-high letters: WIN THE CHAMPIONSHIP. Whoever wins a Super Bowl is naturally going to tell you that he's dreamed about it since his youth—do you think any kid ever dreamed of winning the AFC Central Division? And although it's admirable to finish on top, it's a lock that *someone* is going to finish first. As sweepstakes ads promise, there will be a winner.

But in real life, we're faced with an infinite array of possible home plates, baskets, and end zones. And there's no guarantee that anyone will be or has to be a winner. We all decide the game we play—and how we feel about it when we see it on instant replay.

This is not to say that there aren't circumstances in life that absolutely dictate a long-term goal. Muzaffar Afzal felt it was essential to live in the United States. That is an experience that he could not have duplicated in his native Pakistan. Muzaffar could have lived on Coke and fries, worn a Raiders cap all day, and watched *Baywatch* every night, but he still would have been in Pakistan. If you want to be a doctor, your goal is to graduate from medical school.

When circumstances dictate a goal, there's usually a moment when we recognize and fully embrace it. We just *know*. After this moment, our pace quickens, our motivation soars, our concentration intensifies. If we willingly ignore this goal or even refuse to recognize it, we are inviting financial stress.

But what if a big, clearly defined, long-term goal isn't staring you right in the face and shouting "Follow me!"? Some people are able to pick out goals as if they were ordering from a menu. But for the rest of us, a big, nagging question exists: How can you be so sure that *this* goal is *the* goal?

I once had a manager sit me down and tell me that my problem was that I didn't have a ten-year plan. Pointing to a rising corporate star, he assured me that he had a one-year plan, a five-year plan, and a ten-year plan. I suppressed my urge to say, "Gee, didn't Mao and Stalin have them too?"

Seriously, I found something awry and even depressing about the whole idea of setting a long-range goal with the certainty that this goal was exactly what I wanted to have happen to the exclusion of all other experiences. How can you be sure, and what if you're wrong? Had my life really come down to this, I asked myself, building a cattle run toward an arbitrary bale of hay on the horizon? In my heart I knew that any goals I set under these circumstances would not even be halfhearted: "You want a plan, here's a plan, and you can keep my copy." (By the way, Mr. Ten-Year Plan ended up in corporate Siberia.)

The thing was, I also knew that I wanted to do things. Was there a way that someone without any goals could be a first-rate contributor or even a leader? Weren't there people who zigzagged rather than zigziglared along and yet still ended up in incredible places?

The answer, of course, is yes.

What really matters is knowing what you want to have occur in your life: the daily experience. Because once you know that, you are then able to use the most potent vehicle for smashing through the barrier between doing and not doing, even if you can't see ten years ahead.

OBJECTIVES: THE GENERATORS OF TRUE WEALTH

Countless people have accomplished a lot of nifty things in life without setting lofty long-term goals. What they did have was a clear vision of what they wanted to experience, some ideas as to how they might begin to create the experience, the will to take action, and the flexibility to handle change. In the process of creating and nurturing that experience, they did something that just took off and propelled their lives across an extraordinary distance that they themselves might not have thought was possible to traverse.

Their secret? An easy-to-use, power-packed tool that can generate more value than all of the long-term goals in the world: *an objective.*

An objective is an immediate action that generates tangible results. It is something to do, even if for only a few minutes a day, that will create part of the day-to-day reality of your essential needs. Here are just a few examples of some adventures launched by modest objectives:

Jennifer Barclay, the founder of Blue Fish Clothing, didn't set out to create a multimillion-dollar company that reflects her environmental and social concerns as well as her artistic vision. Rather, she sought the experience of creating colorful and expressive clothing.

After discovering that a linoleum block cut made an appealing print on fabric, she set an objective: Make some T-shirts and sell them at a local festival. Their immediate acceptance was the beginning of an unforeseen adventure—one whose yields can be found in hundreds of retail outlets coast to coast. And through educational outreach programs, the talent of the Blue Fish staff is shared with others, extending the adventure beyond the mere business.

Bill Langejans is the owner of Lange Audio in Grand Rapids, Michigan. As long as I've known him, he's been tinkering with self-designed audio systems. No matter what his day job, he always found a way to have the experience of bringing sound into people's lives wherever they wanted it—whether in a boat, an office, or a family room.

Several years ago Bill set an objective: to install built-in speaker systems in new homes on evenings and weekends. As he adapted to the needs of his growing customer base, he set new objectives. Today Bill runs a successful custom home-entertainment systems company. Instead of fooling around in his garage, he has his own showroom and production facility. A single objective transformed Bill's hobby into a burgeoning career.

I guarantee that Jennifer and Bill have former cohorts who to this day shake their heads and wonder, How did that happen? I mean, one day he or she was doing just what I'm doing, and then one day, whoosh! There he or she was . . ." That "whoosh!" may well have been the sound of objectives generating value.

WHY OBJECTIVES GENERATE VALUE

Objectives help you generate value in three ways:

1. *Objectives focus your energy on the present—where the battle against stress is won or lost.* They are based on the principle that whatever you can do today is better than what you think or hope you'll do tomorrow.

Concerned about your kid's future? Quit dreaming, and worrying, about sending him to Princeton in ten years. Pull the plug on your television set today, make sure he does his homework tonight, and put some bucks in a jar every day this week. These are can-do objectives that punch through the mega-stress barrier between "not doing" and "doing."

Want to have your own houseplant shop someday? Quit thinking that you have to start with a storefront and a minivan. In your spare time start raising plants for profit—even if it's only for a church or school fund-raiser. Once you're in business, the entire landscape will change.

Whatever is important to you, you can make it an immediate part of your daily life in some way, shape, or form.

2. Objectives enable you to experience what has been missing from your life. And a positive experience is the most effective way to plant a seed of growing motivation.

Consider the Pohl and the Hudy families: two representative families with identical incomes. The Pohl family can't save a dime and struggle under the financial weight of their charge accounts. The Hudy family sock away 12 percent of their income without strain.

What's the difference? It could very well be that long ago the Hudy family simply found a way to save just enough to experience the positive benefits of saving. They may have started saving in amounts far less than their current rate, and it may have taken a concerted effort—even a struggle—at the beginning. But at some point, a situation arose where the benefits of preserving value hit home. After that, the Hudys found that increasing their savings rate became progressively easier while the Pohls are still relying on debt to deal with financial stress—a surefire loser.

3. Objectives change the backdrop for future decisions. You don't need to be a Shakespearean scholar to have heard the phrase "All the world's a stage." What is the backdrop for your current scene? It is largely the decisions you've made to date. Only if you make decisions today that improve the backdrop for decisions that follow can you go from being an extra in a vaguely familiar grade-B melodrama to the lead player in the story of your life.

I'd like to illustrate the backdrop concept with a common worry today: job skills stagnation. Isaac has an uneasy feeling that he's not keeping current—that new kid at work threw out some ideas that went by him like a rocket. He knows that he needs to be able to do more. But when Isaac asks himself what, exactly, he needs to be able to do, he can't make a sound decision, let alone take action. His backdrop is a big blank that, unless he changes it, will leave him stuck in the same scene with the same single line of dialogue: "I dunno."

How might Isaac improve his backdrop? By setting an objective to gather his available options. If he obtained information on all of the continuing education programs in his area, asked people throughout his company and even his industry for suggestions for skill development, and considered potential lateral moves that would offer a "skill raise" rather than a pay raise, he would certainly be well on his way to creating a solid backdrop for choosing a skill-enhancing objective.

PUTTING OBJECTIVES IN THE TRUE WEALTH EQUATION

We're now going to make one last addition to our evolving equation, placing objectives right where they belong: in the middle of the True Wealth generation process:

True Wealth = (Time × Energy × Resources) → Objectives → H2O

Objectives can be thought of as the vehicles that enable us to combine our time, energy, and resources in a way that allows us to focus our value generation on things we want most to have happen—to make our H2Os our daily experience rather than a distant or deferred dream.

Thinking in terms of objectives, in effect, helps us reduce the infinite number of possible actions to a number that is humanly manageable—or at least comprehendible. It sets the stage for this simple question:

"This is what I want to have happen. What might be some possible ways to get going right now?"

TWO OBJECTIVES TO PURSUE RIGHT NOW

So where do you begin? Right here, with two objectives that apply to everyone, including you. Ready?

1. Put the Framework of Your Life on the Table

The more I talk with or read about people with serious financial stress, the more I believe that a goodly portion of their stress can be traced to their belief that the structure of their lives—house, geographic area, job, occupation, and so on—is written in stone. They cannot imagine themselves living in a different house or in a different neighborhood, city, or state; working for a different company or in a different field; or doing much of anything different than they currently are. This unwillingness to reconsider the framework of their lives sends a contradictory message: "I'm unhappy, but I wouldn't change a thing."

"We don't want to move . . . we really like it here."
"There aren't many openings for someone with a degree like mine."
"I don't know what else I could do except the job I just lost."

"We hate living here, but Todd has a really good job in the Snack
Food Marketing Division. We've got to stay put."

"Our lives are hectic, but the money lets us do things we couldn't
do otherwise."

Statements such as these are often signs that people's lives might be less
stressful and more rewarding if they took a step back and reevaluated
the framework they've built (often unknowingly) for themselves.

So here's your first objective: *Reevaluate the basic framework of
your life.*

Before going any further, spend some time, with your spouse if
you're married, reevaluating where you stand. Block out a couple of
hours where there'll be no distractions, have a pen and paper ready to
record any interesting thoughts, questions to explore, or conclusions
at the end of the session (don't go jumping straight to them right off
the bat).

Toss around possibilities. Play "What if?" This is not a decision-
making summit, merely a brainstorming session—a stretching exercise designed to increase your flexibility. Throw everything out the
window and see what you'd bother to pick up and bring back inside.
Don't get defensive—let your imagination roam. Daydream about
adventure!

Some questions to get you started:

Why do we live here? What are the trade-offs? If we moved, why
would we want to and where might we go? Across town, out of
town, or out of state?

What are we missing that we want in our lives?

Why do we do the work we do? What attaches us to it? What else
could we do? What if we looked into doing _____ ?

If we could restructure our lives, what would we change, include,
add, or get rid of? Why? What seeds of possibilities lie dormant?

You may very well arrive at the conclusion that the basic framework of your life is fine and dandy. That's great to know—you've got
a sound foundation for future decisions. But you may end the discussion with questions—some "hey, what ifs?"—that you want to mull
over. Write them down, think about them for a week, and then have
another discussion. *Repeat your conversations until you either
(a) are satisfied that your current framework is not causing you
undue stress, or (b) have articulated the big question(s).*

A *BIG QUESTION* is one that begins with "WHAT IS IT REALLY
GOING TO TAKE TO *[fill in the blank]*?"

While you're working on formulating your big question(s), we're going to get started on some other objectives.

Do you have your blinders off? Are you thinking about life's possibilities? Good, because now it's time to . . .

2. Turn Off the Television

There is probably no single greater act you can take that will enable you and your family to generate more value, individually and collectively, than pulling the plug on your televisions.

Any complaint about not having enough time to do the things we want to do in life has to be weighed against the truly extraordinary amount of time we find to devote to television. An average person watches an average of over two and a half hours a day—seventy-five hours a month! Habitual viewers log at least four or five hours a day. No time? Get real! Every hour of television your kids watch is an hour of time they'll never get back.

Television is a 100 percent passive activity—your brain is more active when you're sleeping. A good way to unwind from the stress of daily life, you say? What you're actually doing is letting your stress pile up through inaction while your "wants" get pumped up (and, no, you're not immune to it). "Do less! Want more!" Relaxing for sure.

Look, I like *The Simpsons* as much as the next guy. I'd be lost without the Weather Channel and C-Span. I enjoy *Biography* on A&E. But whenever I find myself scrolling through the channels, clicker in hand, I try to remember that channel surfing and value generation are mutually exclusive activities.

A good place to start the battle of the boob tube: *Get the televisions out of the bedrooms.* Right now. C'mon, just get up and do it. In a few days you won't miss them, and you will notice the difference. You will have more time and will be pursuing more worthwhile activities—how about sleep?

With your eyes opened and disengaged from the television, let's now begin to look at choosing objectives that target your impact H2O.

HOW DO YOU KNOW AN OBJECTIVE IS A GOOD ONE?

Although there's no magical formula for determining exactly which objective(s) will work best, there are some guidelines that will help ensure that what you do will be worthwhile—and leave you with less financial stress.

A good objective will accomplish at least one of the following:

1. Make the Obvious a Growing Reality

More often than not, a big piece of our financial stress puzzle is staring us right in the face. We know what it is, and we know that if we fit it in our lives, our lives will be a more complete reflection of our needs. Nevertheless, we leave the piece sitting on the table: often for years, sometimes for a lifetime.

When you think about fulfilling your impact need, did an objective leap right out at you? Is there some potential objective that you've pondered for a long time that would really make a positive difference in your life if it ever got off the drawing board? Do you feel as if your whole life is being held back simply because you haven't taken action in one specific area? Well, guess what? *You have to get to it.*

2. Remove a Deterrent to Generating Value

It might be possible that the reason you haven't taken stress-reducing action up until now reaches beyond not knowing what exactly to do. Have you ever heard yourself think or say any of the following:

"I don't know how I could ever find the time."
"I just don't have the energy."
"What's the point?"
"I've tried everything."
"I just can't deal with . . ."
"If only I had _____, then I could . . ."

The truth is, we often think we can't do anything more or do anything differently than what we are doing right now. We're stuck, gunning our engines in neutral, waiting for the tow truck of life to pull us out. We let ourselves get into this ditch for several reasons:

We believe we are lacking in at least one of the elements necessary for generating value: time, energy, or a basic resource.

We let ourselves undermine our value generation. We can be our own worst enemies sometimes—working hard to get ahead and simultaneously torpedoing our own efforts. Would you walk around with a sign that said, "Don't take me seriously," "Avoid me like the plague," "Running on empty," or "I'm a certified drag"?

So right off the bat, you might consider an objective that will free up some time, boost your energy, rustle up some spare change to fund additional objectives, or generate more personal value. If you feel that you've neglected your spiritual life, for example, now would be a good time to get reacquainted or even to open the door.

You don't have to initiate a massive self-improvement program to generate value in your life. But you might have to break a habit, or a jam of inaction, and get some positive momentum flowing that will help you address your impact need.

3. Increase Your Most Vital Resource: Ability

Through learning—combining knowledge, practice, and experience—we increase our most vital resource: ability. And whether you're self-employed or employed by the federal government, when it comes to developing your ability, you are an entrepreneur. You just might not fully realize it yet.

One of the seismic shifts in the workplace is the transference of the ultimate responsibility for the development of one's ability from institutions—public and private—to oneself. The days when a degree and osmosis could carry you for decades are over. Wherever you work, the responsibility for increasing your ability rests with you. If your employer helps you out, that's a bonus, not a right.

Ability is more valuable than money. It takes ability, after all, to make money. So just as you see making money as an ongoing activity, so must you see that which makes earning possible.

Any objective that increases your ability will always be of value in some way. An objective that increases your ability to generate value toward your H2O will leverage your time and effort even further.

4. Develop and/or Convey Your Character

Through action we make who we are a part of other people's lives—hopefully to positive effect.

We do this through a two-part process. The first part is developing, refining, and strengthening our character. As children we (hopefully) learn the basics of good character and develop who we are as individuals. As adults our character is put to the test and forged in ever more demanding situations: work, marriage, parenting, and any number of crises. We also have the opportunity to refine who we are—to add beneficial personal skills and habits and get rid of bad ones.

The second part of this process is to convey our character to others through our actions. This is an absolutely critical aspect of generating value in our families and communities as well as in the workplace. Children don't care about what we say—they learn from what we do. As we've already noted, most of what we believe will enable our kids to become happy and productive adults rests on our ability to convey *our* character. If we honor our commitments, our children will be far more likely to honor theirs.

A strong community has yet to be crafted from hot air and duplicitous self-interest. And although the business world is not lacking in those who will shave corners and stretch the truth, strong character is the one product we can offer to others that will never lose its market share or its value.

Anything you do that either strengthens or conveys your character will generate value. As we deal with others, we are in turn dealing much of our own hand.

THE ONLY FINANCIAL GOAL YOU'LL EVER NEED

In the next chapter, we're going to examine a range of potential objectives. But before we do, let's resolve one last issue that might be bugging you.

Some of you may not have taken too kindly to our willful ignoring of long-term goals. You can't go on without one.

So here's the only financial goal you'll ever need: to live a financially neutral life—one in which your decisions are neither severely restricted because of a lack of money nor driven by a perceived need for more money.

If you must have a goal, try this one.

Practical Strategies for Achieving True Wealth

6

Seventy Low-Cost, High-Efficiency Ways to Generate True Wealth

Now let's look at a variety of possible objectives for addressing your impact H2O. Far from being platitudes, these time-proven objectives are low-cost, high-efficiency value generators with few, if any, barriers to getting started.

1. *Get the answer to your big question.* We're surrounded by the most easily available information and resources ever, and yet we often let our initial hunches be the last word. Leaving big questions unanswered for months or even years turns them into roadblocks. Yet the answers are at hand if you're willing to do even a little digging.

What's your big question? It is the one for which knowing the answer would not only rid you of the stress of uncertainty and inertia, but also point the way to further stress-reducing action. You may have already identified a "big question" by reevaluating the framework of your life or by examining your needs in terms of value:

"What do I really need to know to be able to do that job?"
"Where can my son get a good college education for a reasonable cost?"
"What would it take to start a business on the side?"
"How much will we give up in income if one of us stays home with the kids?"

Remember the two-income family that was pushed to the limit? Instead of getting tips on efficient grocery shopping and meal prep, they should have been sitting down and asking these questions:

"What do we get from both working?" The answer: "A bigger house, miserable kids, a disconnected marriage, time-impaired careers, and a punishing daily routine."

"What would happen if one of us was able to devote him/herself to his/her career and the other one stayed home with the kids and developed a part-time income?" Answer: "A smaller house, happier children, a calmer environment, and more time for everything, including each other."

Granted, there are many households where two full-time incomes are an absolute necessity. But I've also observed numerous families where having two full-time incomes is the *cause* of major stress, not the antidote, yet the framework of their lives has become so ossified that no one can consider moving an inch. However much you think your current framework is carved in stone, if you're able to take a step back and view it from a distance, you might find it only to be written in sand.

If this is your big question, the answer may surprise you: *It will cost you less than you think.* In fact, you may be losing money on your second income. First of all, you have to begin by looking at the *net* pay of the lower of your two incomes. Most people have no idea of how big their tax bite really is. Add up all of the costs of going to work—day care, transportation, clothing, lunch, and snacks—and the potential savings. And, if you end up in a lower tax bracket, you'll be able to keep more of your remaining income.

The key: managing your housing and automobile costs. Many two-income families are paying a huge price to be overhoused and ride in style.

You may have already identified a "big question" in reevaluating the framework of your life. Whatever it is, commit yourself to getting a definitive, informed answer.

2. *Play on an open field.* One of the hallmarks of a low-stress life is unstructured leisure activities that are driven by curiosity and passion. In fact, many ethologists believe that just plain ol' goofin' around on an open field of inquiry is what makes us true human beings.

The benefits of an active interest are many. First, the "flow" of the activity is a great stress reducer in and of itself. Second, no matter what interest we pursue in the world, it heightens the sense of balance in our lives. And finally, our interest can serve as the springboard for a great adventure—one that might lead to the pot of gold at the end of our personal rainbow.

It doesn't matter what our active interests are—model ship building, knitting, bird-watching, collecting bottle caps, camping, studying architecture, playing guitar, reading history—so long as we have them. And it's up to you to actively develop the things in the world that turn you on. You can't just pay your money or plop down in a chair and say, "Entertain me."

I'm convinced that the key to developing an active interest is staying with something long enough to develop the basic skills or vocabulary. As with learning to ride a bike, there's a period of fumbling and frustration and then, suddenly, a rudimentary, clumsy competence. Not long after, you're flying down the block.

As a kid, you had a powerful built-in motivator to learn to ride a bike or play basketball: You didn't want to be left out. As an adult, you're on your own. There's not anyone around to push you to stay with something long enough to turn a spark of interest into a pastime or avocation. Just remember, if you ever find yourself bored, it's your own fault.

3. *Do that something you've always meant to do.* What's that one thing you've always meant to do: Learn how to paint or sculpt? Study a foreign language? Play harmonica? Learn to juggle? Catalog those antique bottles you collected as a kid? We all have a small packet of unplanted seeds of genuine or unexplored interests and potential adventures, often carrying them around in our pockets until we're laid to final rest. You'll never know how they might grow unless you take one out and plant it in a time frame, water it with energy, and cultivate it with your other resources.

4. *Read to be challenged and to learn.* It sometimes seems as if the basic American home library consisted of worn copies of *Shogun; Our Bodies, Ourselves; In Search of Excellence;* and a sampling of the works of King, Grisham, Clancy, and Steele. There's nothing wrong with reading to be entertained or to keep up with the latest opinion trends, but when was the last time you read "off the road" of the best-seller list and tackled a book that challenged you, or even read an article that was outside of your usual habits?

If broadening your horizons for the thrill of it doesn't grab you, try this: A research study has shown that the higher your literacy level, the greater your job and income potential, whether or not you're a college graduate.

Here's some good advice: "It is pretty unlikely that people will become knowledgeable without being excellent readers. . . . I make it a point to read at least one news weekly from cover to cover because it broadens my interests. If I read only what intrigues me, such as the science section and a subset of the business section, then I finish the magazine the same person I was before I started. So I read it all." That's a startling recommendation from someone who virtually symbolizes the age of electronic media—none other than Microsoft multi-billionaire Bill Gates. If he has the time to read, you probably do too.

Looking for a place to get started? Read *The Wall Street Journal,* the *International Herald Tribune,* or the *Christian Science Monitor.* If you don't think you have time to read two papers, read your local newspaper a day late. Entire sections, particularly sports, will become irrelevant. Want to fill in the gaps of what you never read in school? *The Lifetime Reading Plan* by Clifton Fadiman is an excellent guide to the classics.

5. *Learn how to read.* Even in the age of technology, much of our ability to learn depends on our ability to process and absorb information through the eyes and brain. If you don't read as much as you'd like to because you find reading too slow, tedious, or difficult, enroll in a reading course at your local high school or college. It may very well be your key to True Wealth. A word of encouragement: There's no need to be embarrassed—even many college students have mediocre reading skills at best. If you've ever said, "I don't like to read" or "Reading is boring," you should seriously consider this objective.

6. *Let your brain explore beyond your beliefs.* The search for truth is different from the search for more of what you already believe.

It's easy to fall into a trap of accepting a common opinion as gospel or assuming that the way you've always done something is the best possible way, and then processing only information that reinforces your belief. In your business life, your success or even survival may very well depend on your ability to recognize a shifting reality while others still embrace the old. Two motivating words: buggy whip.

New isn't always better—many a new business theory has produced more losses than profits—and history often repeats itself. But a rigid belief that the future will be no different from the present and that present methods will succeed until further notice is a guaranteed stress generator in business (not to mention investing).

Suggested applications: Identify something in your work that has been done a certain way for so long, no one can remember why. Start over from scratch, identifying the purpose of the task (if, indeed, there is one) and then determining the best way to get it done based on evidence and observation, not opinion or emotional ties.

Warning: If you have a strong personal belief that sets the tone for your entire worldview—like the existence of a secret global government conspiracy—be on guard: The more one-sided and hysterical your information intake, the greater your stress.

7. *Start something.* That oft-delayed, ignored, or even dreaded project or task is almost always harder in theory than in reality. Whether it's shopping for the right insurance or clearing a decade's accumulation of stuff from your basement, if there's something that you *know* would generate value in your life, breaking through the barrier between doing and not doing may be all it takes to boost your energy level enough to see the project through. And in the event it's not . . .

8. *Finish something.* Whether at work or home, we're surrounded by the half fruits of our labor. These unfinished projects stand in mute and mocking testimony to our failure to see them through. And although we may have generated some value in whatever we did, the real value boost comes from being able to put the punctuation at the end: FINISHED!!

Make a list of all of your half-finished projects. Decide which ones you're going to pursue further and which ones you're not. For the no-goes, get rid of the evidence. That half-sewn jacket? If you're not motivated to finish it right now, out it goes. Now you've got a short little list. Pick one and get going.

9. *If you work with your mind, learn to do something new with your hands. If you work with your hands, learn to do something new with your mind.* People have a tendency to become either "mental"—adept at using their minds but all thumbs when it comes to using their hands—or "physical"—skilled at using their hands but on extended vacation when it comes to using their minds. You can see it in the defensive posturing of the professor who doesn't want to get his hands dirty changing a tire and the assembly plant worker who pokes fun at a coworker who studies on breaks.

If your work is either primarily mental or physical, you still have to develop your "other side" to some degree or you'll feel out of balance. Show me a professor who enjoys fixing a faucet or a roofer who likes to read, and I'll bet you they have less stress than their counterparts. So if you use your hands only to press the hold button, learn something physical: carpentry, bricklaying (Winston Churchill's favorite), picture framing . . . whatever. And if your mind sacks out on the job, stimulate it; take it to the library or to a night class for a workout.

10. *Focus on the craft of your job.* Whatever your job, think like a craftsman. There is an essence to any job, a core product or service that must never be ignored. Yet we often don't give a flashing thought to what that essence really is. If we can stay focused on the essence of our work, even the swirling winds of management demands and office politics can't blow us off course.

One of my favorite craftsmen is Earl P. Howze, Jr.—known in Buffalo as the Earl of Bud. When minor-league baseball returned to Buffalo in 1979, Earl—a fireman by trade—took a part-time job as a beer vendor. At the outset, it did not appear to be a gold mine. On many nights, a mere few hundred fans might have been scattered throughout the cavernous and crumbling "Rockpile," once the home of the Buffalo Bills.

But Earl had intuitively made a key observation—his job wasn't just to sell beer. People came to the ballpark to be entertained, to forget about their troubles. And as someone with a winning personality, Earl cast himself in the role of entertainer. It began with a smile and friendly conversation for all—a running dialogue with the audience. Soon he had a trademark punchline: "You got it!" Then came a white tuxedo emblazoned with his stage name: The Earl of Bud. Legend has it he was selling as much Budweiser as any vendor in the country.

When the Buffalo Bisons moved to a new ballpark, Earl was elevated to star status. His dance atop the visiting dugout became a ritual at each game. He landed a radio segment, made personal appearances, and did commercials for charities. Throughout it all, he's remained the same friendly guy. "I've watched people grow up in the ballpark," he explains. "The fans are like a big family."

Whenever I go to a Bisons game and watch Earl work the crowd, I think: "Beer vendor. Minor-league ballpark. How many people have done the work without understanding what the real job was or seeing the opportunity?"

So what is the essence of your work—your real job? When all is said and done, what pivotal role do you play in the workplace? What is the ultimate value that you provide? Once you know what it is, your work will take on a previously unrecognized dimension that can make all the difference between a daily grind and a lifelong adventure.

Two hints: (1) An important clue as to the nature of your craft will come not from your perspective, but from that of your ultimate customer—the people for whom your goods or service has the potential to have a positive impact. (2) Any craft is *proactive*. For example, there's not a craftsperson in the retail world who perceives her job as merely "*waiting* on customers."

11. *Build a learning network*. There are two ways you can view each person whose work is connected to yours: as a mirror that reflects back on your job or as a window to another endeavor. Showing a genuine interest in other people's work—not only from the perspective of how you can do your job better, but also from that of how you can help them do their job better—is one of the time-tested ways of generating personal and work value.

Here's how to get started. Make a list of everyone you come into contact with in your work and what they do (so much for not knowing anyone). What don't you know about their work? How does what you do fit into what they do? Have a list of questions for each person. Don't interrogate everyone, but be conscious that every time you interact with an individual, it is a chance to learn about his or her work—and to gain a different perspective on your own. If you can weave three extra questions a day into your normal interactions, you'll keep your brain from stagnating on the job.

Perhaps you've heard of the concept "six degrees of separation"—that you are connected to everyone else in the world by a string of no more than six acquaintances. If you apply this principle to your work, your current job is in some way connected to work in any field imaginable. And it's unlikely that you're going to have to take all six steps to get to somewhere previously unimagined.

12. *Put a lid on your time at work*. In a downsizing corporation, it's not unusual for one person to be doing the work of three. The result: a potential seven-day, round-the-clock workweek. Recognizing that these demands are very real, you must nevertheless realize that if you fail to draw the line *anywhere* when it comes to your work, it takes over fully.

Suggestion: Set a limit for the amount of time you are giving to your job on a weekly basis. Be generous to the company but fair to yourself—somewhere between nine-to-fiver and martyr. Setting a time limit will force you to be more efficient. The prolific Duke Ellington often remarked that he didn't need more time, he needed a deadline.

Prioritize your tasks—focusing on the issues that your organization considers most vital. Do the secondary things when and if you can. It's impossible to cover all of the bases, but make sure home plate is nailed down. And don't forget—your personal value to others can end up being what keeps you on the team.

13. *Make a lateral career move.* Careers are like elevators in a skyscraper. The elevator you've ridden to the nineteenth floor may not go any farther. If you want to go higher, you'll have to get on another elevator. In the corporate world, the crowd is always looking up, up, up: Everyone is trying to force themselves into a space that gets smaller and smaller. The term "lateral move" is often looked on as a euphemism for "stalled career." But a lateral move into an area that will allow you to better use your talents or that just plain excites you will enable you to generate far more value in your work—and provide the force for greater things to happen (even if they're in another building altogether).

14. *Learn how to speak in public.* It's often been reported that more people are afraid of speaking in public than of death itself. That's good news—there's less competition for those who can speak on their feet. Good platform skills are valuable not only when you have to talk to a group, but any time you have to communicate your ideas—around a conference table or even over the phone. (Have you ever known a good speaker who made a weak impression on the phone? Me neither.) In addition to local adult education courses, Dale Carnegie offers public speaking training. If you really want to elevate your skills over time, join your local chapter of Toastmasters International.

15. *Learn how to write.* Do you agonize over writing a simple one-page memo or cover letter? Do your great ideas get lost on the page? Is your first draft your final draft because it was just so hard to do you can't contemplate how it could be better?

No matter who you are or what you do, the ability to communicate your ideas in writing effectively will serve you well. And, perhaps even more important, your inability to do so will rule you out of the running for opportunities in more ways than you can imagine.

Start looking for a writing course in your area today. And get yourself a copy of *The Elements of Style* by Strunk and White.

16. *Open your ears.* Everyone demands to be heard. But before you can have something to say that's worth being heard, you have to listen. Some companies provide employees with listening skills training. If yours isn't one of them, don't wait. Check the business seminar listings in your area for a listening skills workshop, or look in the phone

book under "Training and Development" for a company that offers training for professionals.

17. *Listen for and act on valid criticism.* We're surrounded in our daily lives by some of the best and most readily applicable advice in the world. Unfortunately, many adults spend far too much energy defending themselves or their work with a tenacity perhaps more appropriate for the pope or the inventor of the wheel.

Listen to what people say about you—whether at home or at work. Walk around with your antennae up instead of your dukes. Odds are that if you hear something more than once, there's more than a grain of truth to it. And don't reject the message out of hand because you don't care for the messenger. One of the most useful critical comments I've ever received came from a boss I had little respect for—while I was handing in my resignation.

Hint: Granted that you are probably perfect, ask yourself, "If I were doing something wrong, what might it be?" Then look and listen for the answers.

18. *Become a profit center.* Many employees toil along diligently—even for years—without ever pausing to consider how they contribute to the bottom line. If a business can't survive without making a profit, how can you ever be sure of your value to the organization without thinking of yourself as a profit center?

Sketch an organizational chart of your company with you right in the middle, as if you were pivotal to the survival of the company. What role do you play in helping your business to make money? How can you do it better? Is there a way you can quantify it rather than verbally finesse it? Looking from the perspective of being a profit center can be a real eye-opener. The receptionist—the first impression for prospective customers—may very well have more bottom line impact than a midlevel manager who bounces from meeting to meeting.

19. *Take one task and go way beyond what your job requires.* At the core of every job are basic skills that transcend office politics, employer, and, in many cases, profession. Pick one of the basic skills you use on your job—speaking, writing, computing, customer service—and consciously develop your ability beyond what your work currently requires.

20. *Learn to earn.* Yep, I know that "Make more" isn't necessarily an answer. But if you can readily identify a skill that you lack which would pave the way to your moving up a notch in job and pay—or give you one more concrete option—you're crazy not to learn it. And not just for the sake of getting ahead, but to avoid getting left behind.

21. *Volunteer for work no one else wants to do.* The greatest opportunity often lies where there is the least interest or greatest perceived risk.

When an area of operation appears to be boring or mundane, odds are that it has been overlooked and allowed to drift along. That means that someone with a fresh approach and an eye toward generating value may be given not only latitude with gratitude ("You want to do it, more power to you") but also the chance to learn and make a significant impact.

People will stay away from work they perceive as carrying a risk of failure. That creates a chance for you to show what you can do. I'm not advocating that you set out on your personal version of Pickett's Charge—Todd the Snack Food Marketing Specialist wisely stayed away from taking on the Tuna Poles ("the smoked snack stick that comes from the sea") account. But that project you know would be a winner with the right approach might be the right vehicle for you to boost your value. Look for an area in your organization that has confounded others, scope it out, and raise your hand.

22. *Solve a big problem on your own.* Identify a core problem or obstacle in your organization—something that is just accepted as part of the terrain that has to be worked around. Give yourself the special assignment to solve the problem, no matter how long it takes. Do it quietly on your own time. (The framework of my biggest contribution to a former employer was worked out at my dining table on a Sunday night.) Don't pester people with each little potential good idea you have. Wait for the opportunity to present your broader answer— when someone else brings up the problem.

Your idea might take hold or it might be ignored; to a large extent it doesn't matter. The benefits of thinking and learning for yourself— becoming an intellectual entrepreneur—are yours to keep.

23. *Take advantage of training.* If your company offers a course, sign up, and then show up ready to learn. If your employer will pay for a class that's related to your work, you have no excuse not to take one.

Need added incentive? It has been estimated that employees who take advantage of company training earn on average about 10 percent more than their counterparts. Exception: If the course in question is some touchy-squishy drivel-fest, you're excused.

24. *Learn to use a computer to generate value.* Forget about the gadgetry or entertainment value—for many the Internet is an updated CB radio—and think about how using a computer can help you generate more value, both in and out of your workplace. If you are able to determine what you need or want to do with a computer, it's easy to learn how to do it.

Librarian William B. Collins has used his computer skills to increase the demand for his services, even during a period of public sector cutbacks: "The key is not to be dazzled by computer tricks, but to focus on practical application and content. A computer is a bunch of objects we all know how to use—calculator, file cabinet, telephone, typewriter—all tied together. You've got to know enough about whatever's hip so you don't get blindsided, but you've got to concentrate on how you can use this box to do your job better. My ability to come up with an accurate budget and store vital information has gotten me a lot further than my ability to set up a Web site."

Adult education courses are an inexpensive way to acquire basic computer skills and to get your questions answered patiently without trying for hours to get through to a toll-free number. Or you might be able to arrange for private tutoring from your neighborhood computer whiz (and to think we used to hire kids just to mow the lawn).

If you don't own a computer, perhaps a friend has a spare he'd be willing to loan you or rent out for a few months. Technowhizzes may tell you that you need all kinds of memory and the latest bells and whistles. Ignore them. A used machine that worked just fine for them a year or two ago will more than suit your purposes for now.

25. *Use your talent.* Once we discover an innate talent, there's no guarantee that it will propel us farther and faster ahead in life. We have to muster up the courage and perseverance to develop and use it, even when there's no readily apparent financial opportunity to do so.

I believe that most adults know where their talents lie. Far too many choose to ignore them. Take another look at your "value generation" résumé from the end of Chapter Three—those accomplishments in your life that you are most proud of. What particular talent(s) do you have that made them possible? Which one(s) are lying dormant? If you can't find a way to use this talent in your work, you *have* to find a way to use it outside of work.

This is as serious as it gets: If you grow something you're good at, an abundance of True Wealth will be yours.

26. *Learn to read a financial report.* The health of a business is in the numbers, not glossy pictures or zippy words. Knowing how to read a financial report can enable you to better understand what's really going on with your company, your competitors, or a company you are thinking of investing in. Otherwise, you may be stuck relying on the interpretation and recommendation of others. Less control—more stress potential.

Learning to read a financial report is best accomplished in a classroom with a teacher who can make the material come alive with examples of everything from hidden fraud to buried financial treasure (accounting needn't be dull) and who can answer all of your little questions along the way. Many business schools now offer seminars on this specific topic for the nonfinancial professional.

27. *Read what your manager or competition should read (and probably doesn't).* Ask yourself: "If I were in her shoes, what streams of information would I consider absolutely essential for keeping abreast of our field?"

Whether it be in finance or the arts, I've found all too often that people have an astonishing lack of curiosity about their own fields beyond that which they perceive as necessary to do their jobs. Even setting aside the obvious need to understand your competition and the marketplace, there's this question: If you don't have an active interest in what's going on beyond your field of immediate sight, can you really expect someone out there to take an interest in you?

On the other hand, if you continually expand your horizons, you never know what you'll come across—or leave behind. There's additional value to broadening your horizon beyond the edge of your desk. It can heighten the sense of balance in your life. You're not just working away in some little nook, you're tapped right into the action.

28. *Make a dollar from your hobby.* Figure out a way to make *one dollar* from your hobby. Remember, for everything that you think is fun or merely a pastime, it is someone else's livelihood. Once you've done that, try to make one hundred dollars.

Once you've figured out how to make money from your hobby, determine how you can keep generating income on an ongoing basis. Before you know it, you'll have a second income doing something you love—and another option in life.

29. *Learn how to sell.* There will always be a place for the person who knows how to sell a product—who can develop, facilitate, finalize, and follow up on a transaction. For without the transaction, everyone else can stay home.

Sales has a loud-blazer, fork-tongued reputation. But sales is really the art of learning and listening—finding the square peg for the square hole—and service—not disappearing before the ink is even dry. A word of caution: There are far more sales training courses than there is useful information on the subject. Everyone who has ever sold anything is an expert. Start by reading the book *Consultative Selling* by Mack Hanan and finding a way to learn from someone in sales whom you admire as a person as well as for his or her success.

Helpful hint: Don't pay too much attention to Number One. Top salespeople are often riddles unto themselves—and are sometimes not who they pretend to be.

30. *Get active in a trade group or professional association.* If there is a trade group or association for people in your field, join it and get active. Many people look at these groups strictly as a chance to do some cosmic networking—a hybrid lottery and chain letter where, if you meet enough people and hand out enough business cards, some fabulous unspecified opportunity will find its way back to you. But a trade group can be best thought of as an "annex" to your job—another venue for learning and a chance to broaden your horizons in your field.

31. *Publicize your niche.* How is one deigned an "expert"? After all, there is no official Expert Certification Program. One of the best ways is to get your insights into print. Whether in a trade magazine or your local paper, the printed word has the ability to direct a spotlight toward your expertise outside of your workplace.

Let's say you work at the jewelry counter in a store at the local mall. Not exactly a high-profile gig, you might think. Yet your local paper—or even a women's magazine—might welcome an article titled "The Ten Biggest Mistakes Women Make Buying Jewelry," "What Every Woman Needs, Dahling: The Basic Jewelry Wardrobe," or "How to Fake It in Style: The Best Buys in Costume Jewelry." (An alternate approach would be through public speaking—giving a talk to a local men's group at the beginning of the holiday shopping season, for example.)

With experthood bestowed, you can enjoy the benefits, which might include a greater sense of independence, increased business and enjoyment from your work, and new opportunities.

32. *Create your dream experience in the real world.* Some friends recently had the mandatory "What do you plan to do with your life?"

talk with their soon-to-graduate son, a photography major. When asked what his ideal situation would be, their son answered, "Win the lottery and travel around the world taking pictures."

As unrealistic as that answer might be, it contained the seed of a realistic solution: working as an international tour guide, scheduling time off overseas rather than at home. The core experience—taking pictures of foreign sites—was identical to his dream scenario.

The lesson is this: There is virtually no experience you cannot create in your life if you concentrate on *what it is you really want to do* rather than the ideal environment in which to do it.

33. *Befriend the competition.* Sure, your competitors are inferior in every way, having to rely on unsuspecting consumers to get by with such a substandard product. They're the enemy, waiting to be wiped out. At least all this is true according to the well-worn script—probably the same one your competitor is reading from.

But take a moment to consider that maybe, just maybe, your competitor is doing some things right, and doing some things you could benefit from knowing. By having an open, inquiring mind about the competition, you'll broaden your expertise within your field. Suggestion: Identify a means (legal, mind you) for obtaining the most up-to-date information on your competition.

34. *Reactivate an interest.* When you're cleaning out your house or apartment (that's coming up), pay special attention to reminders of past interests. Take a moment to reflect, "Gosh, wasn't that fun?" Ask yourself why your interest faded. It may have been for good reason—been there, done that—but perhaps it just got pushed aside in the shuffle. As an adult, there's no reason why you can't pick up the thread of an interest that goes back to high school.

35. *Help those who help you.* Like you, I've worked for all kinds, including the manager who introduced himself to his staff by saying "Your number one job is to make me look good." It proved to be an impossible task.

But I've been fortunate enough to work for several managers who took a sincere interest in my development—who I believed (cliché be damned) really cared about me as a person. Yet here's the clincher—almost everyone else who worked for them felt the same way I felt.

These special individuals (who, in addition to offering encouragement, had an uplifting way of informing you that you were goofing up) treated everyone who reported to them with this guiding principle: *If you help those who help you, everyone wins.* Needless to say, this approach inspires loyalty and effort on the job. But there's also a sense of value in your life that money can't buy when there are dozens upon dozens of people who, long after they've parted company with you, remember you and are thankful for the positive impact you've had on their lives.

36. *Explore that good idea.* What's the difference between those who find adventure and those who don't? Often it's not the lack of ideas, but rather the unwillingness to explore and possibly implement the ideas they have.

How many times have you told yourself, "Hey, that's a pretty good idea," daydreamed about runaway success for a minute, then stopped right there. Maybe you can't believe that no one else has ever thought of your idea—someone has to have already tried it and failed. Or maybe you're afraid to take the risk yourself. Don't be! A single idea—your idea—has the potential to take your life into an experience that would otherwise have been impossible to create.

Not all "good ideas" turn out to be good in practice. But you never know until you set an objective to find out for yourself. And just checking them out is a learning experience.

37. *Lead by example.* There is a far greater chance that your children will treat others with respect, eat right, be thrifty, read for pleasure, or display whatever other behavior you believe will serve them well in life, if they see you doing it. Almost any desirable behavior you can think of needn't require a penny, merely an honest and consistent advocate. Pick a behavior, get yourself up to speed if need be, and then convey the message by example. Like parent, like child: You go first.

38. *Volunteer as a family.* Doing volunteer work in the community—as a family, as father and son, mother and daughter, or any other combination—is a terrific way to convey character. It is an inexpensive activity with tremendous returns for all. Look for a spark of interest from your child and feed it with enthusiasm and direction.

39. *Get involved in your child's education.* Do you know what your children are really learning in school—beyond what it says on their report cards? Are you going to send an A student off to college and find out he has D writing skills? It's happened to several parents I know.

Involvement in your child's education is not to be confused with doing her homework or becoming the relentless mastermind of

Superchild. Being involved is making sure that he is learning what he should be learning at his age—and taking whatever steps are necessary to ensure that a solid educational bedrock is in place.

Involvement also includes contributing to the school in a way that suits your talent and interests—whether it's helping with an extracurricular activity or serving on the budget committee. Children whose parents are involved in making their school better do better in school.

Word of advice: If you're a technophobe, you're going to be impressed with anything your kid can do on a computer, even if it is useless or passive. (A CD-ROM is often an inferior substitute for a book.) As a parent, it is up to you to ensure that the computer is a practical experience rather than a disconnection from reality.

40. *Recast your family leisure time.* Does your family leisure time center on consumption or marketing vehicles that drive consumption? Most "collectibles," for example, are really just collectors of your money. If that's so in your family, it's time to rethink and resist.

In addition to volunteer work there are endless avenues to explore, no matter where you live, indoors and outdoors, in any season. Set an objective—a new experience every weekend or every other weekend. Hint: Virtually every newspaper publishes a weekly entertainment guide. Look past the movie listings and you'll find a host of different and unique things to do: museums, free concerts, readings, nature walks, demonstrations, exhibitions, and so on.

41. *Eat dinner together.* Eating dinner as a family is a proven way to generate family value: Exchange ideas, impart values, and identify and solve problems.

Although the decline of the family dinner hour may have something to do with busy schedules, I believe it has at least as much to do with a lack of will on the part of parents. Eat late or eat early, but eat together. Don't let your family become a house full of strangers who occasionally bump into each other in the kitchen.

42. *Set and enforce limits and standards of behavior for your children.* In years gone by, when a college education was the exception and teenagers often shouldered financial responsibility within the family, the most potent factor in a person's moving up the socioeconomic ladder frequently was personal behavior.

When you read the biographies of great men and women who rose from humble origins, invariably you will find that whatever they lacked in material wealth was more than compensated for by their having adults in their lives who set limits and standards, encouraging behavior that would be recognized and valued by others in almost any situation.

When today's parents complain about their children's lack of responsibility around the house, it is often a result of the parents' having never spelled out just what they expect of the kids or having failed to ensure that these expectations are met. Doing so requires time and effort, but (never forget) doesn't require money. And if you think that a person's sense of responsibility isn't at least as important as where he or she attends college, go talk to a few small-business owners who do their own hiring.

43. *Volunteer to use your talent in the community.* If you have a talent you can't express through your work, volunteer work may be the ideal vehicle to let it shine. If you know that you'd be a good sales manager if you only had the chance, prove it to yourself by heading up a local fund-raising drive. Want to organize a direct-marketing effort or work with the media? Get involved in a local political campaign. The opportunities to use your talent are myriad. And remember Jonas Gadson's advice: "You've got to love something so much that you'll do it for free, and that's what will make you good enough to get paid."

Volunteer work is also a great way to use your artistic talents. I have a friend whose work involves extensive travel and who never goes anywhere without his guitar. Instead of spending his evenings in his hotel room, he calls a nearby nursing home and schedules an impromptu concert for the residents. He is always "on tour."

44. *Take the lead in improving the quality of life in your community.* It has been said that ordinary citizens can accomplish extraordinary deeds. But these "ordinary" citizens are really just *active* citizens.

Have you ever looked at a problem or an opportunity in your community and said, "Someone ought to . . ."? Change that to "I'm going to . . ." Speaking from experience, I can tell you that if you're willing to take on responsibility, you'll soon find that you'll be given all the responsibility you can handle.

45. *Give up a bad health habit.* Whether it's smoking, drinking, a strained relationship with fruits and vegetables, or treating fat as a food group, you can identify a bad health habit of yours. And you've probably had it for so long, you accept it as part of your unalterable self. That's a choice you don't have to make.

The benefits of giving up a single bad health habit are not only physical (you'll feel better and be less prone to serious illness) and financial (bad habits cost money and lead to higher health care costs) but, and perhaps most important, psychological.

I recognize that, say, giving up Camels is harder than giving up Clark Bars. But beating a bad habit can give you the confidence and strength to take on the rest of the world. "After I quit smoking," a successful freelance artist told me, "I found myself knocking on doors that had once intimidated me. My business just skyrocketed because of my change in attitude about myself and what I could accomplish."

46. *Take the first steps toward fitness.* This is not to be confused with losing weight nowfastforever, alchemizing your buns into metal, or becoming a weekend triathlete. Rather, it is simply making sure that you get twenty to thirty minutes of exercise three to four times a week. If you can maintain this objective, additional health-generating habits will follow.

47. *Drink water.* Water is both a necessity and a luxury we take for granted. Yet drinking six to eight glasses a day will not only help you feel and look better, it will also save you hundreds, if not thousands, of dollars a year otherwise spent on sugar water and chemical punch. If you think that you don't have dollars to spare as a resource for generating value, here's a good place to find them.

Hints: Don't rely on trips to the drinking fountain. Keep a glass or water bottle nearby throughout the day. If your tap water is truly awful, invest in a basic filtration system. It will pay for itself many times over, especially if you're in the habit of buying bottled water—a needless expense given that most of it is tap water to begin with.

48. *Plan your day and defend your time.* Do you want to get more out of your day? The best way to do it is to spell out exactly what it is *you* want from that day—not just what circumstances dictate you have to do to keep up. If you spend a few minutes each morning planning how you are going to generate value, you are far more likely to make the decisions that will keep you a step ahead of the present.

Defending your time means blocking out a time frame for taking a specific action and keeping the obvious time thieves at bay while you get it done. Biggest culprit on the job: idle or irrelevant chatter. Biggest culprit at home: You guessed it, television.

For excellent training in planning and managing your day, I highly recommend attending a Franklin Covey time management seminar (see Appendix B).

49. *Clear the deck and organize a value zone.* Whether it's starting a new activity or approaching your work with a renewed spirit, you might already have a good idea of an objective you want to reach. But you can't picture yourself doing it because you don't have a space to do it in. If your office is a modern-day Augean stable, spend a Saturday shoveling it out. Organize a space in your home that is conducive to generating value: a desk or a reading chair in an out-of-the-way corner or a cleaned-out work area in the basement or garage.

Word of caution: This is not an excuse to spend money outfitting a home office or a workshop. Start with what you have.

50. *Stop doing the one big stupid thing that could wreck your life.* If a part of your life is a candidate for a bad country music song—whether it's drinkin' and drivin', lyin', cheatin', foolin' around, gamblin', or stayin' out partyin' all night long—change your tune before you're singing the real-life blues. Actions have consequences—a lesson better learned through theory than through practice.

51. *Read* Learned Optimism *by Martin Seligman.* Almost anyone can benefit from the ideas and exercises in this book. Pessimists may find the key to a brighter future.

52. *Quit whining.* Take out a sheet of paper. Write down every person and condition that you believe is holding you back in life and how you believe they are doing it. Your boss, coworkers, family, company, government, people you don't know: Tie everyone into your conspiracy theory. Now pretend for a minute that nothing on your list is ever going to change—no amount of complaining is going to make a difference. You could stop it for an entire day, right? How about a week?

Write these words at the top of your list: "I will not complain about . . ." Refer to the list as often as needed to remind yourself to quit whining until you are ready to throw out the list and the complaints for good. Bonus: This objective does not take a single penny or second of your time to pursue once you get started, but the payoff can be astronomical.

Listening to others whine diminishes your opportunity to generate value as well. Hints: Until you're in the habit of forestalling whiners, post a little note to yourself: "I am not the complaint window." When a coworker starts in—you know the likely candidates—cut him off politely and hang up or walk away.

53. *Don't accept pain.* As we enter middle age, our bodies begin to collect aches, pains, and ailments. So what do we often do? Ignore them or accept them until they become chronic limitations. Between traditional and alternative medicines, the powers of the mind and the body, and simple exercise, there is a host of potential solutions costing little or no money. Many people will attest to the long-term benefits of yoga, tai chi chuan, and/or meditation in helping to keep their bodies relatively free from pain.

54. *Go to bed early and get up early.* Here's an interesting concept: One hour of sleep before midnight is equal to two hours of sleep after midnight. I don't know what the scientists think, but my personal experience is that there's more than a grain of truth to the matter. Ask yourself this: Has there ever been a bit of information on the local nightly news that has given you a jump start on what you want to accomplish the next day?

Whether it's catching up or getting ahead, you'll be amazed at what you can accomplish in a single hour of morning solitude.

55. *Get a makeover from your neck up.* If you've been wearing the same hairstyle or glasses for years and years—a pair of disco secretary frames or a "usual trim" hair helmet—it probably looks like it. The problem: A significant number of people don't take you as seriously as they should. People do react to how you look, and a fresh look is an inexpensive way to generate more physical energy, even among longtime colleagues.

A word of caution: If you think this suggestion is dumb or doesn't matter a hoot, you probably need to take it seriously. If you want to rush right out to the optometrist or salon, you probably don't need to.

56. *Sit in the front row of life.* An interesting phenomenon: Students who sit in the front row in class get higher grades. Why? Because the location virtually demands a higher degree of mental engagement, if not active participation, than a seat in the back row or on the perimeter.

I think that the same principle applies to almost any gathering—whether it's a conference, meeting, or seminar. If you're near the center of the action, you're going to get more out of the event, even by sheer osmosis. Yet I can tell you from years of observation that the front row is usually the last to fill up. If you're going to spend the time and/or money, why not position yourself to get the most value out of your investment?

57. *Try to understand things you've never understood.* How does electricity work? Why do bond prices go down when interest rates go up? What's with the sport of curling? We all have blind spots in what we know that have a nagging way of popping up over and over. Yet filling in our blanks may take only a minute.

For quick reference, I recommend keeping a basic "What the . . . ?" library, consisting of a good dictionary; *The Way Things Work* by David Macaulay; *The Dictionary of Cultural Literacy: What Every American Needs to Know* (Houghton Mifflin Co.); *The Larousse Desk Reference* (Kingfisher Books); and *How in the World? A Fascinating Journey Through the World of Human Ingenuity* and *The Reader's Digest Book of Facts* (both Reader's Digest).

For in-depth exploration, if there's something you've always wanted to know, there are plenty of ways to learn without going to class, let alone getting a degree. My wife, Linda, who hasn't taken a science course since high school, has been studying physics on her own for several years. Using an excellent audio course (see Appendix B) and several books, she's reaching her primary objective—to understand at a layman's level the latest developments in quantum mechanics. The unexpected benefit, she explains, is that "Now when I speak to a group of scientists, I feel a lot more confident, and I think my respect for their work comes across."

58. *Stop placing people on a ladder.* One ill effect of using money as the currency of your life can be that you immediately size people up using a vague formula based on their job, income, and possessions and then position them on a mental ladder. If someone is a rung below you, they are part of the faceless mass that must be tolerated as necessary and dismissed without haste; if someone is a rung above, their favor must be curried through the full range of assumable postures. Remember: Any stress caused by social climbing is, at its root, financial stress.

Objective: Treat everyone with whom you interact—whether it's the pizza delivery person or the president—as a person of equal standing, and you'll be surprised at how your own circumstances will be elevated.

59. *Tune up your sound.* Pretend for a moment that you are a saxophonist or a trumpeter. When you talk, what sound do others hear? You may be projecting a bunch of jumbled discordant notes or a flat-out screech and expecting others to hear them as a mellifluous melody.

An observation I've had of great jazz musicians is their understanding that the *sound of a single note* communicates as much to an audience as all of the notes played. Listen to yourself. Tape-record your portion of a phone conversation or let a recorder run during meetings or around the house. How do you sound on tape compared to how you would like to sound? Keep practicing until the sound that leaves your mouth is the same as the sound in your heart and mind. As Louis Armstrong said, "If you ain't got it in you, you can't blow it out."

60. *Make the easy change.* We all have little annoying habits that bug others—and turn into the equivalent of the assassination of Archduke Ferdinand. One incident and, next stop, total war. Why should anyone make a big deal out of a little thing like leaving wet towels on the floor or dirty dishes around the house? Who cares if making that clicking noise with your fingernails or slurping a beverage drives a coworker to distraction?

Look at it the other way: If it's such a little thing, why not cut it out and save everyone the annoyance and yourself the animosity?

61. *Do what you say you will when you say you'll do it.* Remember when you had an appointment with a repairman and he actually showed up on time—not three hours later or the next day? You hailed it as a minor miracle and told your friends about the experience as if you'd accidentally bumped into Elvis. Now imagine the goodwill you'd generate toward yourself if you did the same: Do what you say you will when you say you'll do it. The secret: not biting off more than you can chew and managing your time well.

62. *Get your résumé updated.* What single piece of paper has the power to hold back millions of people from taking even the first step toward stress-busting action—sometimes for years on end? An outdated résumé. Even if you don't plan on looking for a new job in the foreseeable future, having an updated résumé stored in your computer makes possible an instant response to an unanticipated opportunity.

63. *Vote in every election that you are eligible to vote in.* If you don't exercise your right to vote, you have no right to complain. Federal, state, local, school board, fire district, whatever: Fill out a ballot or pull a lever. If you're uninformed, a few blank minutes in the booth may provide the motivation to pay closer attention.

Added motivator: I've been told that, early in his rise to power, Hitler won a crucial election by one vote. I've never confirmed this because, even if it's not true, it is worthwhile pretending that it is.

64. *Slow down for a day.* Perhaps you're old enough to remember that one day a week when the stores weren't open? Or when national holidays weren't celebrated with storewide bargain bonanza blowouts?

There certainly was a different tone to those nonshopping days—one that put the emphasis on generating value in ways that might have been overlooked during the week. In other words, an opportunity to balance your life. Recently my family decided that just because stores were open on Sunday, it didn't mean we had to go to them. Just as with pulling the plug on television, you'll adapt quickly and be surprised at the positive change.

65. *Mend a fence.* Sure, there are people who do horrendous things, and after we've forgiven them, we want to write these people out of our lives. But other times we let past events or differences become lifetime grudges that take on a life of their own—working their way into our thoughts and conversations like bionic termites. It's almost as if we're compelled to live in our own soap opera.

By mending fences with estranged family and friends, you're not trying to go back to the way things were before. But you will be getting rid of a lot of toxic baggage that can absorb too much time, energy, and resources that could be better used in generating value than sticking pins in voodoo dolls.

66. *Practice human ecology.* On a camping trip, one way to generate value is to leave nature better than you found it. As we negotiate the wilderness of human interaction, a simple guide for generating personal value is to leave each encounter having enhanced the lives of others—even if it's just an appreciative word to the harried airline ticket agent who's been blamed all day for the blizzard outside, or a friendly "hello" to a service worker toiling away in a state of near invisibility to others.

67. *Look up for a minute every day.* We see the world for the most part at eye level—everything and anything important is within six or seven feet of the ground. That can be suffocating. Even if it's just when you're walking across the parking lot or going out to get the mail, pause for a moment. Take a deep breath, look up at the sky, and try to soak up a little bit of the majesty of the universe. Put your trials and tribulations in perspective.

68. *Learn about what other people believe.* Approach other people's spiritual beliefs from the perspective of "What do they believe?" rather than "What should I believe?" Approach religion as a topic like history or science: something you need to know about in order to come close to an understanding of the world you live in.

69. *Decide to believe.* To anyone who comes up blank in the spiritual values category and who is pondering how and where to begin, allow me to offer a few brief words of advice: Don't act like a consumer and think, "I'm going to wait until the right thing to believe in comes along before I put my heart and soul on the counter." Rather, you'll find that first making the decision to believe will help you discover what to believe.

70. *Make your faith a part of your everyday life.* You live through all seven days of the week. Why make your faith part of only one of them? Suggestion: A few minutes of reading, contemplation, and prayer before you turn out the lights at night is a great way to clear your mind and sleep in peace.

FOUR GOOD QUESTIONS—FOUR GOOD OBJECTIVES

So faced with both a single H2O and life's infinite options, how can you quickly narrow the possibilities to a manageable few objectives that will effectively address your need? I believe that if you can set an objective that answers each of the following four questions, you'll have a solid blueprint for reducing your financial stress.

OBJECTIVE QUESTION #1: **What do I absolutely have to be doing that I am not doing right now to make fulfilling this H2O part of my day-to-day reality?**

OBJECTIVE QUESTION #2: **What ability could I increase that, when learned and put into action, will help make my H2O a part of my day-to-day reality?**

OBJECTIVE QUESTION #3: **What could I do that would remove a deterrent to generating value toward my impact H2O?**

OBJECTIVE QUESTION #4: **How can I address this H2O by strengthening and/or demonstrating my character on a daily basis?**

TIPS FOR PICKING OBJECTIVES THAT WORK

Here are some guidelines for selecting objectives that will maximize your value generation:

Spread Your Value Generation Across the Full Spectrum

The obvious place to begin choosing objectives is within the primary type of value for your impact H2O. If, for example, your impact H2O is work-related, the situation demands that you generate work-related value in a way that addresses your need head-on. There's no mystery to that—or at least there shouldn't be.

You've got to face reality and directly do something about what's bugging you. (Refer to the discussion on pages 103 to 116 if you're unsure about what type of value relates to your H2O.) But although that may be where you begin to set objectives, that's not where it should end.

Your life is not a bunch of little framed portraits: work, play, family, neighbors. Think of it instead as a large mural. Ideally, each scene not only is pleasing to the eye but is harmonious with and enhances the other scenes. If you've got an area of your life that is the equivalent of a dark gray picture of tortured squirrels, it is going to shade the rest of your life in a negative manner. Try as you might, you can't block it out.

So you also want to think of ways to generate value not directly related to your impact H2O that nevertheless can play a key role in fulfilling your need. When you generate value across a broad spectrum to fulfill a specific need, not only are you accessing the full range of solutions, you are also broadening the web of cause and effect in your life—that one good thing will lead to another.

Here's how I suggest spreading your four objectives throughout the value spectrum:

- Choose two objectives that generate the type of value directly related to your impact H2O. Pay particular attention to Objective Question #1, i.e., doing the obvious.
- Choose one objective that will generate personal or spiritual value.
- Choose your remaining objective from a type of value different from your first three objectives.

Look for Objectives That Will "F.I.T." into Your Daily Schedule with Reasonable Amounts of Focus, Initiative, and Time

Don't try to cram all of your objectives into the same time frame—a surefire recipe for failure. One way to increase your value generation is to make sure that your objectives don't compete against one another for your time and energy. That can be accomplished by spreading your objectives throughout the day—before work, during work, after work, and in the evening. By spreading your objectives throughout the day, if you're unable to tackle a given objective at its designated time, you'll still have other opportunities to generate stress-reducing value. The entire day won't be a bust.

Make sure that you can properly focus on your objective at the selected time. You might find it easier to study computer programming early in the morning when you're rested rather than at the end of a long day. On the other hand, the evening might be the perfect time to pursue an outside interest where your passion will serve as a reserve of energy.

Pick at least one objective that doesn't run on time. One way to generate value is to *not* do something. For example, it takes no time *not* to carp about your boss or your company at every turn—and not complaining gets rid of a stress-creating barrier. And by *not* doing something, you will free up some additional time *and* some additional resources (bad habits often cost money).

Make Sure You Know You're Getting Somewhere

To keep your objectives going, you've got to feel as though you're getting somewhere.

Some objectives have readily identifiable means of measuring your progress—learning how to do something new or increasing your number of sales calls, for example. Other objectives are more subjective—setting a good example for your children or sharpening up your appearance.

Whatever your objective, choose whichever one of the following measures will help you best gauge your results:

- At the end of the day you can say you did (or didn't) do it.
- There is something that you can see as a result.
- There is something you know or can do that you didn't know or couldn't do before.
- There is something you've done that would have never happened otherwise.
- Other people let you know how you're doing (referrals, unsolicited comments, performance evaluations, grades, etc.).

Put the Two Types of Decisions—Cumulative and Sequential—to Work for You

One way of looking at an objective is as a means of organizing and making decisions.

Although financial stress is ultimately a big pile of little decisions, we don't have to make an equally big pile of little decisions to make it go away. Rather than just heap together decisions and hope that they add up to something different, we can proceed much more efficiently and effectively simply by keeping in mind how decisions can work together to change the backdrop of life.

Decisions work together to weave objectives into your daily life in two ways:

1. *Cumulatively,* that is, your decisions add up. By repeatedly making the same decision(s)—daily, weekly, monthly—your objective becomes a growing part of your life.

> Spend fifteen minutes planning your day and you'll become more efficient.
>
> Put aside $5.50 a day and you'll have $2,000 for your annual IRA contribution.
>
> Practice something every day and before you know it, it will be second nature.

Cumulative decisions are the foundation work for True Wealth. There's no mystery and often little glamour to them—they just add up. You don't need even to think about them too much. Once you've made the initial decision, say, to exercise regularly, you don't have to carefully evaluate each subsequent decision. You simply get into the habit and then allow the force of habit to do the work while you reap the rewards. Once you're on a roll, the objective doesn't need much maintenance or attention.

2. *Sequentially,* that is, your decisions move you ahead. By making a series of different but related decisions, you get from point A to point B and beyond, each decision pointing the way to the next.

> If where you live isn't where you want to retire, you'll use sequential decisions to determine where you move—whether it's across town or halfway across the country.
>
> If you're looking for a new job, you'll pound the pavement with sequential decisions.

Sequential decisions add greatly to the distinctive character of your life. They require a more active combination of thought and judgment than cumulative decisions do. Each decision may point the way to the next, but because each decision is unique, sequential decisions require more concentration and effort. You can't go on autopilot. One potential benefit from the extra effort: Sequential decisions are the catalysts for adventure.

You are going to want to pick objectives that give you a mix of both cumulative and sequential decisions. When you weave both types of decisions together toward creating a desired experience, the habits of your cumulative decisions complement and reinforce the progression of your sequential decisions. The result: The fabric of your life is strong and true to your needs, a vibrant and appealing backdrop for future decisions. Visually, here's how the change is made:

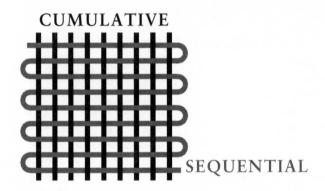

ASSEMBLING A BLUEPRINT FOR TRUE WEALTH

1. Gather your resources and plan your decisions for each objective, using the questions and worksheet on the pages that follow.
2. Prioritize your four objectives based on immediate impact.
3. Begin acting on your highest-impact objective today.
4. Record your value-generating decisions each day (this is where a day planner is particularly handy).
5. Add one additional objective every week until you are taking value-generating, stress-reducing action toward your impact H2O with all four objectives.
6. Keep making those decisions until they become permanent habit or reveal the next logical objective.

WORKSHEET: THE OBJECTIVE PLANNER

H2O:

OBJECTIVE:

Time:
Which days of the week am I going to work on this objective?

What time(s) of day?

For how many minutes/hours?

Energy:
Do I have the necessary physical, mental, and emotional energy to work on this objective?

If not, what objective(s) will enable me to raise my energy to the necessary level?

Resources:
What abilities—knowledge, skills, and experience—do I have that I can use to accomplish this objective?

What information do I need to accomplish this objective, and where can I get it?

What people do I know—or know of—who might help provide me with an insight as to how I might accomplish this objective?

What organizations or institutions—schools, businesses, community, church, government, nonprofit, cultural, civic, or private—might offer resources that I can use to accomplish this objective?

WORKSHEET: THE OBJECTIVE PLANNER

H2O:

OBJECTIVE:

Time:

Energy:

Resources:
Ability

Information

People

Organizations and institutions

Resources:
What do I already own that I can use to accomplish this objective?

What existing opportunities do I have to generate value toward this objective?

What money will be required—if any—to accomplish this objective?

What tools am I lacking that are needed to generate value toward this objective (see Chapter Seven)?

Decisions:
What can I be doing on a regular basis to accomplish this objective?

What series of sequential decisions will I need to pursue to accomplish this objective?

Progress:
How will I measure my progress in fulfilling this objective?

Resources:
What I already own

Opportunity

Money

Tools

Decisions:
Cumulative (A → A → A . . .)

Sequential (A → B → C . . .)

Progress:

How to Never Spend Another Dollar: The Exchange Standard

NOW WE ARRIVE at that part of your value generation that you can take to the store and readily exchange: your income.

By making *value* your basic currency and by phrasing your needs in terms of what has to *occur* rather than what has to be *bought,* a change is already happening in the way you're going to utilize your money. Many of your needs you are now going to address first and foremost by generating value—and to much greater effect.

But as a result of generating work value, you *do* have an income. And that raises a key question: **What do you do with the money you have to help create the life that money can't buy?**

This question appears paradoxical only to the degree that you've disconnected making money and spending money. The moment you get a little loot in your hands is not an occasion to forget about how and why it got there. Rather, it is a critical juncture to align and strengthen the relationship between how you generate and exchange value. Because if you see the two activities as separate and distinct rather than part of a whole, your money will ignore your commands to make you happy. The reason it does so: You think that money is for spending.

Let's go back to the purpose of money. Money is a means of exchange—not a means of expenditure. If you look up the word "spend" in *Webster's,* you'll find: Pay out, use up, exhaust, consume wastefully, squander, give up, sacrifice, waste wealth or strength. In other words, spending money is a lopsided transaction. No matter what your expectations, you will always get back less than you part with.

Unless you shed the spending mind-set, you're going to continue to shell out your money for a jumble of stuff that doesn't add up to the life you want. Let's now explore the spending mind-set. The better our understanding of why it fails us, the easier it will be to scrap it.

"I SPENT IT ALL, AND ALL I'VE GOT TO SHOW FOR IT IS A BUNCHA CHUD"

The road to hell, it is oft reported, is paved with good intentions. It's also lined with billboards that beckon, "Buy now, save a bundle" and "Be the happyzestysmartsexysuccessfulfascinating person you know you really are." Of the thousands of advertising images you see each day, every single image has the same ultimate message: Gimme Some Money.

It's little wonder that whenever you try to travel the path of fiscal sanity—one hand on the wheel and one on your wallet—you're soon swerving down an exit ramp, rationalizing that this upcoming purchase is the momentary missing link between dull existence and downright euphoria. But no matter how solid your reasoning seems before you hand over your money, the chances are significant that you're just getting more chud to cram in your trunk.

What is chud?

Chud stands for Consumable Had-to-Have-It Under Delusion.

Chud is anything you spend money on that, given the benefit of hindsight, you'd give up in an instant if you could have the money back instead. Perhaps the phrase "juice machine," "souvenir straw hat," or "limited offer" just flashed through your mind. It takes only a second to recognize that you've probably consumed a lot of chud in your lifetime—and have a lot less money for doing so.

Chud comes in three distinct varieties:

1. *Visible chud* is the fodder for the occasional game of "Sell, Donate, Chuck, or Keep." The shoes in your closet you wore only three times. The electronic keyboard gathering dust in the basement. The bread maker in the kitchen that cost more bread than it ever made. The toys that occupied your child for less time than they took to assemble. The racks of unwatched videos. The thirty-dollar concert T-shirt.

While driving down a rural road, you've undoubtedly passed a house where the entire yard was crammed with chud—cars, appliances, a lifetime collection of empty bleach containers, year-round Christmas decorations: a virtual theme park of consumer detritus. "Whoa ho ho," you've chortled, "who could ever live like that?"

Here's the answer: *You do.*

The only difference between you and the Turniptops is that you have the good social graces not to store all of your chud on your lawn. You've got closet systems and storage racks and a garage and boxes from basement to attic keeping it hidden from public view.

If you walk from room to room with a mental Chud Scanner, you're going to realize that you've got a ton of chud. And if you added up what you paid for it, you'd experience a wave of borderline nausea. Boy, wouldn't you just love to trade that exercise contraption for a charge card payment?

2. *Invisible chud* sneaks into your life unnoticed and stays just long enough to grab some money and get out, leaving little trace. The money's gone, and you have nothing to show for it.

Invisible chud includes almost anything that comes out of a vending machine or any piece of paper bearing the word "lottery." The food you put in your refrigerator and then toss untouched a week later. A couple of hours of inconsequential on-line wandering. The extra amount you'll pay for something just because it has a designer logo.

Invisible chud is in many ways more insidious than visible chud. You don't have the hard-core physical evidence staring you right in the face for months or years to jar you by saying "Here I am. You bought me and really didn't need me, so when are you going to start rethinking this whole spending thing?" It's more like Chinese water torture, a steady drip of value leaking from your life. As long as you have a continual replacement supply of money, you barely notice the loss.

3. *Big chud* calls the shots each month when you pay the bills. That part of your mortgage that goes for more house than you need or that part of your car payment that puts you behind the wheel of a personal driving machine, not a mere automobile. The vacation property that you have to work seven days a week to pay off.

Big chud is problematic in two ways. The first is that it demands huge chunks of cash in one bite. If your car payment is $499 a month, there's no letting up until the finish line. Every month the hurdle is at the same height. You can't, say, send in $249 without repercussions.

The second problem with big chud is that we think that, once we have it, it's permanent. We can't move it out of our lives—to do so would be an admission of failure. And even if we want to, it takes a lot of effort. Who wants to go through the hassle of selling a house, let alone a camper unit and a couple of jet skis?

THE MENACE OF CHUD

Chud is too often accepted as the natural by-product of the consumer life. You make some money, do something with it, and accept as a given that some of it you're just throwing down the drain. But chud is serious stuff.

Chud siphons value that, if directed toward your H2Os, would dramatically reduce your financial stress. It would probably be fair to conclude that just half of your lifetime invisible chud tab would make for a pretty good-sized nest egg.

Chud distracts you from focusing on your real needs. When you get too much chud, you end up as Chief Chud Custodial Engineer. You're not running your life, you're running your universe of chud. You've got all that chud that begs for immediate attention: sorting, fixing, cleaning, organizing, maybe even using it!

Chud takes on a life of its own. Chud often requires more chud just to keep it going—ask anyone who has a swimming pool. It becomes another mouth to feed, living on a steady diet of time, energy, and money.

With visible, invisible, and big chud at work, it's not too difficult to get to a point where chud-driven decisions add up to financial stress. And when your financial stress symptoms get to be too much to handle, almost instinctually you think first of tightening your grip on your spending, that is, cutting out chud. You muster your resolve and haul out the most common Chud Fighter known to man: the budget.

WHY BUDGETS AND DIETS
HAVE THE SAME SUCCESS RATE

Unfortunately, going on a budget has about the same success rate as dieting. Only the most committed are able to keep a tight grip for long. The first few days you're filled with resolve. A week later, you've been doing so well, one little splurge won't hurt. And soon after, "It was just too difficult to stick to with everything going on. Maybe some time after the holidays . . . or when summer's over . . . or . . ."

How is it that this week's budget turns into next week's joke? The answer can be found right in the trenches.

We have chud because we spend money on it—daily. This ongoing exchange of value for chud is in many ways the front line where the fight against financial stress can be won or lost. In order to begin to control the exchange, we first have to understand how most people make their spending decisions.

Here's the framework commonly used for spending money. It has five levels of consideration for a potential purchase:

The Five Steps to Throwing Money Down the Drain

1. *I want something* . . . Why do we want something? Because we believe that life is going to be better in some way with it than without it. Automatically this tilts our mind-set toward spending. If we don't spend the money, we're going nowhere. Immediate spending is the fastest way to improve our lives.

2. *. . . do I have a means to buy it?* This is not to be confused with "Can I afford it?" or "How does this fit with the rest of my life?" Rather, do you have access to an amount of cash or credit that matches the price tag?

You can spend a lot of your money without ever getting past this step—which is how bank accounts dwindle to $1.32 and charge cards get maxed.

3. *. . . is it a good deal?* If you get to this level, you applaud yourself for being a smart shopper, even if your last "good deal" is already in a box in your basement. When we see the words "on sale" or hear the words "regularly sells for," common sense goes out the window. Suddenly the subversive notion takes hold that by spending money we're somehow saving money.

Here's the truth: If you have less in your pocket when you leave the store than when you walked in, you haven't saved. Unless the owner is paying you to take something out of the store—"Here's a toaster and five bucks for your piggy bank, now beat it"—you're not now and never will be saving. *You're simply spending less,* and often only in theory.

4. *. . . do I really need it?* By this level your money may have a mind and will of its own. All you can do is wave good-bye.

Of course you need it—and you come up with a ready rationale for any purchase. If you have the deluxe leather interior in your car, you'll feel successful on your way to work; and if you feel successful, you'll act successful; and if you act successful, you'll be more successful; and if you are more successful, before you know it you'll be right at the top—all because you sat on some cow skin on the freeway.

And, just to prove that you're not totally reckless, you're willing to push some other want aside to accommodate this one. Unfortunately, until you've framed your spending wants within the context of generating value, you're just shuffling your impulses.

5. And finally, . . . *is there something else I should be doing with the money?* Of course there is. That's why your brain usually shuts down before you get this far. You don't want to think about your "shoulds." So what's wrong with this picture? The big problem with this typical spending framework is that your wants are right up front calling the shots. When your spending is driven by your wants, you are putting yourself on a perpetual treadmill where everything you desire appears just out of reach.

It is a *100 percent certainty that your wants will always outpace your resources.* And it is a constant danger that you'll try to make up the difference with debt or ignore more pressing needs.

When you put yourself on a strict budget, you are, in effect, attempting to turn the entire framework upside down—pushing your wants underground and hoping that you have the willpower to keep them there. Your wants still exist—you're just trying to pretend they don't. Before too long, they are bubbling up to the surface, undermining your commitment—which may indeed be tenuous—to your budget. In the tug of war between wants and shoulds—guess who has more emotional pull?

Trying to twist this want-driven framework into one that enables you to effortlessly determine how to exchange your money for your H2Os is like trying to do Rubik's Cube wearing a blindfold. So let's scrap it altogether for a simple guide that *begins with* all of your needs, rather than *gets around to* some of them some of the time.

THE FOURTH COMPONENT OF TRUE WEALTH: EXCHANGE YOUR MONEY FOR THE TOOLS YOU NEED TO FULFILL YOUR H2Os

---

In *Webster's* you'll find this entry for the word "exchange": "to part with, give, or transfer in consideration of something received as an equivalent."

This meaning takes us beyond the surface financial transaction ("This costs $4.99 and I have $4.99 in my pocket to spend"). It directs us to think not only about what we're giving or transferring—value—but also balancing that value with the other side of the transaction—getting back an equal amount of value. In other words, making sure you have a good solid answer for this question: "What's in it for me?"

What's mostly in it for you is a means to generate value that brings your H2Os into your day-to-day life. Money may not obey your commands, but it is always willing to do something along with you—if you take the lead. To paraphrase JFK: "Ask not what money can do for you, but rather ask what you can do with your money."

People with True Wealth understand that when you exchange your money, generally the person on the other side of the transaction makes a financial profit (or at least hopes to). That's a given. To the degree that what you get back enables you to generate value in your life, *that's your profit*.

If you use your money to make your H2Os your day-to-day reality, *the value of your dollars never leaves your life*.

In other words, if money is exchanged for a form of value that fulfills your needs, then that money isn't gone for good. Quite to the contrary: *Your money has become a permanent part of your life*.

This concept is one of the keys that makes it possible for one person to have far less financial stress than someone with two times, ten times, or even one hundred times greater income. It is how people who consistently exchange their money for their needs can end up with True Wealth regardless of their income. It is what makes it possible for there to be little relation between income and happiness.

THE PRACTICAL TOOLS OF EVERYDAY LIVING

We exchange an overwhelming percentage of our money in order to fulfill H2O #16: Providing ourselves and our family with the basic necessities of life and a reasonable level of comfort. *Practical value* is the value you generate by exchanging your money for the daily needs of you and your family.

A household budget is a compendium and reflection of the tools we believe we need to make our daily lives manageable, pleasant, satisfying, and rewarding. So let's look at where the money goes.

Now, right off the bat, I'm going to acknowledge the legitimacy of all of these needs. If you want to argue that you don't need electricity or that personal care products are a trapping of oppression, fine. There's an empty shack in Montana that has your name on it. But, by and large, these needs are embraced by the overwhelming majority of households. The critical issue is how they are interpreted—and the relative weight given to each.

Your practical needs, for starters, are the basics: *food, clothing, shelter, furnishings, utilities,* and *transportation*.

You need to take care of what you own. *Maintenance* keeps your things in good shape, preserves their working order, and extends their life.

You feel better when your surroundings are pleasing to the eye. Some *decor*—a picture on the wall or a planter on the porch—gives your home a personal touch.

You need to protect yourself from a calamity or unforeseen event turning your world upside down and shaking every last cent out of your pockets. *Insurance*—life, medical, property, auto, liability, and disability—provides a line of defense against a serious disruption in your life.

Whether it's baby-sitting, income tax preparation, or trash collection, there are *services* for hire to take care of those needs you cannot or do not want to do. I am thankful for the fellow who plows my driveway in the winter.

You need to take care of your body and your appearance. Soap, shampoo, vitamins, exercise accessories, haircuts: These are all *personal care* items.

When your body goes on the blink, you incur *medical care* costs: eyewear, dental work, prescriptions, and everything and anything not covered by insurance.

It costs money to go to work to make money. *Work expenses* are those needs that arise from the logistics of going to work: clothing (the difference in cost between the jeans you wear around the house and the suit or uniform you wear to work), day care, commuting costs, and food (the difference in cost between what you could take out of your refrigerator and what you spend for lunch).

You need to have a positive impact on the world beyond your direct value generation. *Charitable donations* are a direct reflection of those priorities.

Now we get to the final two categories: *entertainment* and *exploration and development*.

Entertainment is any activity that is largely a diversion. It is a pleasant or even dazzling way to pass the time, but when it's over you are essentially the same person you were before it began. There's been no discernible increase in your ability. Some examples include attending a sporting event, attending a pops concert, or watching a story on film.

Exploration and development encompasses those activities that increase your ability—you've added to your knowledge or enhanced a skill—or generate additional value. Some examples include participating in a sporting event, playing a musical instrument, or writing a story on paper. If you are a parent, probably the most financially significant of all exploration and development needs are those of your children—tuition bills being at the top of the list.

There is not a clear dividing line between entertainment, and exploration and development. A computer can serve both needs. A movie like *The Bicycle Thief* or *Schindler's List* might serve as entertainment, but also leave the viewer changed in a profound way. Something pursued for pure entertainment can transform itself into an avenue of exploration and development.

Likewise, an expenditure can straddle several categories. Eating in a restaurant is part food, part service, and part entertainment. And if, after sampling a style of cuisine for the first time, you are inspired to prepare it at home, eating out can even be exploration and development.

Is entertainment frivolous or a total waste? Absolutely not! As the saying goes: "All work and no play makes . . ." Pure entertainment can be the source of some of life's truly memorable experiences. And it can also provide a setting for generating value. A nice leisurely dinner with your spouse can be a great way to rekindle the fire that's been stamped out by Big Bird. That being said, when you consider all of your needs of value, exploration and development plays a much greater role in generating True Wealth than entertainment does.

Entertainment and exploration and development compete for the same time, energy, and money in our lives: the hours outside of work, sleep, and household obligations, the dollars in our pocket, and our mental focus. If you computed how much a person spends on each category, you'd have a quick and approximate indicator of his or her relative financial stress.

Show me someone who believes that entertainment is fun and that exploration and development is a chore—and I'll show you someone with financial stress.

Show me someone who believes that exploration and development is fun and entertainment is a change of pace, and I'll show you someone with a head start toward True Wealth.

EXCHANGING YOUR MONEY FOR TRUE WEALTH: HOW TO NEVER SPEND ANOTHER DOLLAR

Trying to steer a want-driven spending framework toward your needs with a budget is like trying to stop a car from rolling down a hill . . . when you're not in the car. But if you begin with a need-driven framework that is based on exchanging your money for the tools you need to generate value, you will always be in the driver's seat.

Here's the basic framework that will ensure that you get maximum value in return for your money from every exchange:

1. Determine your "have-to-haves."

2. Understand what you're really exchanging your money for.

3. Apply the Exchange Standard.

Now let's look at these three simple steps for exchanging money one by one:

STEP ONE: DETERMINE YOUR "HAVE-TO-HAVES"

Have-to-haves are the basic items that you absolutely have to have to either:

1. *Directly fulfill a basic need.* The bottom line for each of these have-to-haves is that there is no lesser acceptable substitute.

Housing that is safe (inside and outside) and keeps out the elements. A car that is reliable. Food that provides proper nourishment. A refrigerator to keep your food cold and a stove to cook it on. Appropriate clothing for work. Lightbulbs. Major medical insurance. A bar of soap. With all of these needs, either you have them or you don't. And once you have them, the need is, by and large, fulfilled.

2. *Generate value that fulfills an H2O.* For have-to-haves that enable you to generate value, the line of demarcation is this: If you don't have it, you cannot act on your objective. If you do have it, the rest is up to you. Examples:

If your objective is to exercise four times a week, a have-to-have might simply be comfortable walking shoes. There's not a single piece of fancy exercise equipment that can make you get off the couch or a health club membership that can force you out the door.

If your objective is to start pursuing new employment options, you need an up-to-date résumé, not a new computer.

If your objective is to prepare more meals at home, you need some basic pots, pans, and utensils. You don't need to outfit your kitchen like Julia Child's.

If your objective is to learn more about astronomy, you need a basic guidebook, not a fancy telescope. Man navigated by the heavens for centuries before the first lens. And you could learn quite a bit about the stars before spending a cent.

Once in hand, a have-to-have is a resource—one of many. So in determining a have-to-have, it's important to keep focused on the first two parts of the value generation process: your time and energy. Because ultimately, how you apply your time and energy will determine how much value you generate.

This might seem simple and obvious, but many people go through their entire lives in search of magic things—possessions that will somehow prod or inspire their owner into action and make up for their inaction. I consider myself fortunate that I comprehended the futility of this belief relatively early in my adult life. Here's how I figured it out.

The Big Lesson I Learned from Hound Dog Taylor

After I graduated from college, I did what any young man serious about making his way in the real world would do: I joined a rock group. Actually it started as a band of high school friends getting together a few nights a week and making some noise. But then an enterprising member booked an actual engagement and—suddenly—we were professional musicians.

Thus began our quest for the deluxe equipment that would speed us to our rightful destiny at the top of the charts. We emptied our wallets in search of the magical instrument that would awaken our inner Claptons. A guitarist of no apparent skill, I nevertheless thought I had to have both a vintage Fender Telecaster and a Gibson Les Paul. The irony—not to mention ludicrousness—of all of this was lost on me until I went to see the legendary Chicago bluesman Hound Dog Taylor.

Hound Dog Taylor played the blues in a particularly joyful and raucous style. On the night I saw him, he ambled up to the stage, sat down, and proceeded to burn the house down with a constant barrage of the most low-down-and-off-the-wall guitar I'd ever heard. The clincher: Hound Dog was doing all of this on the cheapest guitar imaginable—a hunk o' junk that my buddies and I wouldn't have deigned to use as firewood.

Somewhere in the middle of Hound Dog's romantic paean "Gimme Back My Wig" the light went on: It's not the tool that matters anywhere near as much as the desire and persistence of the person using the tool. Here was a man in his late fifties (he was to die within the year) who did what he did as well as anyone on the planet—and not only did he not need anything fancy, he had turned the limitations of his instrument around and made them work for him.

Soon after that night, our little combo discovered its actual destiny—oblivion—and I sold my guitars. Years later, when I got another urge to fumble around, I remembered the lesson of Hound Dog Taylor: If I wanted to play guitar, all I needed was some semblance of a guitar. After that, it was all up to yours truly. I bought a used Sears guitar for forty dollars and made a promise to myself that I would play it until I was absolutely chafing at its limitations. I still have it.

There's Still a Place in Life for "The Real Deal"

Concentrating on have-to-haves doesn't mean that you are being asked to commit to a spartan existence.

The truth is there's a place in your life for the luxurious, the frivolous, or the "real deal." There may be every reason why you should drive a '55 Chevy, take a trip to Tibet, wear an Armani suit, or collect whatever it is that summons up your passion. Your kids should have some things that are special to them—regardless of how silly they are—if for no other reason than that they're kids.

But you are going to be in a much better position to judge where indulgences belong in your life after you've put your have-to-haves into action throughout your life. This is . . .

The Secret of How Your Parents (or Grandparents) Managed: Avoid the Sponge Syndrome

Over and over the media remind us that "this is the first generation of Americans not to have as bright a future as their parents." This has in fact been said of no less than three generations: boomers, X-ers, and Next-ers. Let me put my cards right on the table: This belief is a pile of hoogysnackle.

What this pessimistic viewpoint really means is: "This is the first generation of Americans who expect to start out where their parents ended up—or even a few steps ahead." They want to have a kitchen that costs more than their parents' home and still be able to dine out more in a month than their parents did in an entire year.

There are many myths and misnomers regarding the social and economic trends of the 1980s and their possible connection to financial stress—the misguided belief that things are perpetually getting worse, for example. But there was one trend rooted in the '80s that has undoubtedly cranked up financial stress from coast to coast: the proliferation of what I call the Sponge Syndrome.

The Sponge Syndrome is the futile stress-creating notion that you have to work your way up to "the best" of every consumer item in your life. Once you buy something—anything—that's not the end of the story, it's just the beginning. You are a sponge that will not be satiated until you've soaked up all that the marketplace has waiting for you. You need a pen, you buy a pen; then you can't rest until you're the proud owner of a gold-plated fountain pen the size of a billy club.

Imagine for a moment that everything you own is spread out over your lawn or parking lot. Think about how stressful—and, in the end, irrelevent and meaningless—your life would be if it were somehow your calling to keep spending money on replacing each item until you owned the best of everything. An elusive and fruitless proposition? You bet. Yet that's precisely the life's mission of millions, pursuing a course on which they might barely reach the first turn by the end of their lives, all the while worshiping those who've reached sight of the imaginary finish.

So here's the secret of how your parents or grandparents raised a family on one income when today it takes two: *Right down through their budget, they focused on have-to-haves.* They worked to cover the bases—all of the have-to-haves for all of their needs. When a have-to-have was in hand, they were satisfied. Before they ever entertained the idea of moving up to something fancier, they made sure that all inconspicuous or mundane needs were fulfilled. Adequate insurance across the board took priority over the latest fashion. (When you were a kid, do you recall ever seeing an adult festooned with expansion team logos—except for the occasional cap?)

In the standard-issue middle-class neighborhood where I grew up, no one went on weekly or biweekly trips to the toy store. Most of what we did was free and within the range of our bicycles. But when we showed an interest in something that involved the outdoors or the imagination, the have-to-have tools were made available.

This focus on, and contentment with, have-to-haves was forged in the Great Depression and World War II. Both of these cataclysmic events served, in effect, as the financial equivalent of near-death experiences. When you've had to do without basics or lived on the edge of losing everything—and not just your job or house but your freedom, your loved ones, or your life—a three-bedroom, one-bath house with a fully stocked pantry is a palace.

Now, granted, today's senior citizens have had some advantages that subsequent generations won't have. They've taken far more out of Social Security than they ever put in and been handed Medicare and Medicaid. They enjoyed a huge run-up in the price of real estate and two major bull markets in stocks. They were able to keep more of their take-home pay while saddling subsequent generations with debt. But they also had a sense of restraint. The house they paid $20,000 for might have appreciated to $200,000, but they didn't flip it and trade up to a bigger pad.

Too often people go way beyond their have-to-haves in a few areas of their lives—house, car, clothing, and entertainment being the most likely candidates—before even meeting their basic needs in other areas—insurance, maintenance, medical care, and exploration and development frequently coming out losers. Unfortunately, it is precisely the bypassed areas that are breeding grounds for financial stress.

I don't know of anyone who suffered terribly because he drove a used Taurus or Accord instead of a spanking-new Limited Edition Sport Utility Vehicle. But I'm sure you'd have no trouble finding people whose vehicles in the garage have left no room in their budget for disability insurance.

If you focus on fulfilling your have-to-haves across the board, you will still have want-to-haves. And you should have them. Our want-to-haves play an important role in our enjoyment of life. But they can never add to your happiness for any real length of time—nor will you ever have a true picture of what your want-to-haves really are if they're expected to make up for a lack of have-to-haves.

By concentrating on your have-to-haves and generating value, your want-to-haves will not only be more sharply defined, they will add to the character of your life beyond merely being things you own. And you'll avoid having a lawn covered with chud and charge slips.

STEP TWO: UNDERSTAND WHAT YOU'RE REALLY EXCHANGING YOUR MONEY FOR

Everything for which you exchange money has four aspects: *basic function, quality, enhancements, and image.* To get the maximum value in return—value that is tailored to your needs—it helps to know what your requirements are in each aspect.

Let's look at each aspect in depth.

Basic Function: What's the Point?

Basic function is, when you get right down to it, what something does (or is supposed to do). In other words, what the @#$%* purpose does it serve?

Basic function is the foremost determinant of whether we have to have something or not. Because if we don't have an existing need for the basic function of something, then—however much we want it—we don't need it.

Concentrating on basic function gives you solid grounding, a firm and clear starting point, when you consider any potential exchange. And by doing so, you are in a much better position to fulfill all of your practical needs. For example, consider how much money you might save over a lifetime (the total could easily run well into the six figures), simply by understanding and acting from the vantage that the basic function of:

A car is to get you from point A to point B safely and efficiently, not to impress strangers at stoplights.

A house is to provide comfort and safety for you and your family, not to signify your relative economic status in your community.

Workday clothing is to look appropriate enough to be taken seriously by others, not to advertise your detailed knowledge of changing-by-the-minute fashion trends.

Food is to provide proper nourishment, not to exercise your jaw while the rest of you does nothing.

Again, this is not to advocate a bare-bones existence: living in a box, driving a box on wheels, wearing the same blue suit every day, and living on brown rice and broccoli. But it is critical to remember that basic function is what largely fulfills a practical need—and leaves you with enough value to fulfill all of your needs throughout your life, both present and future.

Quality: Can It Do *Your* Job?

Whatever we exchange our money for, we don't want it to quit on us, unravel, fall apart, break down, fall short, or wear out before our need no longer exists. Equally important, we don't want it to fail to measure up to reasonable performance standards right out of the gate. If you buy some glue, you expect it to stick.

Quality addresses one or both of these two critical questions:

1. How well will something serve its basic function right now?

2. How long will it continue to do so?

An oft-repeated rule of thumb is to buy the most quality you can afford. Ah, but if it were so easy. The truth is: *We don't always need the most quality we can afford. We simply need enough quality to meet our needs.* Stretching to buy the highest quality we can afford right now is how you can end up with a $500 watch and no savings, when a $50 watch would have met your needs. You don't need the best watch you can buy, merely one that performs well enough to fulfill its basic function. A Rolex does not somehow give you a *better* 2:30 than a Timex: 2:30 is 2:30.

When determining the degree of quality you need, the fundamental question to ask is this: *How long and how often am I going to need the basic function of this item?*

The longer and more frequently you're going to use something, the more quality becomes a good investment. Look at a simple item—a picnic cooler—and the quality needs of three different parties:

Doug the Construction Worker carries his lunch and bottled water to a construction site every day. He needs a thirty-dollar high-quality cooler that will hold up under the constant heavy use. The Shecky family uses a cooler several times a year for tailgate parties. A basic fifteen-dollar plastic cooler fits their needs just fine. Alice is going to the beach for the first time since she can even remember. She can get by with a $1.49 Styrofoam job. In each case, a different need was exactly filled by a different level of quality—and not one extra cent was wasted.

Now, a few general guidelines to help you zero in on quality:

If something is built to last, it is likely to perform its basic function quite well. A well-made pair of shoes, for example, will be more comfortable than a pair that will fall apart the first time you wear them in the rain.

There is not necessarily a direct relationship between price and quality. I've known people living in brand-new $500,000 homes that were falling down around them. I've witnessed friends throwing away thousands of dollars on "the best medical care money can buy"— only to find the solution to their ailments in a low-cost alternative. And we've all eaten at least one horrible meal served by a surly waiter—and paid through the nose for it.

The absolute cheapest is usually cheap for a reason: It's junk. Unless you plan on using something just once (à la Alice's picnic cooler) and you might not even make it that far, the cheapest available version is usually a waste of value.

The more you spend, the smaller the incremental increase in quality you get for each additional dollar. There's usually a big jump in quality from the cheapest-priced of any item to a midpriced version. For example, there's a noticeable difference in quality between a $100 pair of stereo speakers and a $200 pair—and that difference is much greater than the difference in quality between the $1,000 pair and the $2,000 pair.

After a certain point, the quality received in return for each dollar exchanged diminishes and you have to plunk down more and more bucks to get a smaller and smaller increase in quality.

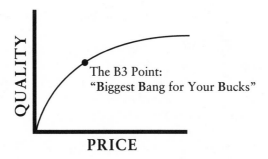

The bottom line: Try to make the most of your exchanges around the "B3 Point": the price range where the quality curve bends and you'll get the Biggest Bang for your Bucks. Finding the B3 Point should take only a little amount of comparative shopping.

Save going out along the flat part for those special situations where you are certain to get a full return on the extra quality. For example, if you're a marathon runner, your feet will get the full benefit of the best-quality running shoes you can afford. If you're strictly a dog walker, a pair of shoes around the B3 Point will do.

Enhancements: For Your Benefit— or Someone Else's Profit?

Enhancements are the features, extras, doodads, and details that are added on to basic function. They often serve a real, everyday purpose—air-conditioning in your car can prevent it from becoming Hades on wheels in July. But many enhancements look a lot handier than they really are or ever could be—they are the flash that entices you to part with your cash.

Take the case of a wristwatch: What enhancements do you really need? Waterproof to twenty leagues under the sea? When was the last time you dived deeper than the bottom of a pool? Accuracy to a tenth of a second per year? You certainly don't want to be a tenth of a second late for an appointment. The ability to time three events simultaneously and program a simulated NASA space launch? Okay, Mr. Wizard.

There are certainly professions or activities that demand extraordinary features. But beyond wanting a feature because it sounds nifty, what is your existing need for it?

Try this little experiment: Walk around your house taking a look at your electronic gear and appliances one by one. And while you're at it, take a look at your car. Your assignment: Count up all of the features you've never used or, for that matter, never even figured out how to use. I'll wager that you have more unused features than ones that you find truly indispensible or even useful. How many doodads do you really use on your VCR? Unless you have a degree from MIT, probably about two.

Each of us has a personal portfolio of modern conveniences that enhance our lives. But here stands the hurdle: Will an enhancement actually make it easier for you to generate value or . . .

. . . do you think you have to have it merely because it exists and, hey, if it wasn't a good thing, they wouldn't have made it? Next time you watch a car ad, ask yourself how many of the new features you thought were missing from your life.

. . . is it another thing to fiddle with to no net effect? Whatever time you spend fiddling with it is equal to any time supposedly saved. But many supposed time-savers are merely alternative time-spenders. A lot of kitchen gadgets take just as much time to set up, operate, and then clean up as using a good sharp knife in the first place. And what percentage of the time do computers actually save time?

A few additional tips:

Break out the cost of that extra feature. Once we make the initial decision to spend money on something, we can lapse into a "what the heck" mode and pile on the extras. The result: an extra 10, 20, 30 percent or more added on to the final cost. If you added up all of your outstanding credit card debt, it could very well be attributed to the total cost of the extras you've tacked on to your purchases over the past few years—from an extra appetizer to an extra gigabyte. Before you spend the extra bucks, ask yourself: "Would I buy this enhancement if I had to pay for it separately?"

Any enhancement that is apt to be first described as "cool" is probably one that you can do without. The thrill of whatever seems "cool" usually fades with time, leaving chud in its place. Remember, he who dies with the most toys doesn't win diddly. He just stops shopping at The Sharper Image.

Be aware that some enhancements can work against quality. The more parts there are to something, the more things there are that can malfunction. For example, adding an ice maker to your fridge considerably ups the chance that it will go on the fritz. And the fewer gizmos involved, the easier—and less costly—an item is to repair.

"State of the art" can be simple. Look beyond all of the available features for any given item and you might see something truly useful: that what is considered "the top of the line" or "state of the art" has very few extra features above its basic function. For example, it's not

unusual for a piece of audiophile stereo equipment that sells for thousands of dollars to have only one or two control knobs.

Image: The Slippery Slope

Image is that part of anything you own or do that shapes the impression that you make on others: that you're young, old, hip, successful, interesting, smart, beautiful, sexy, handsome, athletic, intellectual, wealthy, bohemian, ethereal, earthy, ethnic, WASPy, artistic, rebellious, sophisticated, rugged, powerful—you name it.

The challenge is that paying for image is a slippery proposition at best—like picking up mercury from a tile floor.

Image is dependent on the interpretation of others. Try as we might—and no matter how much we spend—we can end up looking goofy, phony, idiotic, wasteful, pretentious, ugly, dumb, juvenile, useless, stiff, silly, desperate, insecure, ludicrous, and just plain moronic. The wristwatch that looks like a big psychedelic pickle might speak directly to your quirky self, but to your division manager it might say "goofball." Mr. Homeowner believes that the six-foot statue of a stallion on his front lawn gives his digs "a touch of class," but a passerby might conclude otherwise.

Nevertheless, we are willing to spend billions and billions of dollars on image. Entire industries are image-driven—cashing in on our relentless search for the right image. Closets are stuffed with out-of-style clothing (that will unerringly be discarded a year before it comes back into fashion). Hair is chopped, greased, fluffed, and dyed according to an ever-shifting Look. Every day in commuter parking lots there are billions of dollars of image losing value by the minute. And then there's the entire concept of the tennis bracelet.

This is not to imply, however, that image is a waste of value or that it can be ignored. Quite the contrary: Image can be your friend—a useful tool in generating value. If you told David the Frugalist that his recycled, half-fitting wardrobe is protecting him from any consideration for advancement, he'd probably snap back that it shouldn't matter. But he'd have a lot less stress if his basic wardrobe approximated the look of his manager's rather than that of the part-time clerk at TofuWorld.

This is not to say that we should suppress our unique personalities and become mindless drones 'n' clones—although that's the reaction many people have at the first whiff of a suggestion to alter their image. The truth is that between the worshiping of image and the ignoring of image, there is a middle ground that permits the most powerful form of image to shine though loud and clear: value.

Value Generates Its Own Image

If the value we generate is the strongest statement of who we are, then our first and foremost concern when considering image is not to let our image obscure our value. Let me illustrate what I mean using one of the most admired men in the world: the Reverend Billy Graham.

Picture in your mind the Reverend Graham standing alongside world leaders—including the president of the United States. What words come to mind that you might use to describe the Reverend Graham? Dignified, showing moral strength and courage, a powerful leader? Does he look as though he belongs with the surrounding company? Absolutely.

Now try to remember any specific characteristics you've ever noticed about the Reverend Graham's clothes. Drawing a blank? I thought so.

The Reverend Graham's value is what you focus on—not the fact that his suits are off the rack and cost a mere fraction of the cost of the custom-tailored suits worn by world political leaders. But if he wore a flashy designer jogging suit and gold chains, or had on a plaid sport jacket that looked like a horse blanket, you'd be distracted from the value generated by the man—cracking jokes instead of listening to his message. As long as the Reverend Graham reasonably looks the part, he is free to develop and perform his role unfettered by a dissonant image.

This is the crucial concept when grappling with image: *Value generates its own image.* Avoid letting the packaging undermine or obscure your substance. Or to put it a different way: Make sure that as you paint the picture of your life with value, the value doesn't have to fight just to stand out on the canvas.

Here are several additional observations that will help you turn image into a value-generating tool rather than a sinkhole for your money:

A little carefully chosen image goes a long way. A well-chosen, understated image speaks more clearly and effectively than piling the image on. The right tie or scarf can make an entire outfit look perfect for the occasion, without requiring a head-to-toe overhaul. A few strategically placed plants and shrubs can improve the looks of any house, without your having to annex your local nursery.

The louder and broader the image you try to project, the more money you risk blowing. It is costly to both create and sell an image—ask any small-business owner who's ever paid for an advertising campaign. That's why if you lifted the lid on the lives of the suburban couple trying to project an image of landed gentry to the world at large—"Hey, look at us, everybody! You may not know us, but we're . . ."—you might find empty spaces marked "savings," "retirement," and "tuition."

You cannot buy enough image to cover up a shortage of value. The reality of your value generation (or the lack of it) will eventually overpower any and every attempt to disguise it. It doesn't matter what house you live in; if you're a creep, people are going to figure it out.

You cannot become an image, only dress up in it. Image can't make you what you aren't. If you're not a twenty-five-year-old professional athlete or supermodel, dressing like one won't change that fact.

The right image for your needs needn't cost more. It's often just a matter of making the right choice. You can spend an equal amount of money in a clothing store to look like a total dork or a totally self-assured individual. There's no tariff on the exercising of good taste.

STEP THREE: APPLY THE EXCHANGE STANDARD

The issue of basic function raises a practical concern: Is there any way of quickly determining if a potential exchange fulfills a real need? Otherwise a simple trip to the store could become an extended philosophical dialogue—"Behold! A pair of socks! What do they mean, I ask you; what purpose do they serve?"

Some years ago I found myself in a hardware store wrestling with a potential purchase. I had gone into the store to buy a few screws, had wandered into the tool section, and had become enamored of a gadget that I was certain had the power to turn me into Bob Villa, Jr. As I stood in the store deciding whether or not to part with thirty dollars for something I had no immediate and concrete use for—although I could imagine many—a simple two-pronged question hit me over the head:

What would this enable me to do, and what can't I do without it?

I didn't have an answer. I put the item down and walked out of the store—with a tool that has proven to be infinitely valuable.

I call this tool the *Exchange Standard:* "What would this enable me to do, and what can't I do without it?" If I don't have rock-solid answers—free from the hollow ring of rationalization—for both questions posed by the Exchange Standard, then I know that there is almost no chance that I'll be receiving an equal amount of value in return for my money. The exchange will be a value loser, and one not worth making.

On the other hand, if the Exchange Standard can be met with a response that has the sure footing of common sense and existing need, then I know that I have an excellent chance of receiving at least an equal amount of value in return.

I've used the Exchange Standard virtually every day since I discovered it—and every time I consider a new or different potential exchange. I don't, for example, bother to ask myself why I'm buying gasoline every time I fill up. But I don't enter a store without having the Exchange Standard at the ready. I've applied it to the biggest exchanges—a house—and the smallest—a newspaper—to equal effect.

What I've found is that the Exchange Standard not only helps me exchange my money wisely—with fewer regrets and less chud—but also greatly reduces the tension of self-discipline. I feel as though my best interests are in control and not forced to constantly wrestle with whims and wants.

I became so excited by the immediate effectiveness of the Exchange Standard that it was some time before I even began to examine why it worked so well. After time, though, the reasons became very clear:

1. *The Exchange Standard puts the responsibility for generating value where it belongs: on you.* In asking yourself what a potential purchase will enable you to do, the emphasis is squarely on *you*— and even more to the point, on *your* action. The question is not "What is this going to do for me?" That's often a subtle way of asking "How can this do for me what I can't seem to get in gear and do for myself?"

By keeping the focus on your action, the Exchange Standard helps you avoid the false belief that inanimate objects have a gravitational pull—that they can overcome our inertia and yank us into action. For example, in studying the lives of great athletes or musicians, one thing that has struck me is that their desire to play often overcame even the severest of limitations of their equipment (often homemade).

Action—time and effort—will always overcome even the most limited of resources. When you relate "What does this enable me to do?" to an already established pattern of action, the possibility is greater that you will exchange your money for a tool that you'll put to immediate and stress-reducing use.

2. *The Exchange Standard keeps the spotlight on your needs.* When you ask yourself what a potential purchase will enable you to do, you will ask yourself almost simultaneously something like "And you need to do that because . . . ?" or "And that would fulfill what need?"

3. *The Exchange Standard jogs you to focus on what you already own.* By asking yourself what you can't do without the potential purchase, you may very well discover that you already have a similar or perfectly acceptable resource.

Have you ever contemplated a purchase—even convinced yourself that you really needed it—only to conclude that "the one I have is perfectly good" or "there's really nothing wrong with what I have"? If you're like me, you felt a sense of relief from that quick shot of practical sense.

That's a feeling you'll experience frequently by using the Exchange Standard. Can you still go attend the upcoming conference if you don't have that new outfit? It's highly likely. Can you still watch television if you don't have a twenty-five-inch screen? As long as your nineteen-inch model shows a picture.

Almost everyone has something that they are constantly buying more of—way ahead of their logistical ability to actually put it to reasonable use: clothes, videos, shoes, software, hardware, gadgetry, or whatever. I guarantee that if you make a sincere effort to apply the Exchange Standard, you'll get a grip on your spending. Perhaps more important: The enjoyment you get from what you already have will be greater than the thrill of buying more.

Beginning with the moment I plunked down $2.99 for *Meet the Beatles*, I've been a serious, lifelong record collector. There were years when I purchased on average at least one new recording a day (I've just confirmed my parents' longtime suspicions). But no longer—I've used the Exchange Standard to cut my expenditures by over 80 percent. It really does work.

4. *The Exchange Standard nips chud in the bud.* Finally, the Exchange Standard can point out just how plain stupid some things really are. If you ask yourself the two-part simple question before opening your wallet, you'll nip a lot of needless expenditures on chud in the bud.

Try holding a can of Cheez Whiz in the grocery store and telling yourself, "Without this, I will be unable to enjoy pressurized snack paste at will."

LOOKING FOR VALUE IN A WORLD OF CHUD

For your consideration, I'd like to offer a compendium of tips and suggestions that have been shaped by my observations and experience exchanging money for value:

Focus on the people, not the place. A house is first and foremost a place to live. It is not your life or your family's life. *What goes on within the home is far more important than how big it is or how fabulously it is furnished.*

Our perceived need for more living space is similar to our perceived need for more money in two notable ways: (1) It is all relative to our current amount of living space. (2) No matter how much space we have, we always think we need more. Our "need" is elastic—always stretching ahead of the reality of the present.

Take a basic living space: three bedrooms, one bath, a kitchen, a living room, and a dining room. In New York City, that space could easily cost $5,000 a month in rent—well beyond the reach of most of its inhabitants (and former inhabitants). You don't even want to think about what it would cost in Tokyo.

But in Middle America, three bedrooms and a bath is considered a "starter home"—the first step toward bedrooms and bathrooms for all. If you live, say, in Ohio, your first home in all likelihood will be bigger than your ultimate home would be if you lived in New York City.

So here's a basic question: Are people who live in a suburb in Middle America a different species from the East or West Coast urban dweller—somehow needing way more square feet to survive? Of course not. But just as people automatically think they need 10 percent or 15 percent more income to be all set, they also think that they need another 500 or 1,000 square feet to have "enough room."

If you want to put a more manageable price tag on your dream home, ask yourself how much that extra 500 square feet is going to cost you a month. Is it space you are going to actively live in every day or is it "show" space? Is it worth the potential stress?

Look for unused space in your current home. Running out of space? Look again. A formal dining room is an architectural relic in most instances—being pushed aside by the eat-in kitchen. With entertaining becoming an increasingly informal affair, you may be using your dining room only on holidays. Turn it into a study/home office for yourself or the kids. If you have a living room and a family room, how often do you use the living room? And who should care if you turn your living room into an art studio? It's your space—use it!

Would you rather have outer prestige or inner peace? Ask yourself this: "Would I be happier in my day-to-day life if I lived in a house that made me look as if I had money or actually had the money to fulfill my needs throughout my life?"

Flip through your local real estate ads and you'll find adjectives like "prestigious," "executive," and "desirable," aimed at buyers for whom perceived status is one of the most—if not *the* most—important factors in choosing a home. Yet the average millionaire won't be found in these neighborhoods. What does he know that others don't? Money that goes to the mortgage department is not money in the bank. Having a closet bigger than a mobile home and pillars out front is far less important to him than avoiding financial stress.

Chuck the chud. Your house may seem too small because you have too much chud. The cheapest and fastest way to have more closet space is to clean out your closets. A guaranteed way to make any room bigger—without knocking out a wall—is to eliminate visual clutter. If you have things you don't use but can't bear to part with—extra furniture or your college textbooks—consider warehousing them in deep storage (often a cheaper alternative to storage spaces that allow access).

A few thoughts about the game of "Chuck, Donate, Sell, or Keep":

○ Recognize broken-down, worn-out chud for what it is: junk. Throw it out. Don't insult charitable organizations by donating what is essentially garbage. It makes their work harder.
○ The most efficient way to pass along still-useful items is to donate them to a worthy cause or organization. Selling takes time and effort and the money you get back might not be equal to the value of getting the job done quickly and helping others.
○ A garage sale is a great project to get your kids involved in. But make sure that you don't hang on to what you don't sell. Plan to chuck or donate whatever doesn't sell immediately.
○ Store the items you decide to keep where they are readily accessible. Those books you are finally going to read or those clothes you're going to wear: Put them right out on your reading shelf or hang them in the front of your closet. Test your judgment.

Eat at home. Americans spend over 40 percent of their food budget eating out. If you're eating out (or ordering in) more than once a week, you're throwing away money. "Fast-food" restaurants won't provide a meal faster than fixing it at home—don't forget to factor in travel time. And there are none where you can get a meal cheaper. But, I know, you don't like to cook, don't know how, or don't have time. Keep reading. . . .

Learn how to cook. People who say they don't like to cook usually just don't know how to cook. Cooking is a wonderful way to relax, treat your body well, make others feel good, and cut costs. So what's not to like? As a committed cook, I can assure you that with a little practice, you'll be able to whip up tasty, balanced meals in minutes.

One key to everyday cooking is to forget fancy: Think simple. Fancy meals are nice to eat in restaurants or fun to read about in magazines. A good guidebook to culinary efficiency: *Recipes 1-2-3* by Rozanne Gold (Viking).

When you do cook, maximize your effort: Never prepare a meal without making at least half as much more than you'll immediately serve. The leftovers can be tomorrow's lunch or the starting point for tomorrow's dinner. If everything's all gone after one meal, you've wasted time.

Buy simple food. As a rule of thumb, the more preprepared, processed, and packaged a food, the more it costs, the more chemicals and/or fat it likely contains, and the less real nutrition it contains. Eating right costs less. Compare the cost of a bag of apples to that of a bag of corn chips. Rule of thumb: If reading an ingredients label reminds you of a high school chemistry test, leave the item on the shelf.

Eat your vegetables. Fewer than 30 percent of meals prepared at home include a vegetable. When you consider both the minimal prep time for most vegetables (many can go from the grocery bag to the dinner table in ten minutes) and their nutritional value, one might surmise that some portion of whatever health care crisis we have is behavior-driven.

Exercise your power of the purse. Parents who complain that their kids don't eat right usually have no one but themselves to blame. Who do they think buys the junk and brings it home?

Use your grocery budget for actual food. Is there a way to cut your grocery bills if you don't want to clip coupons or study grocery ads as if they were stock market listings? There certainly is: Restrict your grocery budget to actual food.

Consider that, after meats and fresh produce, the top ten supermarket categories (in order) include:

- Carbonated soft drinks. A big gulp of wasted money.
- Cigarettes. A killer in the cart. Certainly not a food, unless you are prone to pouring milk in a full ashtray and eating a bowl of butts.
- Chips and snacks. A sophisticated delivery system for salt and fat foisted upon a witless public by Todd the Snack Food Marketing Specialist.
- Beer and ale. Ceases to be a food group upon graduation from college.
- Juice (nonrefrigerated). Check the label—a lot of what gets marketed as juice is mostly water and sweetener.
- Frozen dinners and entrées. It's amazing how much people will pay for cafeteria food if it's frozen into a brick and packaged in a box with a nice photo. An informal observation at my supermarket: Senior citizens seem to really go for this stuff. Don't they have time to cook when they're not complaining about the cost of health care?
- Also among the top twenty: ice cream, cookies, and candy. No comment necessary.

Look classic. There's a reason why rich people tend to dress in a classic style, and maybe it's one reason why they're rich. Free from being slaves to fashion, they don't have to overhaul their wardrobes from year to year. The Brooks Brothers/L.L. Bean/Talbot's–inspired look (adjusted for your region and your profession, of course) never goes out of style—and you can wear it almost anywhere. I've worn the same shirt to sweaty dives and upscale corporate functions and looked equally appropriate. And actress Sharon Stone wore a twenty-four-dollar Gap T-shirt to an Academy Awards ceremony to much applause.

Fashions come and go, but all fashions cycle back to the same classic look. Ralph Lauren has made a fortune on this one simple fact. You might not make a fortune like Ralph, but you can save a small fortune if you adopt the classic look as the basis for your wardrobe. And with the look thoroughly democratized—available at local malls as well as exclusive shops—there's little effort and no additional money involved, merely focused selection.

Buy your clothes off-season. With rare exception, I shop for clothing twice a year. After Labor Day, when kids are back in school and the stores are bringing out the winter merchandise, I buy summer clothes. And after Spring Break, when the sun is out and everyone is wearing shorts, I buy winter clothes. There are several big advantages to this strategy:

1. The savings are huge. I recently purchased $600 worth of top-quality winter clothing (wool blazer, sweater, slacks, two shirts) for $125—on an eighty-degree day.
2. You have a much clearer idea of your needs—what clothing is worn out and could be replaced or what you could use more of—because you just went through the season.
3. You have to wait. Because you don't usually get to wear your new threads right away, there's no instant gratification factor to hasten a transaction. This forces you to do some serious thinking as to what you really need and channels you away from the latest fads that will look plain silly in six months.

Find a skilled tailor. A skilled tailor can work wonders, enabling you to get far more mileage out of your wardrobe than you imagine is possible. A jacket can be let out or taken in, pants turned into shorts, a skirt shortened, or buttons replaced, giving the clothes in the back of your closet a new lease on life.

Put the smallest, not the greatest, amount of money you can in a car. Seemingly half the tyros in the investment world profess to emulate

Warren Buffett: buying stocks the "Warren Way." But there's another aspect of Buffett's financial dealings—far removed from Wall Street—that could make them, and you, far more money over a lifetime. What kind of car does the multibillionaire drive? A nondescript older sedan. Why? Because he understands that a car is a guaranteed money loser—the only question is how little or how much is lost.

If you knew that a mutual fund was certain to go down, would you buy as much of it as you could afford? Of course not. Then why do it with a car? Once you've determined your needs in a car, your objective should be to spend as little as possible in fulfilling these needs, not the most.

Don't be the automaker's favorite customer. There's about $1,000 to $2,000 profit margin—at most—in the price of a car that lists for $15,000 to $20,000. There is as much as a *$10,000* profit margin in a car that lists for $35,000. Paying more for a car doesn't mean you get proportionately more car. It means that, although you're getting some extra features, you're mostly paying out the wazoo for the image of driving a more expensive car. Or spending $15,000 for $5,000 worth of extras. The operative word that comes to mind is "chump."

Keep your car clean, inside and out. Baseball Hall of Fame slugger and car enthusiast Reggie Jackson once told an interviewer that he'd never owned a car that didn't ride better when it was clean. He's right.

Program your thermostat. The energy it takes to heat up (or cool off) your house a few extra degrees can really inflate your utility bills. And a lot of times those extra degrees are unnecessary—whether it's because your teenage daughter cranks the heat up to seventy-eight degrees when she comes home from school or because you leave the air-conditioning on when you go to work. A quality programmable thermostat (around $100) will enable you to set the right temperature for your daily needs—without constant readjusting on your part or by others. It will pay for itself many times over.

Appreciate the joy of maintenance. Fix a window frame. Polish a pair of shoes. Paint an old piece of furniture. Check the air pressure in your tires. Sharpen a knife. Activities that address the maintenance of everyday life may seem fairly mundane, but over time they create value in your life that goes beyond merely saving a dollar or two. They add to your peace of mind and your appreciation of what you already have. And they provide a sense of satisfaction that can't be achieved by paying someone else to do it. There is as much pleasure in maintaining what you own as there is in getting something new.

Maintenance might not be sexy, but over time the rewards sure add up.

Consider renting. Renting is often thought of as what you do when you don't have enough money to buy. But there are a number of situations where renting can save you a bundle in the long (and short) run:

- ○ Renting real estate in a stagnant or declining market is less costly than buying if you are not willing to make a long-term commitment to the area.
- ○ Renting a big-ticket leisure item—a vacation home or a boat—might seem costly when you consider the daily or weekly tariff, but when you total up the costs of owning it year-round (and how little you might end up using it), it can be a bargain.
- ○ Renting the gear necessary for a new activity, until you know you're going to stick with it, can make more sense than a big outlay up front.
- ○ Renting a piece of equipment for a household project can save you a bundle if you're not likely to need it again in the future.

Word of caution: Avoid "rent to own" stores. They're rip-offs.

Word of advice: Browse through your local rental center just to acquaint yourself with all of the possible things that can be rented. You'll be surprised.

Buy something on sale only if you'd buy it anyway—and then buy a bunch. Sale can be a code word for "How cheap do we have to price this before you stop thinking about whether you need it?" I'm willing to bet you that a lot of the things around your house that you've never used were "really good bargains."

So how do you avoid getting tricked into buying chud by the word "sale"? By following this simple guideline: *If something is on sale that you already use or for which you have a preestablished need, buy it. And if it's something you use up, buy a lot of it.* You use a certain brand of shampoo? Buy a year's supply when you see a good deal—you're not going to stop washing your hair in six months (one hopes).

Word of encouragement: Buying a quantity of a sale item that you use constantly offers a better "return" than virtually any investment you could make. If you buy a year's supply of kitchen garbage bags when they're marked down 50 percent, in effect you've doubled your money.

When something works, stay with it. Some products are virtually interchangeable—I've never lamented the poor performance of a dish detergent, for example.

But some products *do* work better for us than others. If you look through your closets and cabinets, I'm certain you'll find a lot of chud—whether it's cosmetics, panty hose, soup, or razor blades—that is similar to something you use all of the time, but just isn't as good. Get rid of the chud, and from here on out go with what works best for you. You'll throw away a lot less money.

Buy presents as you see them. When you wake up on New Year's Day, several things are certain: the gift-giving holidays are at the end of the calendar, and everyone in your family will have a birthday before the end of the year. So it makes no sense to rush around at the last minute throughout the year, trying to find the right present (translation: something, anything) for each person and often overspending time and money in the scramble.

Given that throughout the year you will be in stores for one reason or another, why not keep your eyes open for suitable presents that just happen to be screaming bargains? Father's Day might be in June, but when you see a sharp tie that's marked down in February to 75 percent off retail, grab it and be done with it.

Money-saving tip: Wrapping paper and a greeting card can add five dollars to the cost of a last-minute present. You can buy a year's supply at a discount outlet for a third of the cost—and save yourself a lot of time.

Avoid onetime event purchases. When you hear yourself say, "I need something to wear to . . . /take on the trip to . . . /do this one thing . . . ," stop for a moment and ask yourself if this is a onetime event and, if so, if there is any acceptable alternative, such as using what you have, renting, or borrowing. The fewer onetime-ever purchases you have to make, the less chud you'll have.

Do business with the little guy. This advice isn't born out of any anti-big-business let's-stop-Wal-Mart-from-ruining-our-idyllic-town watered-down-elitist-socialist hissy fit. There's a good reason for patronizing a small business—and even paying a premium for doing so: potentially better service.

A small-business owner is likely to be passionate about his work and eager to share his expertise. For example, I've shopped at all of the various Humongo Home Improvement Barns. None offer close to the quality and service that's available at my local lumberyard. Is it worth the extra dollar or two? You bet.

Who makes a better pizza: Pizza Chain or the local shop on the corner? If it's Pizza Chain, the little guy deserves to go under.

Understand the basic function of insurance. Most of us have two common feelings about insurance: We don't like to deal with it, and we don't like to spend money on it. Nevertheless, you do need insurance—and the whole topic of insurance becomes more manageable and less costly if you approach it with its basic function as your guide.

The basic function of insurance is to provide you and your family with reasonable (not complete) financial protection against the consequences of unforeseen losses, accidents, illnesses, and deaths. In other words, when life hits the fan, you don't want to get completely wiped out and tossed into the street.

Let's sharpen that picture by looking at what the basic function of insurance is *not*.

- ○ *Insurance is not supposed to smooth all of the bumps and bruises out of life.* That's what savings and budgeting are for. If your camcorder gets stolen and you're $500 out of pocket, it's a bummer, man. But that's life.
- ○ *Insurance is not an investment.* Repeat. Insurance is not an investment. People who purport otherwise have allowed their logic to be replaced by a commission structure. Insure what you need to insure as simply as possible. Invest the savings elsewhere.
- ○ *Insurance is not a right.* In the past fifty years insurance has gone from being an individual responsibility to an employer- or government-provided benefit. The result—along with soaring costs—is that we now believe that insurance is a right. We just don't want to spend money at the dentist when we could spend it at the mall. The belief that insurance is a right creates stress in several ways. You may believe that your compensation has stagnated because you haven't factored in the rising cost of your insurance benefits. And you might pass up tremendous opportunities in life just to avoid paying for insurance—or even a prescription—out of pocket.
- ○ *Insurance is not a lottery ticket.* There are much more personally rewarding and less dangerous ways to get a big check in the mail than from an insurance settlement.
- ○ *Insurance is not a way to play Game Show Host from the Great Beyond.* Let's say that tomorrow you get hit by a truck. Does that have to mean that your family wins the Grand Prize: enough money so that no one ever has to lift a finger again—house and college paid for, with a lifetime income to boot? Is that in anyone's best interest? Maybe so, if there's a child in your family who requires special care or your spouse will be unable to work. But three to five years of net living expenses with some additional funds for education should be plenty for everyone to readjust and get on with their lives. Buy term insurance—and read the next paragraph.

Don't bet on your life that you won't need disability insurance. Depending on your age, you have a three- to four-times-better chance of being kicked onto your back—disabled and not being able to work for an extended period of time—than you do of kicking the bucket. Yet many people buy (or get sold) life insurance without giving a moment's thought to disability insurance or feel that they don't have enough money to purchase both.

Simple suggestion: Buy term life insurance equal to three to four years of your after-tax income and then shop for disability insurance that will provide a level of support that will keep your head above water after you've used up your emergency fund (that's what it's for).

Don't skimp on liability coverage. The most common means by which Americans believe they have a chance of getting rich are winning the lottery, receiving an inheritance, and winning a lawsuit. And there's a legion of trial lawyers egging on people to go for Door Number Three and sue whoever is in sight, no matter how ridiculous the premise.

Heaven forbid you should be on the receiving end of litigious lunacy, but keep this in mind: You can handle covering a high automobile collision deductible if you get in a fender bender a lot easier than a jury settlement that's six figures more than your liability coverage limit.

High-quality appliances are a bargain. Household appliances are one area where quality definitely pays off. If spending more for high quality enables you to avoid even one or two extra service calls over the life of the appliance, the extra cost of quality and every extra year of use from an appliance beyond the norm is money in the bank. Must do: Consult *Consumer Reports* for estimated repair frequency. Must avoid: service contracts. They're big moneymakers for the sellers, which means that they're a losing bet for you.

When you exchange money for furniture, sit on it or sleep on it. People often sink a lot of money on "good" furniture that barely gets used—a dining room set that's treated like a museum exhibit or a couch that's covered in plastic—and then skimp when it comes to the furniture they use the most. For starters, you spend more time in bed than anywhere else: A great mattress and box spring are the best investment in furniture you can make. Not far behind: A chair or couch that provides proper support for reading and watching television.

You're going to scratch it anyway, so why pay to be the first? A terrific way to buy high-quality furniture at a low price is to buy furniture that's already been scratched or dented. Look for a furniture store in your area that specializes in closeouts and damaged furniture. You may very well find a choice piece with only minor damage that can be either repaired or overlooked. Our dining table has what we refer to as the "$1,000 scratch"—a four-inch mark that dropped the price from $1,200 to $199.

Word of admonishment: If you pay full retail for furniture, you're a moron.

Learn a decorative art. Expertise in a single decorative art—painting, wallpapering, refinishing, upholstering, landscaping—can make a world of difference in the appearance of your home (and its appeal when you try to sell it).

Must avoid: "buying a look." A sure way to waste value is to spend money decorating your home in the latest look. Sooner or later, every hot look takes on the appearance of red velvet Mediterranean (which is fine, if you like it in the first place). The most appealing and comfortable homes usually have owners who have a firm grip on their personal tastes—"I like what I like"—and decorate over time.

Recognize that there is no genie in a bottle. There is simply no health or personal care product that can take the place of regular exercise, proper diet, enough rest, and a good attitude. You cannot spend enough money to compensate for a lack of any of the above.

Understand that talk is cheaper than drugs—and usually more effective. It is my experience that the best doctor is the one most likely to prescribe changes in behavior and least likely to prescribe drugs or surgery. But we want the magic bullet, and the medical profession knows that it is easier to get us to swallow the bullet than to change our ways. You can get your health costs down, and keep them down, if you seek out physicians who look first at the whole picture and prescribe changes in *behavior.* I've greatly reduced chronic, crushing neck pain, conquered my pollen allergies, and become a father by following this route. Yet the initial physicians consulted in each case asked few questions and quickly recommended either drugs or surgery.

Give a little and see what you get in the mail. Whenever you feel motivated to contribute to a charity for the first time, try this little test: Donate a modest amount of money and see how little or much you are deluged with mailings requesting more. The fancier and/or more frequent the requests, the less is being spent on the cause. I regularly give to the Salvation Army and receive only several modest mailings a year. I've given twenty dollars each to several charities and been rewarded with forty dollars' worth of junk mail.

Don't let the Big Day get out of control. What gathering usually includes cocktails, live music, dancing, and dinner—and is followed by a vacation? A wedding. I don't know about you, but it sure sounds like an entertainment event to me. When the lovely couple announces their intention, be ready with a figure that doesn't eat up all of your savings or put you into debt. Let them handle any overrun. And if they get divorced, ask for a pro rata refund. Just kidding . . . sort of.

Don't work half a year paying for one week off. There are two purposes to a vacation: (1) to relax and spend some time together, and (2) to see a part of the world you haven't seen before. In neither case is the purpose to leave you paying off debt over the months that follow: "I've got to relax so I can get stressed out about money" doesn't make sense.

Want to see a part of the world that you haven't seen before? How about the area within a day trip of your own home? I'll bet you that there are many cultural facilities, historical sites, and outdoor recreation areas you've never been to. And here's a vacation idea that might make you feel better than any trip in the world: Stay home, unplug the phone, and tackle some of those projects you've been putting off forever. Organize or redo a room during the day and go out to dinner at night.

Word of clarification: I'm all for seeing the world—a week in Florence, Italy, was one of the greatest experiences of my life. But the key is to see that part of the world that you have an active interest in—not merely to add it to your portfolio of vacations or to go somewhere for the sake of going somewhere.

Follow your team on the radio. There's nothing wrong with being a sports fan and following your favorite team. But if you're watching every game on television, that's a lot of time watching other people who are actually doing something. Why not join them? Listen to the games on the radio while you are generating value in some way around the house. You can catch all of the action while you're taking action—whether it's pursuing another hobby or working on a home business.

Use your real *gold card.* Your *real* gold card is not a piece of plastic with an unlimited credit line—it's your library card. Your library card is your passport to the greatest (and many of the latest) books in the world plus some of the videos, compact discs, and even CD-ROMs you might otherwise spend money on. Suggestion: Substitute a trip to the library for your weekend trip to the mall.

DETERMINING YOUR PRACTICAL
TOOLS FOR EVERYDAY LIVING

What are your have-to-haves in each category of tools?

In what category(s) are you not currently fulfilling your basic needs?

In what category(s) do you spend money on chud?

In what category(s) do you spend more on quality than might be dictated by your needs?

In what category(s) do you spend money on enhancements that don't add significant value to your life?

In what category(s) do you spend money based primarily on image?

In what category(s) might you be able to spend less and still fulfill your basic needs?

In which of the categories you've identified in the previous six questions might it be possible to decrease your current expenditures and exchange your money instead for unfulfilled have-to-haves? What money spent on wants could be exchanged instead for fulfilling your needs?

What have-to-have(s) are required for each of the objectives you've chosen to fulfill your impact H2O?

Which of these have-to-haves are you lacking?

For each of these missing have-to-haves, answer the following:

What would this have-to-have enable you to do?

What can't you do without it?

Can you borrow or rent this have-to-have until you've proven your commitment?

How much quality do you need?

What enhancements—if any—are vital to your value generation?

What role—if any—will image play in your specific selection? Is it possible to approximate your desired image without spending additional money?

How much money is required to exchange for your have-to-have?

If you don't have the money right now, which of your current expenditures can you reduce or eliminate?

WORKSHEET: YOUR PRACTICAL
TOOLS OF EVERYDAY LIVING

Food

Clothing

Shelter

Furnishings/Appliances

Utilities

Transportation

Decor

Maintenance

Insurance

Medical

Life

Property

Auto

Disability

Services

Personal care

Medical care

Work expenses

Charity

Entertainment

Exploration and development

8

The Enduring Power to Preserve Value— and Stay Free from Financial Stress

D O YOU EVER feel as if the world is a big treadmill, and you're living the same day over and over? Wherever your little spot, you have got to keep chugging just to stay in the same place. If you pause for even a second, you risk falling behind . . . for good.

How do you turn the treadmill into a long "people mover" that helps you to get ahead? By preserving the value you generate today, you'll automatically start tomorrow a little further along your way.

One of the great advantages of the things in life that money can't buy is that they aren't subject to the vicissitudes of daily events. Things that can be generated only by value generally don't wildly fluctuate or disappear overnight. Rather, they steadily accumulate and compound, taking on a permanence in your life. If you . . .

> . . . put a new skill into action today, you're unlikely to forget it tomorrow.
> . . . consistently practice your faith, it's not going to vanish when you need it most.
> . . . devote attention to your marriage daily, you're hopefully not going to be hit in the face—like a pie you never saw coming— with divorce papers next month.

In each of these examples (and countless others), the value you generate is difficult to "spend." You really have to work at it to go "broke"—almost to the point of being self-destructive. This leads us to a key point:

The things in life that money can't buy stay with us because they can't be readily exchanged. If you've got a close family, you can't blow it on a Jacuzzi. If people respect you, you can't trade that fact for a dishwasher. You can't dump everything you've read in the past year out of your brain and into a time-share property.

There's a permanence to the things in your life that money can't buy that often can be undone only by a cataclysmic event or death itself. But value can't buy everything. More to the point—we can't generate sufficient value today to fulfill some needs way off in the future, some of which may not even be known to us.

THE REAL ADVANTAGE OF MONEY

We may have a value-first mind-set, but there is that part of the value we generate that we can readily exchange: money—that is, financial value. Money is a practical vehicle for exchanging value. That means that right up until the moment it leaves our hands, *money is a storehouse of value.*

A dollar bill or a check is not just an inert piece of paper. Invisible to the naked eye, it is a container chock-full of the time, energy, and resources it took to earn a buck—all ready to be put into action at a moment's notice. And although we've emphasized that value is a more effective basic currency than money in our lives, money does have one distinct advantage over value: *Money makes it possible to delay the final form of our value generation for years, even decades.*

Money becomes whatever you exchange it for, however unrelated it may be to how you have earned it. No travel agent ever handed back cash to a retiree and said, "You earned this money twenty years ago in an auto plant. You can't spend it on a plane ticket." Money serves as a transition between generation and exchange—allowing us untold versatility as to the final form of our value generation. It can be an efficient intermediary between what you do and what you get.

Not only, then, is money a practical means of exchange for meeting our immediate needs, but when used properly it is a powerful tool for shaping our future. Money is a lot like dynamite. It should be stored and handled carefully, treated with respect, and used judiciously. It can move a mountain to make way for a new road, or blow a stressful event right out of your life. Money can perform countless man-hours of work in a flash. Or it can be just a big bang that's for-gotten as the last echo fades.

And if you don't have any dynamite—preserved financial value—you'll be fighting financial stress with a wet firecracker.

THE FIFTH COMPONENT OF TRUE WEALTH: PRESERVE FINANCIAL VALUE FOR THE FUTURE

For people with True Wealth, preserving financial value comes as second nature—methodical, unobsessive, and unforced. They pre-serve financial value with a smile. It's not something they *have* to do, but rather something that they *want* to do. They don't need a fiscal crisis or a financial planner to raise their motivation up to the level of "Okay, all right. I guess I really should save." Their attitude is "Why wouldn't I save?" What is their secret?

People with True Wealth understand that the enduring power to preserve financial value lies in understanding the H2Os that savings can fulfill. If you truly embrace these reasons to preserve financial value, you'll never *have* to save another cent. You'll *want* to save.

By preserving value, you are able to fulfill the following three H2Os:

H2O #22: *Flexibility: being able to change course in life or capital-ize on opportunity.*

The flexibility afforded by savings cuts financial stress in two im-portant ways.

The first way is that it increases the accessibility of life's possibilities. Through the generation of value, anything is possible. Money, though, can make some of those opportunities closer to hand. Whether it's tak-ing advantage of a great deal that won't last (a winter coat on sale in May) or turning an idea with a limited shelf life into a second income, money allows you to seize the moment.

The second way that the flexibility afforded by savings reduces fi-nancial stress is by staving off the feeling that you have no choice in life except to keep doing what you're doing. If we don't feel that we have any options, we can end up hating where we believe we're stuck, even though it would be something we would otherwise choose. You might not have liked spinach when you were a kid because you had to eat it—it was the only thing left on your plate. But given the choice as an adult, it's "I'll have the Sole Florentine and the spinach salad, please."

If you feel as if your life is currently on a six-inch leash, each dol-lar you save will give you a little slack until you feel as if the world is your backyard to roam about as you please. And here's the irony. You may find, for example, that it's not your job itself that causes you stress. Instead, what may be grinding you is the perception that you're tied to your job by financial necessity that causes you to resent your work. Afforded the flexibility to pursue other options, you may very well decide that what you're doing right now is just fine.

H2O #23: *Stability: having the ability to take unforeseen events in stride.*

No one can predict the future. And in the phraseology of the ill-mannered: *@&! happens. Despite our best efforts and intentions:

- ○ Healthy people become seriously ill.
- ○ Outstanding workers lose their jobs.
- ○ Insurance policies cover everything except what just happened.
- ○ Honest people need a lawyer.
- ○ Good kids get into jams.
- ○ Mother Nature goes on a rampage.

When anything like the above happens, it's bad enough that it is *happening*. But Bad Fortune likes to bring along his close friend, Financial Stress. So whenever an unpredictable predicament pops up, it helps if you can *just write the check* that will take care of the financial obligation without a second thought and send Financial Stress on his way. Yes, your money market or bank balance is going to take a hit. Yes, you'd rather have the money than not. But you've already got enough to worry about without having to take on a financial burden. It is a great benefit to be able to tell yourself, "This is what it's for," and exchange your money for peace of mind.

There is a constant stress in your life when you live on the financial edge: when a single unexpected expense or drop in income—whether a broken exhaust system on your car or a broken ankle that keeps you out of work for a month—can set you back for the foreseeable future. A financial cushion—money in the bank—prevents the bumps and bruises that are a natural part of life from putting you on the critical list.

H2O #24: *Ability: having the means to do things that are beyond the range of your everyday value generation.*

Thanks to money, you can transform hours, energy, and resources into something completely beyond your range of capabilities or impossible to fit into your daily life. You have the ability to:

○ Perform a thousand acts of labor in a few seconds. How many people do you know who live in a dwelling they built with their own hands? It can be done, but most of us don't have the skills or know-how to pull it off, let alone the time.

○ Teach your children the things that you can't. Try to teach your daughter engineering. Go ahead.

○ Assemble complex machinery. If you had trouble assembling Junior's tricycle last Christmas Eve, how long do you think it would take you to put together your own set of wheels? Fortunately, you can "build" a car or a computer with the single stroke of a pen.

○ Be in two places at once. While you're doing something you enjoy around the house, your savings can be off somewhere working for you, whether at your local bank or on Wall Street. This is the basic concept behind retirement.

○ Explore the world. For a few thousand dollars you can take a trip that once would have put you in the history books.

Throughout your life you will make major exchanges, significant expenditures that can't be covered out of your paycheck. These big-ticket items most notably include the down payment on a home, a home improvement, an automobile, a business start-up, and college education. If you don't have enough preserved value to cover their cost, you or your family will have to do without or go into debt.

Later in life, if for no other than physical reasons, we want to be free from being financially compelled to have a full-time job. This is commonly known as retirement—a relatively new and still developing concept (it may be that more people have died from retiring too early than working too long). Nevertheless, even if the entire notion of retirement is anathema to you, at some point you're not going to want to—or possibly not be able to—punch the clock.

SAVINGS IS A MIRACLE PRODUCT— WHY DON'T YOU ACT NOW?

Each and every one of us has a need in our lives for financial ability, flexibility, and stability. These three H2Os are a given. And whatever our specific personal needs, they can all be addressed with the same thing: savings.

Add up the positive benefits of preserving value, and you'd think that it would be at the top of our financial priorities. But instead it's down near the bottom—somewhere after buying snack food and paying the cable bill. So let's phrase the benefits of preserving value within the typical linear "earn-it-and-burn-it" framework.

Imagine that your boss came to you and said, "I'm going to have to reduce your salary by 10 percent. But here's what I'm going to do for you in return. I'll help pay for your retirement and your children's education. I'll protect you against uncertainties and help you sleep at night. However you want to improve your life, I'll back you. Whatever opportunity you want to pursue, I'll be your partner. And if you want to walk out the door and try something new, I'll give you a check and wish you well."

You'd think, "This guy is doing me a favor." After all, most of us pay a lot more than 10 percent in taxes and get back far less in return.

Or what if you saw an advertisement for a super new product that offered all of the wonderful features above and then some? The financial equivalent of a Bonzoo Pocket Slice-O-Matic could be all yours for one easy monthly deduction from your pay. You'd want to get one right away and show it off to your family and friends: "Hey, look at all the things I can do with my new thingamadoodle."

In either of these cases, you'd find a way to make it happen. If your boss cut your pay, you'd adapt. If you thought the miracle product was worthwhile, you'd find a way to pay for it. Well, guess what?

Savings is a miracle product. And you have the ability right now to take it home. "But how?" you ask. "I'm just making ends meet." And obviously borrowing to save does not compute in your favor.

Remember that, no matter how much you earn, you'll likely think that you'd have it made with 10 percent more. Your Buck-O-Matic—your financial decision-making framework—automatically ratchets upward. But human beings are adaptable in not just one direction; you have the ability to adapt in any direction you so choose. If you don't think you can, think again. If you owe money, you've adapted to the situation you created. And if you change your situation to include saving more money, you will find a way to stop tossing money mindlessly away and instead set it aside for things that really matter.

Recently I read a profile of a midwest family struggling to make ends meet. The point of the article was "Look how tough it is to be working class in Middle America." Heartless corporations and an uncaring society had supposedly conspired to turn out the lights on this family's future. Yet by my estimate, the family spent well over 20 percent of their *net* income on vacations and junk food. They were a few simple decisions away from starting a foundation for True Wealth.

When you decide to preserve more value, you will adapt and find a way to make it happen. Before we look at how to make it happen, we need to examine an important corollary.

THE SWORN ENEMY OF TRUE WEALTH: DEBT

People with True Wealth consistently preserve value. But they also avoid debt like the plague. They probably have a mortgage, but it's not topped off with a couple of car loans. They pay off any credit card debt in a month or two. They subscribe to the same motto as your parents or grandparents: "If you can't pay in cash, you can't afford it." They understand that you can't be preparing for the future when you're still taking care of the past.

Today the pay-cash-as-you-go ethic is often looked upon as financial fogyism. Whereas consumer credit once was available only to the wealthy, today you're urged to "get the credit you deserve." Implicit in this message is that somehow, somewhere we've been cheated and that credit will allow us to quickly catch up. Tales abound of dogs being sent preapproved cards, and it's been speculated that Bigfoot's elusiveness stems from a sizable unpaid balance on an unsolicited MasterCard.

People who avoid debt aren't puritanical skinflints, too uptight to become financial swingers. They understand that there are some very real reasons to avoid debt—and not just that it has to be repaid. These reasons go beyond the mere dollars and cents to the overall dynamics of debt in your life:

Debt is the boss from hell. Most people who work would tell you that one boss is enough, if not one too many. Yet every time you borrow money, you are actually adding one more boss to your life. Someone who has the legal right to tell you what to do walks right in the door along with that new dining room set. He tells you how to spend your money every month—regardless of what you have in mind.

Debt is a pair of concrete boots. Whatever path you want to travel in life, debt is going to slow you down. We borrow money because it gives us the chance to leap ahead rather than take things step by step, that is, pay as we go. But that leap ahead, whether it's taking out a student loan or charging a Saturday night on the town, comes with a price: Wherever you land, you're going to find that you're wearing heavier shoes. You have to be certain that whatever you borrowed the money for will strengthen your ability to generate value—to overcome the weight of the incurred debt.

If you miscalculate, you're eventually going to be stuck, unable to move.

Debt is a nest of termites, eating away at an apparently solid foundation. On the surface, debt problems can be invisible. A loan here, a charge account there: Your paycheck covers it all. You're rock solid. But gradually there are more and more accounts and higher and higher balances. All of a sudden you open your checkbook to pay your monthly bills and find that your foundation is crumbling. And there's not a single exterminator listed in the phone book.

Debt is a killer bacterium that can eat you alive. Compounding interest can be a lifesaver when it's working in your favor. But when interest is working against you, it is more likely a nightmare—an outbreak of financial Ebola. When you're borrowing to make minimal payments on your debt, you're paying interest on interest. With no overnight cure in sight, your financial future becomes a minute-by-minute struggle for survival as the runaway interest payments consume your financial being.

Debt is potentially an addictive drug that can cause you to take leave of your senses and empty out your wallet. Like drug addiction, debt addiction begins with the phrase "I can control myself. It won't happen to me." And just as with drug addiction, dependence on debt accelerates rather than plateaus. At a point where the brakes might still be applied, debt addicts step on the gas and send themselves into a downward spiral that exhausts every available means of support.

Debt is a relentless, punishing foe that answers the bell for each and every round in an endless boxing match. Every month, when the bell rings for bill time, debt is in the center of the ring, ready to take a whack at your assets. It doesn't matter how long the match has gone on or how worn out you are, debt is fresh and ready to go the distance, however long it takes to be paid off. And if you skip a round, you'll have to fight twice as hard just to get back in the ring.

Debt can seal off doors you really need opened. There are times when you *have* to borrow money—purchasing a home is the most common instance. But if the mortgage officer reviews your application and sees that you're paying off a new car, last year's vacation, last season's wardrobe, and last month's meals, you'll only get the rubber stamp that says "reject." At that moment you realize that all of the things you borrowed money for in the past don't matter to you now one bit, but the damage is already done. The door you really needed open is closed for the foreseeable future.

Debt is a magician that steals a lot and makes it look like a little. "No money down! No payments until June! Only $99 a month!" So you think you're getting off easy—that the monthly payment is almost the actual purchase price, not the tip of the elephant's trunk. Almost every enticement to borrow money is designed to make the true costs as obscure as is legally allowable. Just as a magician knows how to distract you just enough to put the hamster in his hat, so does a lender know how to get a hamster through your door and then turn it into an elephant.

Debt sucks. This is not an opinion from Beavis and Butt-head. It is an actual physical phenomenon. Debt sucks value out of your life in the form of interest payments. Like a vampire, it loves to bite your wallet and drain it of dollars that might otherwise be exchanged for a stress-free life.

Debt is a dark cloud on the human psyche. No one has ever felt good about being in debt.

I hope that at least one of these analogies sticks in your mind, helping to build your resistance to debt. If you're already in debt, I hope that they increase your resolve to get out of debt.

As long as you have any significant amount of installment debt, your efforts to preserve value will be severely hampered by both the nuts and bolts of the dollars and cents—debt payments come before savings deposits—and your mental perspective—"I can't even think about saving anything until after these accounts are paid off." That's why getting out of debt is an integral part of the process of preserving value.

THE MECHANICS OF SAVING

Preserving value begins with saving—setting a portion of your income aside. In other words, spending less than you make. That may sound too simple: It looks fine on paper, but when applied to the complexities of your life, it's a nonstarter. But all it takes to save are these seven steps, and theory will become stress-reducing reality:

1. Make the decision to save.
2. Give yourself a low-stress overall savings objective that you can live with for a lifetime—and that helps you live with yourself.
3. Set your savings rate objective.
4. Identify and prioritize your specific savings objectives.
5. Organize and prioritize your savings objectives.
6. Build a pipeline from your paycheck to each objective.
7. Do a value check and take the pressure off.

Savings Step One: Make the Decision to Save

Preserving value begins with the single decision to save. You tell yourself, "I'm going to save. Period." Once you've made that decision with enthusiasm and certitude, every subsequent decision gets easier and easier. The increasing power of the benefits will keep you on course. Think about how much better your life would be if you knew that each day you were taking action to fulfill these needs.

Out of all the money-saving tips in the world, there's only one that really matters: Make up your mind that you are going to save. If you can do that, all the little tips and tidbits will find you and knock on your door. If you can't commit to saving, figuring out the cheapest checking account or the best car deal won't matter a hoot.

Savings Step Two: Give Yourself a Low-Stress Overall Savings Objective That You Can Live with for a Lifetime—and That Helps You Live with Yourself

Now that you're going to save, it might seem that the next logical step would be to set a range of specific savings goals. The problem: These goals—from getting out of debt to financing college and retirement—quickly add up to a figure equal to the GNP of a small Latin American country. Your likely response might be "What's the point?"—and I would agree.

The truth is that a dollars-and-cents tag on a savings scenario can seem completely out of sync with reality—and the dissonance can cause you to tune out the notion of saving altogether, even though you know that's not such a hot idea.

Let's go back several generations, before personal finance computer programs and Hewlett-Packard calculators, and look at how your parents or grandparents approached the entire issue of saving. Did they have specific down-to-the-penny goals for each and every one of their savings needs? I doubt it.

What they more likely had was a commitment to doing overall *the best they could* in regard to fulfilling their financial needs. For example, previous generations didn't have as much personal debt because they had a stronger commitment to avoiding debt, not because times were easier.

I've had many conversations with baby boomers regarding their parents and money. Something I've often heard said with much pride is: "My parents did the best they could." Maybe these people didn't live in a big house and have a new wardrobe for every season. And maybe when they graduated from high school there was only enough money in the college fund to cover a year or two at a state school rather than four years of a private school.

But as long as the roof over their head and the money in the bank represented a *sincere best effort* on the part of their parents, there is not a trace of resentment. Rather, it is accepted as reality—the starting point from which one heads out to make the best in life.

So here's the most effective day-to-day savings objective you can have: *to look yourself in the mirror each day and be able to tell yourself that you are doing the best you can.* You are holding the line where the line can be held, making the right choices when there are choices to be made, and developing a secure sense of balance between today's and tomorrow's needs.

Now at first you might breathe a sigh of relief at the idea that you don't have to save enough money to cover every possible need and outcome in life. But although you might be freed from actuarial absurdity, this objective is dependent on discipline, responsibility, and the ability to be honest with yourself. You have to be able to look at your charge slips and checkbook register and say, "A lot of this chud would be better off in my savings or retirement account."

Are you doing the best you can to save money? If you're like me, the answer is no. But if you're like me, you'll find that the personal objective of knowing in your heart that you're doing all you can do to save is both motivating and manageable.

Each step toward increased saving boosts my resolve and my enthusiasm because I can judge that step in the light of progress, not in the foreboding shadow of best-case numbers.

Each day, look yourself in the mirror and ask: "Am I doing the best I can to set aside money for my future needs?" The degree to which you are taking action will be the degree to which you don't have to squirm and mumble. You'll gradually discover the vital role that making a sincere best effort plays in reducing financial stress. And in time you'll answer, "Sure am, pal"—and be content with the numbers, whatever they may be.

Savings Step Three: Set Your Savings Rate Objective

There is simply no way to avoid this basic truth: *The only way that you can save is to spend less than you earn.* There's no secret strategy of the super-wealthy or cosmic belief system that will allow you to eat all of your cake and have some left over.

So now it's time to set your savings rate—the percentage of your gross income you are going to set aside for a future use.

Because all future financial needs are met with the same item—money—it makes sense to start with the big picture—your savings rate—and then apportion it among your specific needs. Why should you think of your savings rate as a percentage rather than a dollar amount? Because it is psychologically easier to digest.

Let's say you have a household income of $50,000 and spend all of it. If I told you that you have to start saving $417 month, your immediate reaction might well be "That's absurd. I can't even save $40 a month." But what if I told you, "You've got to set aside less than one measly percent of your annual income each month?" Your immediate reaction might be "No problemo." But both scenarios are exactly the same; $417 would be less than one percent of your annual income—and, if set aside each month, would give you an annual savings rate of 10 percent.

What is your current savings rate?

You might have a rough idea, but take a few minutes and figure it out. Add up your retirement plan contributions—401(k), IRA, Keogh, and so on (don't forget any matching contributions), payroll deductions (stock purchase plan, credit union, savings plan), automatic deposits from your bank account to investment accounts (savings account, brokerage account, mutual fund), and any funds (cash or check) that you set aside as they became available (a part of your annual bonus, an excess balance in your checking account, or just sticking money in a jar). Now divide the total by your gross annual income. The magic number is (drum roll) . . . uh-oh.

Relax. We're not going to belabor the present, but rather use it as a launch point for determining what objective you are going to set.

IF YOUR CURRENT SAVINGS RATE IS . . .	THEN YOUR SAVINGS RATE OBJECTIVE SHOULD BE . . .
0–5 percent	10 percent
6–10 percent	15 percent
11–20 percent	Add 5 percent to your current rate

In other words, whatever you are currently saving, you will have less financial stress if you increase your savings. Now, you might think, "Wait a minute. I thought more money isn't the answer." But increasing your savings rate isn't about having more money. Rather, it is simply making the most effective use of the money you have.

A Few Additional Savings Guidelines

If your current savings rate is 25 percent or higher, your savings rate is up to you. Just be sure you're not a poster person for Financial Stress Symptom #6: You can't part with money, even if it's for your own darn good.

If you're a "dink" (double income with no kids), you should be saving at least 20 percent of your combined incomes.

If you are single with no kids, you should be saving at least 10 percent if you're in your twenties and 20 percent thereafter.

If you are (a) starting a new business or (b) taking a lower-paying job in order to either get in the door of a field that excites you or restructure the framework of your life, you're *temporarily* excused. The amount of value you're generating will cover you for now . . . but not forever.

How Can You Possibly Do It?

Looking at the savings rate targets above, you're looking at adding 10 percent to your current savings rate *at most*. Do you have to do it all at once? Certainly not. This is your decision—as long as you stick to your objective long enough to see the results. There are several options you might consider:

- ○ Divide the total amount of your anticipated increase in your rate in half. Add one half of the increase now and the remaining half in six months. Example: If your current savings rate is 4 percent and your objective is 10 percent, raise your rate to 7 percent now and then to 10 percent in six months.
- ○ Identify major cost reduction moves that may take time to implement and add them to your rate as they are in place. For example, when you let that little-used club membership expire, add that amount to your savings rate.
- ○ Boost your rate 1 percent (or even ½ percent) a month. If the devil is in the details, then there is undoubtedly enough chud in your budget to dime and dollar your way toward your objective.

And then again, you might decide to take the plunge and raise your savings rate in one big chunk right off the bat. Many of us respond well to big challenges while letting smaller challenges slip away. If you need to considerably increase your savings rate but haven't even been able to get up to the first rung, you may benefit from a radical approach.

Savings Step Four: Identify and Prioritize
Your Specific Savings Objectives

So now you're going to save a bundle. Do you just throw it all into the same pot and dole it out when you need to? That might sound like the easy way, but it will prove to be less effective in fighting stress.

You'll get the greatest benefit from preserving value if you apportion and earmark your savings dollars among your various objectives. Here are three solid reasons:

1. *You will know that you are addressing each specific objective.*
You'll simply have less financial stress if you know that you are taking

specific measures for each specific objective. If you have a general savings fund on one hand and a number of financial objectives on the other, the best you'll be able to tell yourself is "Well, I *could* use some of the money for that." That's short of being able to say, "I have this definable amount for this specific purpose."

2. *Only if you lay out your objectives can you prioritize them.* As you read through the various potential needs addressed by savings, you may have found yourself nodding at virtually each and every one. And realistically, you could save 50 percent of your income and still not have every future need nailed down tight. After all, how many people do you know who, after buying their first house, were able to fully fund their retirement accounts in that same year and still have three to six months' worth of salary in the bank? I bet not many.

The truth is that we are forced to make choices. And given that fact, it will be helpful both to identify and to prioritize your savings objectives.

3. *If you don't know why you are saving a dollar, you won't be able to invest it properly.* Only if you know what your savings objectives are will you be able to invest your money in ways that help ensure that when you need the money, it will be there. This is vital to the complete process of preserving value.

Now let's take a look at some key points that will help you determine your objectives:

Savings Objective: GETTING OUT OF DEBT

Many people use the phrase "financial freedom" to refer to financial wealth. The problem: How much is enough? Being debt-free is *the first* level of financial freedom—and one within the grasp of all.

If you are carrying any charge account balances for longer than three months, an immediate savings objective should be to pay off the debt. Most likely you are paying from 17 to 22 percent in interest on your charge accounts. By eliminating this debt, you'll be getting a return on your money that exceeds almost any investment you could make in any normal year.

Need further convincing? If you have an $1,800-dollar balance on your charge card (at 18 percent interest) and are making only the minimum monthly payment, it's going to take you over *twenty-two years* to pay off the account. Your payments will total nearly $5,600!! Think about that the next time you're tempted to pay with plastic. Ask yourself if it's something you'd want to still be paying off two decades hence.

Warning light: If your combined charge account balances increase three months in a row, you are headed toward real trouble: a semi-permanent level of debt that will be increasingly difficult to reduce.

Calculate your *debt rate*. In other words, how much are you spending a month paying off consumer debt as a percentage of your gross income? Take a moment and figure it out. Think about how much less stress you'd have if that money could be added to your savings rate instead.

Now here's a question to ponder: What total of what you went into debt for would you, in retrospect, forgo in exchange for money in the bank right now? Quite a bit, I'm sure. Think about that the next time you're tempted to whip out a charge card.

The lesson: If you can get your debt down and keep it down, saving will be easier than you think. You're already accustomed to writing monthly checks—they're simply headed in the wrong direction.

Savings Objective: BUILDING A FINANCIAL CUSHION

Why might you need a financial cushion? Because life doesn't follow a script—and some of its surprises can come with an unexpected tab that, if not taken in stride, can knock you off the path to True Wealth: "Sorry, we don't have enough money to retire because we had to replace the septic tank."

Even if you are consumed by debt and have no money in the bank, you shouldn't wait to start building up a financial cushion until all of your debt is paid off. You should start saving right away, *even if it's just a small amount*. Saving generates a tremendous amount of positive emotional, mental, and financial energy. That is why preserving value is one of the components of True Wealth—and why you need to make saving an active part of your life.

How much cushion should you have? The standard rule of thumb has been an amount equal to *three to six months'* net income at the ready (i.e., not in retirement accounts or nonliquid investments).

If the notion of accumulating even three months' worth of income seems absurd given your other needs, remember that you might consider your cushion as an adjunct to your retirement savings, that is, have it do double duty. The bonus: You might be less tempted to tap into it.

Savings Objective: HOME OWNERSHIP

Let's start with your answering the following question:

I (a) own my own home, (b) don't own my own home but would really like to, or (c) don't own my own home and don't feel particularly compelled to buy one.

If you answered c, then obviously this isn't one of your objectives.

If you answered b, then this need is probably front and center among your various needs. A word of advice: Don't confuse how much mortgage you qualify for with how much you can "afford." The guideline of not borrowing more than twice your annual household income is a good stress preventer.

If you answered a, then I'd suggest that unless your present environment is truly untenable, you focus on other needs before trading up or moving along. And look for ways to generate value by improving your home and neighborhood.

Savings Objective: STARTING A BUSINESS

If you haven't surmised by now, having some form of your own business is an objective I wholeheartedly applaud.

There is almost no business or field in which there isn't a way to start small and let circumstance and success propel your expansion. As your business grows, there may very well be a point where you do have to make a major commitment—using every available cent and borrowing more to boot—to get to the next level of operation. Far better that this commitment be an extension of what you're already doing rather than a price tag for an opportunity in a box.

How much will it cost you to start a business? If there is a business that you have carefully researched as one of your objectives and (1) you are absolutely certain that you lack the necessary financial means to get started, and (2) you have a specific figure, not a guesstimate, as to what it will take to get started, then you have a legitimate savings need. If not, stop the conjecturing and start pursuing the objective through the generation of value.

Savings Objective: SENDING YOUR CHILDREN TO COLLEGE

Not too long ago I had dinner with a good friend whose son was just graduating from a four-year private college. When the subject of college costs came up, he related the following story.

"At the time my son was born, tuition and room and board at a private school ran around $4,000 a year—less than $20,000 for the entire four years. We were told [and reasonably so] that it would take about $12,500 a year—$50,000 total—by the time our son reached college. We dutifully put away the appropriate amount each month, and by high school graduation, we had the $50,000 saved. There was only one problem: His four years of college cost $100,000. We were $50,000 short. So what happened?"

"You got robbed" was my reply. There was no more succinct way to describe what happened to a generation of parents who got stuck with college costs that soared beyond expectation, above the rate of inflation, and well ahead of any increase in the quality of the education received (if in fact there was any increase at all). Colleges raised their tab because parents would pony up, no questions asked.

But just as with real estate prices in the '80s, when the point is reached where there is virtually unanimous consensus that the price escalation is permanent and forever headed to the moon, some funny things happen. The number of potential customers—in this case, students—can decline. Consumers can get more demanding and discerning. A seller's market becomes a buyer's market. This, I believe, is where we are today with higher education.

As the number of potential students declines into the next century, colleges will be forced to compete more based on price and quality just to keep the seats filled and the doors open. In fact, some institutions are already dropping tuition prices. Institutions will compete more for top students, regardless of their economic status.

Bottom line: If your kid is an all-around outstanding student, you have a better chance of cutting an outstanding deal with a quality institution.

Before you get absolutely twizzled over what it may or may not cost you to send your child to college, consider these guidelines:

1. There are far too many variables to predict with any degree of accuracy how much it will cost for an education that will serve a specific individual child well.

2. The best education that money can buy may not be the costliest.

3. That you may not be able to afford the most expensive college money can buy shouldn't bother you if your child is adept at generating value at the college you can afford.

4. Value generated within the home plus a sincere best effort saving for college equals a start in life that most people in the world can only dream about.

Some additional stress reducers:

That common cost figure isn't that common. That much-bandied-about $20,000-a-year tuition bill that sends you into apoplexy (not including room and board, mind you) is nowhere near the typical tab. Fewer than 5 percent of students actually pay $20,000 or more. Over half of all college students pay less than $4,000 per year in tuition.

What your child learns (or doesn't learn) in grades K–12 is at least as important as where he or she goes to college. Virtually any high school graduate today can go on to get a college degree without ever having a solid grounding in academic fundamentals, a genuine thirst for knowledge, and a healthy respect for intellectual discipline and excellence. But you cannot get a good education without them—and the window of opportunity is open right now (it's on the opposite side of the room from the television set).

It's what gets taught that counts. You can cut thousands (and even tens of thousands) of dollars off the cost of a college education if you are willing to focus on what goes on in the classroom—*what actually is taught*—rather than the marquee value of the institution. The difference between a marquee institution and a less well known institution might in fact be the difference between being lectured to by graduate teaching assistants and having close teacher-student relationships with the absolute best professors the lesser-known school has to offer.

Quality is where you look for it and find it. You can greatly improve the quality of education even within the same institution by seeking out the most rigorous and demanding professors who are committed to intellectual growth rather than ideological indoctrination or grade inflation. Consider the range of possibilities that exist at your average Big State University: A degree can signify that the recipient has recycled enough drivel to get by or that she has gained a level of ability that will make her an immediate asset to any pertinent endeavor.

The current Ivy League obsession is an illness. The growing belief in some circles that the only way to guarantee that your child will have a chance in life is to attend an Ivy League or similar-level institution is absolutely ill.

This belief, cultivated by certain elites and perpetuated somewhat unintentionally by the media, not only represents the opportunity-in-a-box mentality, but also, in many instances, a downright neurotic insistence by parents on raising trophy kids. Marquee institutions will still charge top dollar because they can get away with it—just as in any market where people are willing to pay for status.

Yes, a marquee degree will generate contacts and open doors.

Yes, a marquee degree can signify in some instances a body and degree of knowledge not as readily available elsewhere—particularly in the sciences.

But on the other hand, we all know of graduates of elite institutions who could have floundered just as well in life with a generic degree or who, once inside the door, found that their degree was not able to prevent their coworkers from outperforming them.

Simple logic would tell you that in a global economy of billions of people, there is certainly room for any and every person with a sound education who makes generating value the focus of his or her work.

You can save more for college if you have a partner: your child. It is your child who is going to benefit most from a college education, so you shouldn't have to make all of the sacrifices.

From day one, make it an assumption that any gift of money—for birthdays, holidays, or whatever—over a few dollars automatically goes into the college fund. If your kid works after school, a good chunk of that money should go toward college. Why should Tony and Tanya walk around in hundred-dollar sneakers while you're bustin' your tail to save for their education? The bulk of whatever they earn during the summer should never touch their hands in the form of cash.

Start now—switch later. You can cut the cost of a college degree by $20,000 or more by studying two years at a local community college and then transferring the credits to a four-year school.

Many two-year colleges have agreements with four-year schools that allow for earned credits to be fully transferable. You can save considerably on the first two years (more if the student lives at home and/or holds a year-round job) but still have the same diploma as if your son or daughter attended the same school all four years. This is a particularly appealing strategy for the student who doesn't have a clue why he's going to college other than that it is better than not going.

Savings Objective: RETIREMENT

After 227 pages, we now stand face-to-face with the big monster that threatens to devour all of your assets somewhere between your final punch of the time clock and your first purchase of Depends: retirement.

So let's stare the monster down and ask the big question: How much will you need?

Trying to answer this question with any degree of certainty and accuracy is one of the more common yet futile pursuits of recent financial times. After all, your Golden Years are nothing more than the summation and reflection of all of the value you've generated in your life. There is no way any financial planner can measure or ascertain the following:

o To what degree will your faith be a source of comfort?
o Will your siblings or children welcome your company and care for you in a time of need, or will they go to any lengths to avoid putting up with you, even if it means letting you languish until you're warehoused in a low-rent nursing home?

○ Will your kids be financially self-sufficient or hitting you up for bread well into their thirties and forties?

○ Will your body be well maintained to meet the challenges of aging, or a broken-down and abused wreck with a sludge-filled motor?

○ Will you be an active member of a community that values your contribution and takes care of its own, or a phantom geezer, invisible to all?

○ Will your mind be engaged in a myriad of interests, or will your biggest intellectual challenge be extrapolating the *TV Guide* listings into the numerology of your local cable system?

○ Will you never earn another dime, or will you continue to generate financial value long after your official retirement date?

○ Will you truly see yourself as in charge of your life, or dependent on the largesse of others?

In addition to the whole issue of the value you generate, there are the nuts-and-bolts particulars of your life—minor questions like these:

○ How long are you going to live?

○ How long will your spouse live?

○ Are you going to stay married?

○ Are you going to stay in your current job until you retire?

○ Are you going to live in your current house until you retire?

And that's just your personal life!

But even suppose for a moment that your financial planner or stockbroker not only was able to ascertain all of the above (if she can, call the *Star* immediately—they're probably looking for the next Jeane Dixon), but was also able to put an exact price tag on all of your financial needs. Then you'd know how much you really "need," right? Wrong. Because what we're talking about is the future—ten, twenty, and even forty years and beyond.

The dollar you save today has a long journey across the future until the day when you decide to exchange it. So in order to predict just how much money you'll have to sock away each year, you'd have to be able to peer into a crystal ball and figure out what's going to happen in the world as a whole. And here are just a few of the things you'd need to figure out:

○ How are the various investment markets—stocks, bonds, real estate, and so on—actually going to perform?

○ What is the inflation rate going to be?

○ How much in Social Security benefits are you actually going to receive?

○ How much of your income is the government going to siphon off?

○ What type of health care system will the country have and at what cost?

○ As more boomers retire, will All-U-Can-Eat buffets have to discontinue senior citizen discounts in order to stay in business?

Having an inaccurate guesstimate for *any* of the above questions could render any financial plan useless—even one in a faux-leather embossed binder.

YOUR MAGIC NUMBER: IT'S USEFUL ONLY IF IT'S REASONABLE

Even though there's no possible way that anyone could ever even begin to know everything about your life and the future, that hasn't stopped a lot of people from pretending that they can and do. Armed with computer programs that have more built-in assumptions than a federal deficit estimate, the pros are able to tell you right down to the cent how much you need to invest (with them, of course) each year.

At the time I wrote in Chapter One that, according to the experts, you'll need more money than you've ever earned in total if you expect to retire, I was half joking based on my gut instinct that the numbers being tossed out as to what people would "need" to retire were absurdly high.

Since then that impression has been confirmed as fact. Even using software provided by a mutual fund with the soberest of reputations, you can figure out for yourself that you will indeed have to save more money than you will earn over the remainder of your life in order to maintain your present lifestyle.

How do such nutty and impossible "magic numbers" come to be presented with a straight face? Given that fear is a powerful motivator, they might be intended to serve as a cattle prod, shocking people into action. What I suspect is that more often it numbs us into wondering why we should even bother.

It's also worth noting that these projections are fostered within the consumption-driven culture of the financial industry—one in which the Sponge Syndrome is forever epidemic. If you live in a world where making and spending money are your raison d'être, of course you are going to need more than someone whose life is centered on generating value.

Okay, so it's impossible to predict the future—and the people who insist on doing so have an interest in scaring us or a bias toward a cash-driven lifestyle rather than a life. We still aren't any closer to answering the Big Question: *How much money should you save for retirement?* Are we really going to have to be content with vague answers like "a lot" or "all you possibly can"?

Isn't there at least a solid rule of thumb on which we can base a plan of action? This is a question that frankly vexed me as much as it might you. That was until I read a personal finance column in my local paper entitled "Retirement Nest Egg Needn't Be Goose Size." Eureka! A kindred soul!

The article was based on the work of Richard E. Vodra, a certified financial planner in Fairfax, Virginia. Dick approached the issue of saving for retirement—a central concept to the work of any financial planner—with an open and questioning mind (he also holds a degree from Yale Law School). Based on his analysis, Vodra believes that:

You will need less than what you've been told. If your house is paid off, your kids have moved out, and you no longer have work-related expenditures, you can live quite comfortably on about 40 percent (not 80 or 90 percent, as is often purported) of your current gross income after taxes.

Don't forget, you'll also be in a lower tax bracket and won't be saving for retirement once you're actually retired. Factor in some level of Social Security benefit (more on this in a little bit), and that figure is reduced to about 28 percent. In other words, you are going to have to save enough money to generate 28 percent of your current income from your own resources. Any corporate pension you have is included in this.

Two percent is more like it. A reasonable rate of return from your investment portfolio is about 2 percent "net/net"—after taxes (25 percent) and inflation (4 percent)—based on a mix of 50 percent stocks, 35 percent bonds, and 15 percent cash.

That 2 percent might sound awfully puny, but it's based on actual historic rates of return and includes taxes and inflation, two profit eaters all too often overlooked in our rate-of-return mania. You've probably been told that you should have 90 percent of your money in stocks. There will be a time when you'll wish you had 10 percent of your money in stocks.

Over a lifetime, Vodra has assumed a balanced portfolio—thereby reducing the degree to which a retirement is predicated on the return on investment of one specific asset class, that is, stocks.

You should plan on a long life. You don't want to outlive your assets, so you should plan on living for thirty-five years after you retire. This is well beyond normal life expectancy, but it also builds in some slack that can cover a nursing home stay (a far less likely occurrence than the paranoia that surrounds it) or a lousy investment (a far more likely occurrence than investment wizards care to admit).

THE 700% SOLUTION®*

Based on these assumptions, conservative and realistic, Vodra has arrived at what he calls the *"700% Solution": You should have approximately seven times your pre-retirement income saved by retirement date to be financially independent.*

For example, if your current income is $50,000, you will need $350,000 socked away in today's dollars when you retire. If your income is $80,000, your savings need for retirement would be $560,000. If inflation raises prices, your target amount will rise at the same rate.

Now keep in mind that any money you've saved to date will continue to grow, which reduces the amount you'll have to save from now on. Let's say you're thirty-five years old, your annual income is $50,000, and you have $50,000 in your 401(k) already. Assuming a 2 percent net/net return, your savings need is reduced to $260,000—achievable by saving 12 percent of your income per year for the next thirty years (5.2 times your current income).

Twelve percent!! Yikes!! But don't overlook some of the ways your overall need and yearly contribution might be reduced:

- ○ If your employer matches your contributions to your retirement account, his contributions count toward your savings rate—which is why you absolutely *have* to take him up on his kindly offer.
- ○ You may be expecting to receive a pension.
- ○ Your income might grow substantially while you hold the line on your expenses, especially after your kids leave home.
- ○ You might not retire until you're in your late sixties or even your seventies.
- ○ You might continue to generate a modest income in retirement.

---

* The "700% Solution" is a registered trademark of Richard Vodra.

○ You might inherit a sum of money. Caution: Don't hinge your retirement plans on this one.

○ You might move to a smaller residence and save the difference.

The bottom line: If you start saving early, take advantage of your employee benefits, don't ratchet up your lifestyle with every pay raise, and continue to generate value in and out of work, retirement becomes a manageable proposition—a lot more so than the financial fearmongers have made it out to be.

The "700% Solution," too, is a guesstimate—but a sensible one. It is a tool that can help you allocate savings dollars to your retirement need. If you'd like to figure out how much your retirement need might be based on your current income and savings and the number of years until you retire, see Appendix C.

Savings Step Five: Organize and Prioritize Your Savings Objectives

We've just looked at the "big" specific savings objectives. Other savings objectives we've already discussed include an automobile, continuing education, vacations, weddings, and home improvements.

When we think of all our savings objectives together, we tend to put them in one of the following three categories:

The Out-of-Pocket PAST. These are the savings dollars that never make it to a savings vehicle—going instead toward paying off previous commitments. Most of us believe that we would be building more for the future if we weren't so busy mopping up for the past—and therefore any serious savings plan has to include reducing the negative effects of debt.

The At-Hand PRESENT. These are the savings dollars that you set aside (1) for an anticipated expenditure such as a house or home improvement, business, automobile, or other big-ticket item, or (2) as a ready reserve for unforeseen circumstances or unexpected opportunities. Either way, they are dollars you expect to exchange within five years or have available to exchange immediately if necessary.

The Untouchable FUTURE. Dollars in this category are set aside for future needs of such great life-sustaining importance that they are considered off limits for any need that might pop up in the meantime. The two big untouchable future needs: education and retirement.

Organizing these categories as columns and then listing the corresponding needs can help you visualize and organize just what needs you have on the table in anticipation of setting priorities.

For example, a young married couple might organize their objectives as follows:

PAST	PRESENT	FUTURE
Pay off debt	Down payment for house	Retirement
	Start business	College for kids
	Build financial cushion	

That's a lot to handle and still put food on the table. So rather than feel overwhelmed or spread too thin, they should begin by targeting those objectives that they believe will have the greatest positive impact on their lives over the long run.

Here's how they might prioritize their objectives, along with their rationale:

1. Get out of debt—the first level of financial freedom.
2. Start a business—maximize value generation.
3. Save a down payment for house—running out of room.
4. Put money aside for retirement—every dollar saved now is worth several dollars saved later.
5. Build a financial cushion—don't want to live too close to the edge.
6. Save for education—will increase savings as business grows.

Allocating dollars among your savings needs is an art, not a science, and is based on common sense and reasonable judgment.

Our young couple might begin by targeting their debt and starting a business—allocating minimal dollars to their other needs. As their needs to get out of debt and start a business are fulfilled, more resources can be allocated to their remaining needs. As their debt is paid down, dollars are freed up for the down payment on a house. As their business grows, those dollars can be directed to retirement, a financial reserve, and education.

In weighing past, present, and future needs, here are several guidelines:

1. Concentrate first on those needs that will have the greatest overall stress-reducing impact on your entire life: being debt-free, boosting your ability to generate value, creating a business environment for generating value, and providing for your retirement and your children's future.

2. Allocate a dollar amount to each objective based on a percentage of your total savings rate. You can work only with the dollars you have, so divide them up and let the chips fall where they may. If there're not enough chips, raise your savings rate.

A hypothetical example based on a $70,000 income and a 15 percent savings rate:

SAVINGS NEED	PERCENTAGE OF SAVINGS	DOLLAR AMOUNT
Pay off debt	30%	$ 3,150
Retirement	40%	$ 4,200
Education	10%	$ 1,050
Cushion	20%	$ 2,100
Total	100%	$10,500

3. Consider starting at both ends—your nearest-term need and furthest-term need—and work toward the middle. If you are up to your eyeballs in consumer debt, why even think about long-term objectives? Because you have the opportunity right now to turn each dollar saved into a cash machine—and that opportunity will soon pass. Because of the miracle of compound interest, a dollar saved now is the equal of several dollars saved later down the road. And the way compounding works, it's the final few miles that crank out the big profits.

Consider the growing value of a dollar compounding at 10 percent (everyone's favorite rate of return) in a tax-deferred account over a twenty-six-year period:

AFTER . . .	YOU'LL HAVE . . .
7-plus years	$ 2.00
15-plus years	4.00
21-plus years	8.00
25 years	10.84
26 years	11.92

It takes over seven years for a buck to make another buck. Over the years the time it takes to make each additional dollar decreases, until in year twenty-five, your savings hit a flash point and start cranking out more on an annual basis than was saved to begin with. Each dollar saved now—a onetime event—will be worth over a dollar *per year* in twenty-five years. In thirty years it will be cranking out *two dollars per year.* In thirty-five years it will be a virtual printing press: *four dollars per year.*

All the added motivation you need to save a dollar might be right here: a dollar saved this year can be a dollar *per year* later. The sooner you save, the sooner you can get to the flash point. Chop your debt down now, but don't neglect to plant some seeds.

4. *Pay a little attention to each of your objectives.* Allocate most of your savings toward your top objectives, but always allocate at least a little toward every objective. When you allocate an amount—no matter how small—toward a specific need, you have broken through the critical psychological barrier between doing and not doing.

When I snapped out of the sleep-deprived scramble of first-time fatherhood, there was a new savings need on the horizon: advanced education. I tried to ignore it for a while. There were other more pressing financial matters.

But over the months, my lack of action toward this new objective gnawed away at my sense of responsibility. Finally, I set up an account for my son with an automatic monthly withdrawal from our checking account. Immediately I felt worlds better: I was doing something. And since then, I've found ways to increase our contributions that never would have occurred to me before.

Savings Step Six: Build a Pipeline
from Your Paycheck to Each Objective

The most effective way to set aside money is to build a pipeline directly from your paycheck to an objective. Once a dollar touches your hands, the chances that it will be set aside for savings dramatically decrease.

There are only two words you need to know to become a disciplined saver: direct deposit. Payroll deduction and direct deposit will force you to adapt to the reality of increased savings. They are two of the best friends you'll ever make. Virtually anywhere you want to invest your savings will allow you to set up a direct deposit from your paycheck or your checking account: banks, brokers, credit unions, retirement plans, mutual funds.

Arrange in some way, shape, or form for the dollar amount being allocated to an objective to be automatically removed from your cash flow on a regular and ongoing basis. If possible, have a separate, dedicated account for each objective.

If you get a large check—a bonus, for example—deposit the check in an investment account and then transfer whatever portion you need for current obligations to your checking account. You'll save more if you're taking the money out of savings.

Many brokerage firms offer cash management accounts that allow you to draw from your cash balance using a debit card. The card is a wonderful convenience for those times you're making a major purchase or you're faced with an emergency. But it also makes it too convenient to chip away at your savings. My advice: Carry the card, but don't use it. If you can't resist the temptation, cut the card. The same holds true for checks that allow you to tap into your investments.

Banks (and some cash management accounts) also offer the convenience of accessing your savings through an ATM machine. My unscientific observation of the pile of transaction slips left at my local cash machine: An awful lot of people hit up their savings accounts for cash on the weekend.

Decline the option of ATM access to your savings. Out of reach, out of mind.

Savings Step Seven: Do a Value Check and Take the Pressure Off

Even after you've raised your savings rate and set up pipelines from your paycheck to your needs, you are very likely to feel pressure. In the back of your mind, you might still be thinking, "Seven percent here, 2 percent there, 2 percent for this, 1 percent for that: How is it ever going to add up to much?" And everywhere you turn, you're going to be bombarded with escalating predictions of financial doom and gloom. There is no better time to take stock of your most vital asset: value. Here's how:

Write each of your savings objectives on a sheet of paper.
List all of the ways you're generating value toward each savings objective and your H2Os.
Take stock of the progress you've made toward fulfilling each of your objectives.
Make note of how you are planning to generate additional value toward your objectives.

Remember: There's no such thing as perfection in life. Give it your best and enjoy the adventure.

WORKSHEET: ORGANIZING AND PRIORITIZING
YOUR SAVINGS OBJECTIVES

The Out-of-Pocket PAST (% of Total Savings)	The At-Hand PRESENT (% of Total Savings)	The Untouchable FUTURE (% of Total Savings)
(%)	(%)	(%)
(%)	(%)	(%)
(%)	(%)	(%)
(%)	(%)	(%)

Possible objectives

Pay off debt(s)   Down payment for   Retirement
  (list individually)   house   (list each adult)

Financial cushion   College education
    (list each child)
Continuing education

Own business

Home improvement

Automobile

1. List each of your savings objectives in the appropriate category.

2. Prioritize—beginning with #1—your objectives based on stress-reducing potential: "How much less stressful will my day-to-day life be if I know that I am taking action to meet this objective?"

3. Assign a percentage of your overall savings rate to each objective based on your overall priorities (see example on page 234).

4. Prepare to build a pipeline from your paycheck to your objectives—after you read the next chapter.

9

Investing for True Wealth

E ACH DOLLAR you save is the end result of a conscious effort to exchange less money than you earn. But in terms of preserving value, a dollar saved is just a beginning. That dollar must be invested in a way which ensures that it will make the journey from the present to the future. If a dollar saved isn't at hand when you need it, the situation is ultimately no different than if you threw the bill into the trash today.

Here, then, is the final "has to occur" for the value generation cycle to be completed:

H2O #25: *You are comfortable with your investments.*

You're probably thinking "That's it? My investments should be like some old pair of slippers?" After all, the word *comfortable* seems kind of soft to describe a process more commonly associated with precise numbers and certain opinions.

But when you actually look at what it takes for you to feel comfortable with an investment, then comfortable is what really counts. A comfortable investment is one that:

○ You can select to match your objective with a minimum amount of fuss.

○ You understand how it actually works.
○ You don't have to follow every day.
○ Doesn't keep you up at night.
○ Makes you some money (after taxes and inflation).
○ Allows you access to your money when you need it.

Comfortable sounds just right, doesn't it? So let's try to find some investments that fit.

DOES INVESTING ALWAYS HAVE TO BE A GOAT ROPE?

Unfortunately, what should be a relatively simple process has been needlessly turned into a byzantine goat rope—and needlessly so. Now, there's nothing wrong with roping goats—if that's your thing. And there's nothing wrong with spending your spare time tending to your herd of investments, if that's what you like to do.

For some people, investing is like a hobby, a way to generate horizon value, if not extra dollars. These individuals pore over stock quotes like a handicapper on Derby day, treat each prognostication as if it were a pearl of wisdom, and chart a course with the concentration of Magellan (Ferdinand, not Fidelity). If you're one of these people, picking an investment for your 401(k) isn't a chore, it's a downright thrill, diminished only by the fact that you want even more investment options to choose from, not fewer.

But for everyone else—and, I daresay, most people—the prospect of wrestling with investment decisions is fraught with financial stress. You feel that if you really were a responsible adult, you would care more about investing, pay more attention to how you invest, and, in fact, get "really into it."

But the reality is that the idea of picking an investment has all the appeal of doing your income taxes. And even if you have the motivation, what about the time?

Financial magazines abound with profiles of do-it-yourself personal portfolio wizards who compete with the pros in the privacy of their own homes, some of them spending "only" six or seven hours a week. Which is a way of saying that, if you factor out the time you might spend in a few worthless meetings and eating lunch, managing your money could be the equivalent of a part-time *ten-week-per-year* job. And you don't even have to ace the interview to get it.

Right here I'd like you to ask yourself this: *"Is investing something I find relaxing and enjoyable, or does it cause me great stress?"* If you answered "stress," the following pages are specifically intended to clear much of the static and noise from your investment radar screen and help you proceed without looking over your shoulder out of fear or regret. Fortunately, it doesn't have to be that way—you can preserve value (and your sanity) while minimizing financial stress.

And what if you do enjoy investing and believe you have the investment part of your life down pat? Your investments are not only *not* causing you stress, they are a source of great satisfaction. I'd suggest that you still read on—because maybe, just maybe, not all investment roads lead to rosy scenarios. And if financial stress happens to be lurking just around the corner, having a ready response will help you keep the stress from getting out of hand.

STAYING CONNECTED: WHAT'S BEHIND THE NUMBERS ON YOUR MONTHLY STATEMENT?

Once you actually save money, a new stage is set for potential financial stress. You get paid, you deposit your savings dollars somewhere—whether it be a bank, brokerage firm, credit union, or mutual fund—and soon after a statement with some numbers on it arrives in the mail. That's when funny things can happen.

All too often, once value gets translated into dollars and cents, people forget from whence it came. The entire process of generating value—all the time, effort, and resources it took for those dollars to be created—is forgotten. The diligence and discipline that went into saving those dollars fades from memory.

Now you have some numbers on a piece of paper that you have to multiply. Instead of being an extension of a logical process—preserving value for a future need—investing becomes an abstract exercise—a giant video poker game. As a result, people who . . .

> . . . wouldn't think of buying ten dollars' worth of lottery tickets put ten thousand dollars in an investment with not much greater odds of a profitable outcome.
> . . . bettered themselves through hard work and discipline start throwing money around at hot tips and rumors.
> . . . have distinguished themselves by forging their own path in life invest by following the crowd without so much as a second thought as to where it's headed.
> . . . would tactfully refrain from loaning a hundred dollars to a close friend will turn over their life savings to someone who calls out of the blue on the telephone.

How do people with True Wealth avoid such minefields? They begin by seeing each dollar saved for what it truly is: *their value, and therefore an extension of their lives.*

I'd suggest that you take a recent monthly statement from each of your present investment accounts—bank, mutual fund, brokerage, pension, whatever—and spread them out on your kitchen table. Then tell yourself: "This isn't just mine—it is *me.*" To the extent that your money enables you to fulfill important needs of value—retirement, education, a home—*your money is a part of your life.*

When you put yourself in the frame of mind to treat your money with the same care and respect with which you'd treat your own being, the more likely you are to protect and preserve those dollars rather than cast them to the wind—or shove them directly into the pockets of others.

You'll often find that people with True Wealth have their savings dollars in investments that are conservative beyond what even the most cautious adviser might deem prudent. Yet when you look at the total portfolio of their lives, they've invested their value in ways that more than compensate them for their cautious investments.

One such individual explained to me why he invests his savings in simple investments that most professionals would scoff at. "I don't want to be bothered. It's more important to pay cash and stay out of debt than how you invest. Every day is a gift—that's where I make my real investments."

This is a tremendous insight into a crucial difference between using money and using value as the primary currency of your life—and the role it plays in your approach to investing. *With value as your currency, each day is the real "market"—the best place to generate what you want to have happen in your life.*

Your return on your time, effort, and resources will be far greater if you invest them in fulfilling your H2Os than if you chase an extra percent or two return on your investments. No one on his deathbed has ever said, "I wish I'd spent more time managing my portfolio," or had inscribed on her tombstone, "Outperformed the S&P 500 by 2.3% for the five-year period ending . . . " And without the pressure or nagging feeling to make more from your investments, you slam the door shut on a whole lot of potential financial stress.

Using value as the currency of your life emphasizes those things in your life over which you have the most control—how you generate and exchange value and how much money you save—and deemphasizes those things over which you have the least control—the performance of the investment markets and the judgment of others.

Far from limiting your financial resources, this approach can actually increase your bottom line over your lifetime.

It is almost certain that you are going to earn far more money from your livelihood than you ever will from your investments. If you generate more value, at least some of that value will eventually find its way into your paycheck. And by maintaining a high savings rate, you can be satisfied with less from your investments—and will have less stress—than the person who *has* to make money from his investments to make up for his lack of saving.

Now, you might think, wouldn't the ideal situation be to focus your life on value *and* be able to manage your investments for fun and big profits? Sure. But if you are not someone who wants to make investing part of your horizon value, then you are better off accepting your lack of interest and concentrating on the relatively simple task of preserving value for the future. You *do* have the common sense and practical judgment to accomplish that pretty easily. And as long as you invest in the real market—your daily opportunity to generate value—your life's portfolio will yield a return unattainable by even the greatest investment wizards of all time: a life money can't buy.

WHAT'S A GOOD INVESTMENT?

So now you're on your way to becoming a lean-and-mean savings machine. But one big question remains: "What should I do with my savings?"

"Why, make a good investment" would be the common reply. And what would be a "good" investment? If you listen to the hum of the investment world carefully, you'll hear a subliminal message: A good investment is one that will give you more money than whatever you're making now. "Get out your checkbook and follow us!" the Pin-striped Sirens sing.

Now, it may very well be possible to get a little greater return on your savings than what you're getting now without compromising your comfort level. But by heading out on the eternal search for a little more, you're on the entry ramp to the "more is better" road to stress. And no matter how many warning signs about risk and suitability line the road, all but the most disciplined investors begin to ignore them. Before you know it, you'll be chasing after "good" investments such as . . .

> . . . that stock whose price has already rocketed into the stratosphere.
> . . . that piece of barren property that will eventually be at the epicenter of regional development.
> . . . that account that pays 5 percent more than the bank, not guaranteed.

Sure, this chase might be exciting—and so is driving blindfolded the wrong way down the freeway with your seat belt unbuckled. And both pursuits can end up in similar fashion. No, a good investment is not necessarily the one that's going to give you a little more.

People with True Wealth know the real answer: *A good investment is one that delivers an average return with a minimum amount of stress.* We'll look at both average return and stress in detail. But first, it needs to be emphasized just whose stress we're talking about.

YOUR PERSPECTIVE IS THE ONLY ONE THAT COUNTS

When we say that a good investment has a minimum amount of stress, that's stress *from your perspective,* period. No matter what anyone else says or thinks, it is important for you to be comfortable with your investments above all other considerations. It is your money. You're the one who has to sleep at night. And you're the one who's going to use it when you're good and ready to.

A lot of people may know more than you do about investments, and that's as it should be. It's their world. But there is no one who knows more about your world than you do. You don't "have" to be in any investment or conform to anyone's expectations. You aren't obligated to do anything you aren't comfortable with.

You certainly shouldn't worry about hurting someone's feelings. If you ever feel the slightest bit guilty about telling an investment professional "no," just remember this: If the proposed investment doesn't work out, it comes out of your pocket, not his. Even in the event of outright fraud, it's going to take bitter and stressful legal action to get back anything more than a few sympathetic words.

People with True Wealth enter the investment arena with a healthy amount of caution and skepticism. To those who would call them chicken, paranoid, or outright stupid, their response is "It's not your money." This mind-set comes from a combination of knowledge, experience, intuition, and upbringing. Our challenge is this: How can we replicate their low-stress investment results in our lives from the outset—without going through the wringer of trial and error?

SIMPLE TOOLS GET THE JOB DONE SIMPLY

The oft-recommended approach to investing is to sort through all of the available investment options and their attendant strategies, opinions, and hype—the big mountain of financial "what"—and then, bit by bit, narrow the possibilities down to the chosen remaining few that will make up your one-of-a-kind-and-couldn't-be-better portfolio.

But that doesn't sound like a solution as much as a big part of the problem. Do we really have to know and understand everything before we can do anything? Just because an investment exists, does learning all about it necessarily have to be part of the required curriculum of life? No!

Let's start from the opposite vantage point—by approaching the issue of investing much as we'd approach any other project around the house—by asking this question: *What basic tools and knowledge do I have to have in order to get the job done?* I do not believe that investing has to be any different than building a simple bookshelf, working with a small assortment of basic tools and materials—wood, saw, screws, screwdriver, sandpaper, paint, paintbrush—and basic guidelines—painting with the grain, for example.

What we'll focus on in the pages ahead is assembling a set of basic tools and ideas that will enable you to preserve value. We're not going to even attempt to include all of the potentially useful tools—in fact, we're going to willfully exclude some quite common investments that millions of investors have used to positive effect. Just as with any other need, we're going to concentrate on have-to-haves, basic function, and quality—eschewing bells and whistles and, most certainly, image.

By restricting ourselves to a limited number of simple investment tools, we not only make the decision process less stressful, but largely avoid the possibility of our investments taking on a life of their own and becoming a second job. And most important, we stay focused on the mission of preserving value with the least amount of ceremony. Let's begin with two key concepts.

THE FIRST FUNDAMENTAL TRUTH OF INVESTING: THERE ARE ONLY TWO THINGS YOU CAN DO WITH YOUR MONEY

If you peer up at the thousands of investments floating around the financial galaxy—from meteoric hot stocks to the ominous black holes of derivatives—it's easy to be completely overwhelmed. Can any one person ever comprehend them all, let alone find a rightful place among them? Of course not. So right off the bat, you can quit staring off into space and begin your search right where you'd like to end it— on solid ground. Because, in reality, your options are as simple as a fork in a country road.

There are only two things you can do with your money: loan or own.

That's all. You can either (a) loan someone money for a defined period of time and receive interest in return, or (b) buy something and hold it for an undetermined period of time with the expectation of an increase in value.

Every single investment falls into either the "loan" or the "own" category. Among the common forms of loans: certificates of deposit (CDs) and bonds of all varieties. Among the common forms of ownership: common stocks, real estate, precious metals, and all types of collectibles and tangible assets. (A mutual fund can be a vehicle for loaning, owning, or a combination of the two.)

The relative advantages of loaning and owning can be summarized with single words.

The chief advantage of loaning money is *predictability:* It's possible to have at least a pretty good—if not exact—picture of what the future holds. You can size up who you're loaning the money to—your bank, the government, a corporation—and judge their reliability. The terms of an individual loan can be spelled out in advance: how much you can expect to receive in interest and when and how you can get your principal back. Even if you choose to pool your money with other loaners in a mutual fund, the factors that will cause interest and/or principal to fluctuate are known.

The chief advantage of owning is *potential.* Owning is an open-ended proposition: There's not even the whiff of an agreement as to how long you're going to hold the investment or what you'll get back. In return for uncertainty, there is the potential for a significant (theoretically unlimited) increase in the value of your investment.

Speaking from a stress perspective, there are also respective risks to loaning and owning.

The chief risk of loaning money isn't what you might think, that is, getting stiffed. You can largely avoid that risk just by restricting your loans to the highest-quality borrowers. Rather, the chief risk of loaning money is that you will loan money for a period—either too short or too long—that doesn't match your needs, thereby canceling the advantage of predictability.

If your loans are shorter than need be, the invisible rat of inflation may eat all of your income and even some of your principal. If your loans are longer than need be and interest rates rise substantially in the interim, you'll find that the value of your principal has plunged. Either of these outcomes can be avoided by tailoring your loans to match your expectations of your needs.

The chief risk of owning is that you can be wrong. You can be wrong for a long time—the value of your investment goes down and stays down way past the time when you need the money. You can be wrong for good—you buy something that ends up being relatively, if not absolutely, worthless. And you can even be right and still end up being wrong. When the bottom drops out of a given market—whether it's junk bonds or diamonds—it doesn't matter much how choice your specific investment is; the only question to be answered is how much or how little you are going to lose.

Loaning and owning have distinct personalities as financial vehicles traveling into the future.

A loan sets out immediately on a visible—if not precise—course. It marches right down the middle of the road to the regimental beat of days and months, interest rates, and interest payments.

Ownership takes its merry time with unpredictable—but quite possibly greater—results. It wanders along this way and that way, often turning when least expected, sometimes getting completely lost, sometimes discovering fortune. It simply takes more time for ownership to take full effect.

As you'll see, these differences between loaning and owning will play a critical role in selecting the right investment for our needs. But beyond that, "loan or own" plays another important role in low-stress investing—and it's based on the words themselves.

COMMON SENSE: USE IT OR LOSE SLEEP

You make decisions about owning and loaning throughout your life—using common sense and good judgment.

If your brother-in-law asks to borrow a thousand bucks, you'll scrutinize his request. If he's shirking his way toward the deadbeat category, your common sense will give you all the answer you need.

When you're in the market for a new appliance, you'll weigh the pros and cons of the available models to arrive at a decision that feels sensible.

You have a lot of experience loaning and owning—and you'd probably admit to being good at each. Why, then, check these skills at the door when you enter the investment arena (even if you're sometimes asked to)? Be tough-minded, methodical, and inquisitive: Who are you loaning to? What are you really buying? Don't rush to judgment or allow yourself to be intimidated. Get comfortable. It's your money—you'll do the buying or loaning when you're good and ready.

Viewing the investment world through a "loan or own" lens not only will simplify matters from the outset, but will help keep the entire process connected to your common sense and good judgment. The stronger that tie, the lower your financial stress.

THE SECOND FUNDAMENTAL TRUTH OF INVESTING: IF YOU'RE DOING AVERAGE, YOU'RE DOING GREAT

Each year the market for each general type of investment—stocks, bonds, real estate, gold, you name it—puts so much money on the table for the taking. And some years it even reaches into your pocket and takes some back. It's called *average rate of return.*

But not many people consciously aspire to be average, especially when it comes to money. So they reach for more and—more often than not—end up with less.

In a world where the words of Vince Lombardi and Japanese warlords are used to goad you to be a gusto-grabbing victor, it's difficult to adjust gears and actually admit that you're not out to win, place, or even show. But it is one of the delicious ironies of the financial world that aim-to-be-average investments usually end up near the front of the pack without breaking a sweat.

If you approach investing *aiming to be average,* you'll end up with less stress and more money—and leave a lot of professionals who spend seventy or eighty hours a week on the subject in the dust.

Beginning with Burton G. Malkiel's landmark book *A Random Walk down Wall Street,* first published in 1973, the inability of the majority of professional money managers to match the performance of the broad stock market has been well documented. Although the percentage of underperformers varies from study to study depending on the specific time period under review and the benchmark used to measure performance, I don't believe that there is much doubt that over any period of at least ten years, somewhere between *two thirds* and *three quarters* of all professional money managers will *underperform* the stock market as a whole. And are the pros any better when it comes to loaning, that is, investing in the bond market? Nope. Once again, a similar percentage ends up below average, despite all those telephones and computer screens.

Folks, the general mediocrity of professional money managers is anything but a secret. But just as it is widely known, so is it widely ignored. Despite the overall lack of success in just getting to average, average is deemed unacceptable as an objective by the vast majority of "serious" investors. Why?

One reason why we're not content to aim for average is that so many other people seem to be doing far better than average, and without a whole lot of fuss and bother. These wizards have somehow ended up with keys that unlock the entire investment puzzle while the rest of us fumble around and empty our pockets. And they're everywhere we turn—smiling away in financial magazine profiles, opining with all seriousness and certitude on talk shows, and trumpeting their four-star, number-one-with-a-bullet track records. After all, have you ever seen a magazine cover blurb that promised "Five Mediocre Funds You Can Get Stuck in Right Now," or seen an investment ad that beckoned the investor who "seeks the ordinary"? Of course not. What you're surrounded with is a skewed and dissembled take on wishful reality.

The key to profitable investing isn't being able to pick the precise little spot to pile your money on—this fund or that fund, this bond or that CD. It is identifying the broad investment trend or phenomenon that you believe will be profitable, and then selecting an investment or investments quite content to mimic that trend or repeat that phenomenon. In fact, the vast majority of the profits that a given market puts on the table is available just for recognizing the big picture.

If you believe the stock market is going up and want to invest in it, that's the big—and by far, most critical—decision right there. In a long-term bull market, some 80 percent of all stocks will go up in value. Your objective should be to get in the flow and "let the force be with you."

As long as you invest in a way that captures the big trend—*aim to be average*—your savings dollars will likely go much further than if you tried to walk on water. And whatever the going interest rate on the highest-quality CD or bond that fits your needs, your objective should be to say "thank you" and take it. Reach for more and you risk losing both sleep and money.

You may not want to be average in any other part of your life. But with investing, a C not only keeps you in school, it keeps you from paying extra "tuition" out of your pocket to cover big losses. And, if you consciously seek to make average investments, you'll stand out in the crowd.

CUTTING YOUR INVESTMENT DECISIONS IN HALF: THE FIVE-YEAR RULE OF THUMB

Are you ready to make your first low-stress investment decision? Good—let's go back to the savings needs you identified and prioritized in the last chapter. If you are preserving money for a need that either is known and which you expect to fulfill within five years (the down payment on a home or starting a business, for example), or that is unknown, but which you would want to address immediately should it present itself (a family emergency or a loss of employment, for example), then you want to ensure that your money is going to be right within your grasp, principal intact.

You don't want to delay or face being unable to fulfill your need because you are losing money on your investments ("Our high-tech fund just nose-dived, dear, so we've got to rent for another year") or you can't sell them within any reasonable time frame ("I'll fix something to eat, kids, as soon as Dad can sell the vacation property").

Therefore, you can avoid financial stress by following the *Five-Year Rule of Thumb:*

If you'll need the money within five years, stick to loaning and avoid owning.

When you sit down to decide what to do with your savings dollars, if you're looking at need(s) within a time frame of five years or less, you will forgo potential financial stress if you forgo ownership. You will not have to fret over picking an investment that will rise in value in excess of the return generated by a loan, nor will you have to baby-sit the investment and then ponder when to sell (a decision you'll face whether you have a loss or a gain).

Now, immediately you may hear howls of disapproval from invest-ment professionals, many of whom have never experienced a year (or been alive) where ownership proved to be an extended heart-pounding, wallet-beating experience. So when you get bombarded with the 10 percent mantra (stocks have returned 10 percent a year since the be-ginning of time—which is now agreed to be 1926), remember two things: (1) 10 percent is an *average* that includes years when the return was nearly *minus* 50 percent, as well as the boom times, and (2) in the fifty-year prehistoric, pre–Great Bull Market period from 1926 to 1976, half of the time you bought stocks, you would have faced a loss within the first five years of ownership.

Does this mean that when little Zack turns thirteen, you should sell all the stocks in his college account? No. The rule applies to new, not existing, investments (more on when to sell later). But when you are investing fresh savings for a five-year period or less, stick to one of, or a combination of, the following types of loans.

THREE LOW-STRESS WAYS TO LOAN MONEY

Certificates of Deposit

A certificate of deposit, or CD, is a loan to a bank (which in turn will use your money to make loans to other customers).

Convenience and flexibility: Available at your local bank—a place you're in the habit of visiting—in a wide range of denominations (minimums from $500) and maturities (typically one month to seven years) to suit your needs.

Costs: No sales charges or annual expenses. If you cash in your CD before maturity, you'll get back your principal but pay a penalty in reduced interest. If you think that is a good possibility, you might consider sticking with a money market fund.

Safety: Deposits are federally insured up to $100,000 per institution.

Return: What you sign up for is what you get. No mystery.

Things to keep in mind: If you have a significant amount in CDs coming due, your bank may try to steer you toward investing in a mutual fund—a higher-profit transaction for them. This is confusing to some customers, who may not understand that they are jumping into an entirely different pond—with no guarantees—even though it's under the same roof.

Some banks offer free checking and other services if you have a specified amount in a CD. Add up your checking costs, and you may find that the savings will add three quarters of a percentage point to your return.

If you have a long-term CD and interest rates soar, you may find it profitable to cash out your current CD, take the penalty, and reinvest at the higher rates.

United States Treasury Bills and Notes

Treasury bills (up to one year in maturity) and notes (two to ten years in maturity) are loans to the United States government. They are generally considered to be the safest short-term investment in the world.

Convenience and flexibility: They can be purchased directly from the U.S. Treasury during its regularly scheduled auctions. Look in your phone book under "Federal Reserve Bank" and call for details. Treasury bills require a $10,000 minimum investment; Treasury notes require a $5,000 minimum between two and three years' maturity, and a $1,000 minimum for notes maturing in three years or beyond. All are available in $1,000 increments beyond the minimum.

Costs: Commission-free when purchased and held to maturity. If you need to sell before maturity, you'll have to sell through a bank or broker for a modest commission—around $50 or less.

Safety: Backed by the full faith and credit of the U.S. government, Treasuries are as safe an investment as you can expect in the real world (where, need you be reminded, nothing is ever certain).

Return: Varies according to maturity and interest rate on the date of purchase.

Tax advantage: Interest paid on Treasuries is exempt from state taxes.

Things to keep in mind: The value of the principal will fluctuate according to changes in interest rates and the remaining time until your loan matures. The longer the loan you make, the greater the potential fluctuation in the value of your principal.

Should you have to sell before maturity, there are no interest penalties and only a modest brokerage commission. However, the value of your principal will be determined by the current market. If interest rates have risen significantly in the interim, you'll likely get back less in principal. If they've fallen significantly, your principal will likely have increased in value.

A Money Market Fund That Invests
in U.S. Government–backed Obligations

A money market fund is a mutual fund that invests entirely in short-term loans to governments and corporations. Money market funds offer these features:

Convenience and flexibility: Selling in units of a dollar and crediting interest on a day-to-day basis (payable monthly), money market mutual funds are an investment tool that can play a valuable role in virtually every investor's portfolio. Minimum investment varies depending on the fund.

Costs: Money market funds have no commissions, redemption fees, or interest penalties, enhancing the flexibility of this investment.

Safety: Money market funds are not federally insured. What this means is that the dollar per unit value is not guaranteed. Although the actual occurrences of a money market fund "breaking the buck"—paying investors back less than the value of their invested principal—have been rare to date, the steady dollar-per-unit value should not be taken for granted.

The best way to preserve the value of your investment is to use only a money market fund that invests *strictly in Treasury bills and other short-term obligations backed by the full faith and credit of the U.S. government.*

Return: The interest rate fluctuates to reflect the makeup of the portfolio. As loans in the portfolio (often ninety days or less) come due, they are replaced at the current rate. Therefore, as short-term interest rates rise, so should the money market return. If interest rates fall, so should the return on a money market.

Tax advantage: If you invest in a money market fund that invests in U.S. Treasury bills, the income attributable to the Treasuries is exempt from state taxes.

Things to keep in mind: Use a money market fund as the core of your emergency fund in an amount equal to two months of your income. It will provide you with both the safety and the ready access that this need requires. Once you've saved two months of income, you can either continue adding to your money market fund or invest in CDs and Treasuries.

Unless you intend to do business with a stockbroker or financial planner, open your money market account with a no-load mutual fund manager such as The Vanguard Group. Brokerage firms view money market funds as underutilized sources of revenue and are constantly prodding their brokers to invest the money in something more profitable (certainly for the firm, but not necessarily for you). Only the most diligent reps are immune to these pressures.

Money market funds typically have a check-writing feature that allows you immediate access to your funds, sometimes with a $250 or $500 minimum withdrawal. When linked to a cash management account, you are also able to access your funds with a debit card. This can prove to be either an infrequently used convenience or a too-frequently-used drain on your savings. Be careful.

GETTING THE MOST WHEN YOU LOAN WITH THE LEAST AMOUNT OF STRESS

Once you've built up your short-term emergency fund, it's likely that you'll want to know how to increase the return from your loans without undue stress. Your challenge is to loan your money for a longer period of time—staying ahead of inflation—while not locking it up for what seems like forever or subjecting your principal to wild swings in value. Here are several concepts that can help you in that endeavor:

Stay Intermediate

A long time ago I read a profile of a bond portfolio manager whose path to investment success made a strong impression on me. The manager consistently performed ahead of her colleagues—and with much less risk.

Her strategy? Invest in intermediate-term bonds with an average maturity of five years—take the money on the table for the foreseeable future—and not subject the principal to swings in long-term interest rates.

This strategy was not just the right thing to do for a specific one- or two-year period of time. According to Ibbotson Associates, in the period 1926–1995, investors in intermediate-term government bonds actually outperformed investors in long-term government bonds by a shade. In other words, you don't have to be loaning your money for twenty or thirty years to get a good return.

The term "intermediate" means different things to different investors: two to eight years, five to ten years, around five years, around seven or eight years. Here then is what you should keep in mind: If you loan money for a period of time not much longer than the Carter administration—something that almost all of you lived through and, in retrospect, seems to have gone by in a flash—then you'll be getting a good return without undue risk.

Build a Ladder

An excellent way to increase your return as your savings increase is to build a "ladder": Spread your loans across a series of staggered maturities. For example: Using a money market fund as your foundation, you might then invest equal amounts in CDs or Treasuries in maturities of one, three, five, and even seven years. Or two, four, and six years. Or six months, one year, and two years. As maturities come due, reinvest in the furthest-out maturity.

Tailor the ladder to meet your needs—and don't build it past your comfort level. The benefit to this approach is that when rates are high, at least some of your savings will be locked in. And when rates are low, you'll avoid loaning all of your money for what proves to be an inferior rate.

Check the Curve

Whenever you're trying to decide for how long you should make a loan, check the "yield curve," a graph that displays how much interest you'll get for how long a loan. Here's an example:

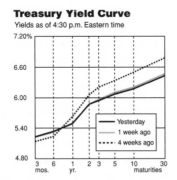

Source: Technical Data's Bond Data. From *The Wall Street Journal*, July 25, 1997. Reprinted by permission of *The Wall Street Journal*. Copyright © 1997 Dow Jones & Company, Inc. All Rights Reserved Worldwide, Inc.

What you'll find is that sometimes a difference in maturity of six months or a year can make a big difference in interest rate—and other times it makes little difference. In the graph above, the difference in interest between a one-year and two-year maturity is nearly one half of a percent. Yet going out another year to a three-year maturity barely increases your return. Looking at this example, if you were considering making a loan in the one- to three-year range, you might well choose a two-year maturity.

Bottom line: You'll often find that the ideal maturity for your investment in terms of getting the most for your money is *right at the top of the steepest part of the yield curve.* At the very least, it's a good spot to begin looking for the right maturity.

The yield curve for U.S. Treasuries is published in every issue of *The Wall Street Journal* alongside the "Credit Markets" column (usually in Section C). If you're investing in CDs, you'll have to plot the rates offered by your local bank.

OWNERSHIP: IT'S MINE, IT'S MINE!! WHAT IS IT??

Now let's turn to the rest of your savings dollars—those set aside for needs at least five years off into the future—and tackle the issue of ownership.

Why, given the relative certitude and safety of loaning, should you even consider owning as a means of investment? The answer is simple—but perhaps not what you think. The immediate response is usually "You can make more." Over time, owning may indeed be more profitable than loaning, but that's the end result.

The fundamental reason to consider ownership is that the investment table is tilted in favor of owning. There are inherent dynamics in the nature of ownership, our economy, and even human nature that favor ownership:

We like to own. Forget the wishes of Marx and Mao: Human beings like to own things. In fact, some things—gold, for example—we've liked to own for thousands of years.

More people with more money are looking to buy more things. As the world population and the economy grow, there is a growing demand for things deemed ownable—from housing to antique cookie jars. And when demand exceeds supply of a certain asset, up goes the value.

We are willing to borrow money to buy things. What do you think the price of real estate would be if people were willing only to pay 100 percent up front in cash?

Governments are willing to print money that is worth less than its purported value. The result? Inflation—and a rise in the nominal value of many existing things.

Some forms of ownership expand in size. A share of stock represents a percentage of ownership in a company. As the company grows, so does the size represented by each percentage of ownership: You can buy 1 percent of a $1 million company and end up with 1 percent of a $100 million company. On the other hand, a loan never becomes anything more than what it starts out as: A $10,000 loan stays a $10,000 loan.

People are sheep—with built-in panic chips. When an asset rises in value, people start buying it for no other reason than that it is going up. It doesn't much matter whether the asset in question is tulip bulbs or Internet stocks. And at some point, many people will panic, buying whatever they can with the belief that if they don't get in on the profits, other people will. This human foible can serve as your financial downfall or, for those well ahead of the herd and able to feed its desire, a once-in-a-lifetime gift.

All of the above factors work in favor of ownership. But the last factor raises a critical point.

When you buy something, you are not buying past and present performance, which is nothing more than a bunch of numbers. You are buying something of value—and, hopefully, good value. But all too often people lose sight of the underlying reality—what it is that makes something valuable in the first place—and don't even try to get a rational sense of the factors and dynamics that might influence future prices.

As of this writing, ownership has become synonymous with one thing—stocks—and the entire range of possible future performance has also been narrowed down to the single number of 10 percent. I don't pretend to know any more about the future than the next guy. But I do know that when future performance is taken for granted with little consideration of the underlying dynamics that are the source of value, I get the creeps.

The reason why the stock market has proven to be a good investment over time ultimately has little to do with what people think or wish. It has everything to do with the profitability of the companies that make up the market. And it is possible, just possible, that the market price of a given form of ownership can get way ahead of the real underlying value. In other words, you can end up owning something eminently valuable and end up losing money.

Indeed, immediately after the Dow Jones Industrial Average closed over 5,800 for the first time, columnist Floyd Norris pointed out in *The New York Times* on September 15, 1996: "For the Dow to show a 10 percent annual gain, excluding dividends, over the 20-year period ending Aug. 13, 2002, it would have to close then at 5,226.73, or

10.5 percent below its current level." However accurate it proves to be, this projection is useful in that it suggests that it might be prudent to take a fresh look at ownership possibilities.

I ask you to put aside all past prejudices and current positions for a few pages while we consider the possible vehicles for the road ahead:

1. Yourself
2. Something you can wrap your hands around
3. A piece of an expanding pie

THE BEST INVESTMENT IN THE WORLD: YOURSELF

Two of the meanings of "own" are "to have control over" and "to possess."

Without treading into metaphysical territory, you most certainly already have ownership and control of a powerful economic engine: *yourself*. One of the best ways to preserve value in your life is to continually maintain and upgrade your means of production. That can mean a financial investment in yourself that provides a "return" of both action and results.

If you walk into a bank or brokerage firm with $1,000 to invest, the last thing any banker or broker will tell you to do is invest in the wellspring of True Wealth—your own value-generating capabilities. That's a decision you have to make by yourself and beforehand—and that's why it's been placed here, ahead of all other forms of ownership.

The next time you get ready to invest some of your savings, it would not be unreasonable to first think, *"Is there anything I can or should be doing right now to maintain or increase my economic viability?"*

Once again, I hear the chorus of "Hey, I thought more wasn't the answer." To which the response is: If you aren't moving ahead, you risk getting left behind in Stressville. And let's say that your $1,000 investment in yourself gives you the tools to increase your income by just $3,000 a year. Over the next decade, you'll be getting a 30:1 return on investment. How many of your other investments have done that well?

There is one big problem with investing in yourself, however: accountability. No one is leaning on you to follow through—to make sure, for example, that you find some ways to put new knowledge into practice, rather than leave it in the "nice to know" category. Taking a cue from the vernacular of politicians, "investing" has come to mean pouring money down a hole and hoping something grows out of it. And everyone has chud lying around his house whose purchase was justified as being an "investment."

Here's an alternative to spending money and hoping for some good results: *Structure an investment in yourself as if it were an investment in a business.* Get a little notebook to use as a ledger and write "Investments in [your name]" on the cover. You can also create a section in your day planner for this purpose. Use one page per investment.

While tracking a specific economic return is close to impossible, you can structure any investment in yourself so that you have a stated return in the form of defined action that is likely to generate value within the economic arena.

Here are some examples of simple investments and stated returns:

INVESTMENT	RETURN
Table saw	500 wooden craft items manufactured and sold
Three-day sales seminar	Five extra calls per day to potential A-level clients for two months
Nordic Track	Exercise four times per week for twenty-five weeks

When you make an investment in yourself, write down the investment vehicle, date, amount, and the specific action that you will generate in return—what, how often, by when.

Then let your alter ego—or, if need be, a family member or friend—play the role of Scrooge Meets Repo Man. Demand without wavering that you live up to your agreement. Don't let the first setback or a minor shift in circumstance call the deal off. Mark down in your ledger each time you generate a portion of your stated return. Let it become a testament to your ability to generate value, not an embarrassment of broken promises.

The best way to invest over time is to expand and put into action your ability to generate value. In tandem with a solid savings rate, it can make all other forms of ownership virtually irrelevant.

A PIECE OF SOMETHING YOU CAN PUT YOUR HANDS ON

A tangible asset is one you can put your hands on. You can see it and touch it.

Ownership of a tangible asset is easy to understand: Here it is, it's mine. That goes a long way toward explaining its basic appeal through the millennia.

A tangible asset can serve a functional purpose: Try living in a hut made out of stock certificates or growing corn in your brokerage account. And some tangible assets serve an aesthetic purpose, adding a bonus return in horizon value: Art and antiques belong in this category. A painting might appreciate in value over the years, and, unlike a growth-fund prospectus, you are able to hang it on your wall and get a little extra return every time you pause to look at it.

One compelling rationale for investing in tangible assets is that their intrinsic value exists independent of the means of exchange used to put a price tag on them. Our fascination with the *Mona Lisa*'s smile has nothing to do with money. By way of contrast, our fascination with Berkshire Hathaway has everything to do with money. The dollar can have less purchasing power than it did yesterday—but an acre of land never shrinks in size.

There are also some significant barriers to investing in tangible assets: They can be unwieldy (you can't keep 1,000 barrels of oil in your safe-deposit box), highly subjective in value, and usually provide no financial return on investment until they're sold. That vintage '55 Chevy might give you plenty of psychic income, but you're going to have to sell it to see any bucks.

That being said, I believe that tangible assets should not be overlooked for two reasons. First, governments have the power of the press and can resort to printing worthless money in an attempt to inflate their way out of a fiscal crisis. Second, our world's financial affairs do not rule out a fiscal crisis. So whatever your current outlook, a piece of something tangible can help bring peace of mind. Here are the three possibilities:

1. *Real estate.* If you own your residence, you've probably got enough money invested in real estate. Unless you have a driving interest in real estate and have developed a feel for it (see #2 below), one property is enough. But if you don't own any real estate, here's something to be aware of: You might have little else in the way of tangible assets. Therefore, careful consideration of the next two options may be warranted.

2. *Something you have a feel for.* Tangibles don't pay interest per se, but they do pay what I call *"interest on interest."* When you have a strong interest in an area—through the generation of horizon value— over time you will develop a "sixth sense" for the economics of that field. This interest makes it possible to uncover and accumulate values while a market is quiet and virtually ignored.

Collectibles of any sort go through extended periods when people with a true passion have the field to themselves. Suddenly, there's an increasing buzz of interest. New collectors enter the market, forcing up prices. During this period, even Bozo the Chimp can buy something and turn around and sell it for a profit. Old-time collectors scratch their heads, say, "Well, if you really want to pay me that much, I reckon I'll just have to let you," and cash in on the interest in their interest. Inevitably the market dries up, and those with a true passion are left alone. A perfect example of the cycle would be the baseball card mania of the past decade.

If you do have an *active* interest in something for its own sake and pursue it over time, it can prove to be a good investment. I know a couple with a substantial nationally recognized art collection who pursued their passion on a shoestring budget and were eventually able to buy a farm by selling a few select pieces. Another acquaintance turned his passion for vinyl recordings into a thriving international mail-order business after accepting an unexpected early-retirement offer.

The key, of course, is not to try to compete against the experts, but rather to be an expert yourself. And that can happen only over time, through experience—the word from which "expert" is derived.

If you really do have an interest in a tangible item that's based strictly on appreciation for the item itself—not on its prospects of appreciation—and pursue your interest on a budget without getting carried away, and take profits when there's a surrounding frenzy, then something you have a feel for can be a good investment. Otherwise, your investment can, figuratively speaking, turn from vintage wine to vinegar.

3. *Gold.* Ahh, gold! A resource of unparalleled beauty to many, a barbaric relic to some. Loved by millions around the globe for thousands of years and hated by central bankers everywhere. Do you comply with the will of a handful of bureaucrats, or bow to the majesty of the metal with the power to silently move mountains? I'll side with the gold, thank you. Three thousand years is a fairly long track record.

I believe that everyone should own a little gold—at least 5 percent but no more than 10 percent of your long-term assets—for the following reasons:

a. If you own at least a little gold, you've partially inoculated yourself against doing something really crazy the next time the price of the metal soars in value. If you're already in the game, you tend to approach unexpected events with more balance and less emotion than if you watch from the sidelines and then rush in and start running around frantically. This is how people ended up owning gold at $700 or $800 an ounce in 1980.

b. There has never been a currency in the history of the world that didn't lose value and ultimately become worthless. Consider gold as an insurance policy.

How would I approach gold? Every now and then when you have an excess balance in your checking account or you get a bonus check, buy a gold coin and put it in your safe-deposit box. You can buy a Canadian Maple Leaf or an American Eagle at a reputable coin dealer for a small premium over the price for an ounce of gold. The coin prices are quoted daily in the *Wall Street Journal*. A little gold goes a long way, but the risk of not having any is as great as the risk of having a lot.

A PIECE OF AN EXPANDING PIE

Our economy can be characterized as a gradually expanding pie of revenue and profits. Through the ownership of common stock, we are able to buy a fixed share of a company or group of companies, and then participate in whatever future growth might occur.

Common stock as a form of ownership combines the ingenuity and energy of people with the possibilities of their available resources and—through free-market economic activity—produces something greater than the sum of the parts. Think of your car, home, or computer—all the miraculous results of man and materials combined to create greater value than the hours of labor or the cost of the materials. The relationship could appropriately be described as "synergistic"—if I weren't trying to write an entire book without using the "s" word.

The economic power of capitalism derives from the fact that *one plus one can equal three.* That's the advantage that stocks have over other forms of ownership—they can grow in size. An ounce of gold remains an ounce of gold, but a share of Small-Co can become a share of Big-Co.

The upside potential of stock ownership might serve as a bright beacon of financial hope to millions, but the downside risks should never be ignored—in fact, they should be fully embraced—if you want to make low-stress investments.

You should not invest in the stock market unless you are prepared—emotionally and financially—to watch the value of your investment drop by at least 33 percent. If the prospect of being "way down"—for a year or even longer—gives you the shivers, then stay out of the water. The stock market isn't for you, no matter how much you're told otherwise.

Patience is a virtue, although one not required in recent times, when investing in stocks as a means of ownership. But if you have the temperament, then owning a piece of an expanding pie can be an outstanding means of preserving value—indeed, all it's cracked up to be. Let's look at three viable means of owning a piece of the pie, working our way from the largest to the smallest slice.

Owning the Big Picture: The U.S. Economy

Your first form of stock ownership should also be the broadest in scope: the U.S. economy. Although its days of uncontested world supremacy are in the past, our economy remains the overall world leader in innovation, the lifeblood of economic growth.

True, we have problems, but so does everyone else. At least we can read about ours and have a chance of understanding them. We're still a long way from sorting out how the economies and markets work in China or Eastern Europe because the participants themselves haven't even come close to figuring it out. So start with what you know.

The best way to invest in the U.S. economy as a whole is with an *index fund.* An index fund is a mutual fund that seeks to match the performance of a specific benchmark group of securities—an index—by owning a representative proportion of each security in the index. It is a "passive" investment—there is no active buying and selling of securities in the portfolio. It buys and holds everything (or almost everything, in some cases) in the index without any fuss, muss, or mystery, and then sits back for the ride—wherever the index might go.

Indexing has staunch proponents and fierce detractors. Detractors argue that without active professional management, a fund cannot sell stocks before a market fall, thereby leaving investors fully exposed on the downside. However, these are often the same experts who advise buying and holding stocks through up and down markets, thereby contradicting their own argument.

Detractors argue that when you buy every stock in sight, you end up owning all of the turkeys. True, but you also own all of the highfliers.

Proponents argue that index funds are a low-cost and efficient way to participate in the performance of the stock market as a whole—or a specific segment. They're right. And there's another noteworthy advantage.

By now you've heard many variations on this theme: "If you'd bought stocks then, and held them until now, your return would be this." This is like saying if you'd bought your first car in the 1930s, and owned a car ever since, your car today would be worth many times over the initial purchase price. What's being left out is that you had to have bought and held on to the *same* car, not just owned any car, trading models throughout the years. My dad may have owned a boss Mercury roadster as a teen, but that doesn't make his Crown Victoria wagon worth one additional cent today.

The rarely heard qualifier is that it's not just the mere act of continually owning stocks that does the trick: You have to buy and hold the *same* stocks. Ironically, the odds of the stockbroker *parroting* the past performance of a buy-and-hold strategy actually *executing* a true buy-and-hold strategy are close to nil. Commissions are in buying and selling—thus the omission of what buy and hold really means.

An index fund best executes the buy-and-hold strategy. Index funds were pioneered by The Vanguard Group (800-662-7447), and they're still the leader in the field.

For many years I've recommended The Vanguard Index Trust 500 Portfolio, which invests in all 500 stocks in the Standard & Poor's 500 Composite Stock Price Index. These are the large, blue-chip companies that represent roughly 65 to 70 percent of the total value of the U.S. stock market.

For years this index quietly lumbered along—cranking out above-average returns without getting much attention, let alone respect. Then, in early 1997, the S&P 500 index became *the* hot investment—with even previous naysayers such as Fidelity Investments rushing to market with products designed to corral some of the billions of dollars investors were pouring into S&P 500 index funds ("You'll buy it, we'll sell it"—the eternal Wall Street motto). This phenomenon, like any other mania, gives one due cause for concern and restraint.

Until the full ramifications of the S&P 500 stampede are known—who's going to get trampled and how badly—I would advise looking at alternatives for participating in the broad market.

For the core of a stock portfolio, I'd recommend The Vanguard Index Trust Total Stock Market Portfolio. It seeks to replicate the performance of the Wilshire 5000 Index, which includes virtually all U.S. stocks traded on a regular basis. In other words, it's the whole shebang. Given that there are times when small stocks do better than blue chips and vice versa, this is a logical way to make a core investment in stocks: Buy 'em all.

Look at it this way: If you aren't psychologically prepared to own the average performance of the entire stock market—where the bulk of the return is on the table for the taking—you probably shouldn't be in the stock market in the first place.

Convenience and flexibility: The minimum investment is $3,000. All transactions can be handled over the phone and through the mail.

Costs: Vanguard index funds are no-load and have extremely low annual expenses. They are the cheapest way to own a large stock portfolio.

Safety and return: The value of your investment will fluctuate right along with the overall market—there are no guarantees.

Tax advantages: Because index funds do not actively sell stocks to take capital gains, annual distributions to investors tend to be minimal and most tax obligations are deferred until sale.

Ownership with Intent: A Mutual Fund That Serves a Useful Purpose

Once you own the U.S. economy as a whole, then you may want to consider owning a mutual fund that serves a useful purpose. And when it's not possible to own a broad-based index fund—it may not be available in your 401(k)—this is where you'll begin investing in stocks.

A mutual fund serves a useful purpose when it adds a clearly defined and desired dimension to your portfolio. In other words, you didn't just buy the darn thing because you thought it was going to go up. A mutual fund can serve one or more of the following useful purposes:

1. *Provide active and superior management.* Although most funds perform no better than average in the long run, there are a small number of fund managers who have established a superior track record, that is, better than average over a meaningful period of time (at least ten years).

These managers are worth considering—if their overall focus coincides with yours. Have a clearly defined objective first, then go looking for superior management. If you wanted, for example, to increase your investment in large-capitalization blue-chip stocks, you'd have reason to consider a fund that focuses on this area, such as the Dodge and Cox Stock Fund. But if your objective were to increase your holdings in small companies, you'd have to rule out Dodge and Cox, despite its track record, and consider a fund such as the Acorn Fund.

2. *Broaden or adjust the exposure of your portfolio.* Once you own a slice of the U.S. economy, you might wish to own a slice of foreign economies in the form of the T. Rowe Price International Stock Fund or one of the several Vanguard international index funds. Or you might decide to add or emphasize a specific area of the U.S. market—value, growth, small cap—by adding a representative fund.

I recommend using the *Forbes* magazine Annual Mutual Fund Survey (published in late August—try your local library if you don't subscribe) as your starting point for choosing a low-cost, solid-performance mutual fund that meets your needs.

Ownership in a Company You Know Inside and Out

Owning stock in an individual company can be a double-edged sword. If the company grows over a long period of time, your small investment can grow into a small fortune. If the company stops growing and atrophies, your investment will wither.

Both scenarios can happen with the same company. The financial pages repeatedly report stories of employees who purchased stock in their companies and at one point were worth a theoretical bundle, only to have their nest egg turn to dust. The day-to-day stress of the stockholders in such a situation packs a particularly nasty punch.

That's why the phrase "inside and out" must serve as a qualifier to any individual stock investment.

Things might look all sunny from the inside at TechnoChud Computer, what with the pep talks, press releases, and coffee mugs with the corporate logo for all. But the world might be rapidly changing around you, with dark clouds looming right beyond the serene landscaping at headquarters.

From the outside, you might see that all the kids at the mall are wearing Sneegee Sneakers, and so you buy stock in the company that makes Sneegees. But the Sneegee management could be making crucially wrong decisions as you place your buy order, which will eventually turn your investment into something to sneeze at.

No one is in a better position to understand the growth potential of the company you work for than you are. That makes it potentially a great investment if you keep your eyes and ears open and are able to draw the distinction between your loyalty to your company and your loyalty to preserving your financial value. They are both admirable qualities that should not be intertwined. Not putting all of your money in your company stock—or selling some of the stock you already own—is not an act of corporate disloyalty. It is your personal business.

If you have enough confidence in your company's future prospects to make a major financial investment, do it outside of your retirement account. You don't want to put yourself in the position of predicating your retirement on the performance of the single company that you're already relying on for income and benefits. That's a huge bet on a single horse.

And as for buying stocks in companies you don't work for? In all but a raging bull market, you have to work to find the winners. So if you don't want to make stock-picking an arena for generating horizon value, accept who you are and ignore the stress-creating pressure to prove otherwise.

THE RIGHT ANSWER IS THAT THERE'S NO RIGHT ANSWER

Here you stand in the kitchen—ready to measure out your financial preserves. Spread out on the counter are your needs, your savings, and a variety of investments. So what is the perfect blend of ingredients? Sorry to say, only time will tell, and right now its lips are zipped.

The right blend of investments for you will be one that matches your needs, puts money in your pocket, and lets you sleep at night. Notice that there's no "the" before the word "one"—it's "one" as in "one of many." There's no game or competition, no one right way, and no specific overall rate of return you must achieve.

You begin by investing in yourself. You build up a portfolio of short- to immediate-term loans to meet your needs of five years or less. You buy a place to live and maybe add to your tangible assets here and there. You continue to save, and soon you're facing the question of what to do with your long-term savings.

Or to phrase the real underlying question: How much should you put in stocks?

Here's where I have to reveal some of my personal financial "what." I've felt uneasy about the stock market for quite some time. It began when an old musician friend, Rock Band Sid, called out of the blue. Sid had scraped together enough money to get into the highest-flying mutual fund on the planet and wanted to tell me that this was the move to make—"Rock 'n' roll will never die" had been replaced by "Stocks forever."

My uncertainty was certain around the time the supremacy of the market became more widely known among Americans than the name of the vice president of the United States. And when politicians floated the idea of investing Social Security dollars in the stock market, my mental marquee read, "From the folks who encouraged savings and loans to invest in real estate . . ."

The truth is that I've been out of the market for some time—and haven't missed a wink of sleep or had a speck of regret for doing so. My focus has been squarely on generating value across the spectrum of possibilities, and as I've done so, the Dow Jones Industrial Average has moved from being a preoccupation of mine to an afterthought.

At some point I'll begin to buy stocks again. Some of the green lights that will turn me on to the idea will be . . .

... when Rock Band Sid sells his mutual fund and buys a new amplifier.

... when a national magazine runs a "Where Are They Now?" cover story on the stars of the Late Great Bull Market.

... when a former bull market cheerleader-in-suspenders asks, "Smoking or nonsmoking?"

... when I wake up one morning and feel comfortable without hesitation with the prospects of stock ownership.

And when I do start investing in the stock market again, it will be with the following concepts fully in mind:

TWO LOW-STRESS WAYS TO INVEST IN STOCKS

1. *Let your loans feed your owns.* For peace of mind consider this: As long as you buy stocks with interest income only, you can never lose money. Even if the entire stock market goes to zero, you still have your original principal in loans and intact.

If you're unsure as to how much to invest in stocks or when to invest, try this strategy: Let your loans feed your owns. In other words, use the interest income from your loans to buy stocks. You'll build up your stock ownership over time, and through dollar-cost averaging— investing a fixed amount on a regular basis—you'll buy more when prices are low.

2. *Make the future a 50/50 proposition.* How much of your long-term investments should be in stocks? The common wisdom is that you can't have enough—if you don't have at least 80 or 90 percent in stocks, you're a gutless slug. But consider this: According to a study by Neuberger & Berman of stocks and bonds over the thirty-five years ended in 1995, a balanced portfolio of 50 percent stocks (S&P 500 index) and 50 percent five-year Treasury notes would have given you 86 percent of the return of a 100 percent stock portfolio with only 59 percent of the volatility. You could have grabbed most of the money the market put on the table without all of the wild fluctuations that might have kept you up nights and even caused you to sell at an inopportune time.

If you make your long-term investments a 50/50 proposition—half stocks, half bonds—you'll have less financial stress than the asset allocators/alchemizers searching for the perfect blend do. And studies have shown that over time you'll do just as well as the average Grand Investment Strategist Pooh-bah at a major brokerage firm.

FIVE WAYS YOU CAN INCREASE YOUR OVERALL RETURN WITHOUT INCREASING YOUR STRESS

People often make the leap from an investment they are completely comfortable with to an investment they have no understanding of, all for an extra percentage point or two in return. If the investment doesn't deliver—or breaks down along the way—they end up kicking themselves right where their wallet used to be. This doesn't have to be. You can increase your return without increasing your stress by remembering these five guidelines:

1. *Save an extra 1 percent of your income.* Whenever you're tempted to reach for just a little more, remember this: It is almost always easier, less stressful, more within your control, and certain of outcome to save an extra 1 or 2 percent than to reach for a higher or above-average return from a riskier investment.

2. *Avoid sales charges.* There may be no such thing as a free lunch, but there is such a thing as a cover charge. The same holds true with investments. Nothing is ever free, but some investments insist on an entry fee—sales charge—in addition to any ongoing fees. And although those that demand a sales charge insist that the tariff makes no difference once you've paid up and are seated at a table inside, common sense would tell you that the money you leave behind at the door isn't working for you.

A sales charge goes to the salesperson—not toward any increased quality of the investment. If you do invest in an investment with a sales charge, make sure it has a long-term top-notch track record. Otherwise, keep walking until you find an investment that allows you to put all of your savings to work.

3. *Keep annual expenses to a minimum.* Investors often get so focused on sales charges that they overlook something that can cost them far more money over the life of an investment than even the highest sales charge: annual expenses. These expenses can include everything from management and advisory fees to marketing expenses.

If you're paying an unnecessary 1.5 percent in annual expenses for a long-term investment, over several decades you will be giving away an amount equal to your initial investment—and for no real promised, let alone guaranteed, benefit.

The average expense ratio for all mutual funds is around 1.25 percent. There's no need to pay more. *Forbes* magazine periodically lists a number of "best buys"—included in its annual mutual fund survey—with considerably lower expenses.

Must avoid: funds that charge their investors 12b-1 fees—the marketing costs of attracting new investors.

4. *Avoid exit fees*. Some investments have a large sign posted out front that flashes "FREE ADMISSION." What you might not see on your way in is the little sign over the exit that tells you how much it's going to cost you to get out.

A modest redemption fee shouldn't discourage you from making an otherwise low-cost investment. It can even be to your benefit if the fee prevents you from hopping from investment to investment. But beware of investments with hefty back-end loads or surrender charges. Should you want to leave earlier than planned, you'll end up leaving a fair chunk of your profit, if not a slice of your principal, behind.

5. *Avoid big losses*. In our race to find the big winners, a vital key to long-term preservation of savings is overlooked: Avoid big losses. This is in fact how turtles who stick to making loans can end up ahead of the hares—they are less likely to make a costly slip. And one slip can be costly.

Here's a simple example. Doreen has her savings—$100,000—invested entirely in mutual funds and individual stocks. She likes the market and keeps track of her portfolio on a daily basis. Most of her moves are smart and informed, and at the end of the year, 90 percent of her investments have appreciated by the now-mandatory 10 percent: $90,000 grew to $99,000.

But Doreen had a spell of hi-tech fever in the spring and invested the remaining $10,000 in Convoy Communications, a company that was developing the technology to access the Internet with a CB radio. Unfortunately, the "big 10-4" turned into an "over and out," and she lost $5,000—half of her investment.

Doreen shrugs off the loss, telling herself, "Oh well, the rest of my investments did great." But overall, for all of her effort and for being 90 percent right on the money, her $100,000 has grown to only $104,000—a 4 percent return. Doreen would have been better off in a CD, although she probably would argue otherwise.

Investors are prone to consider their losses as aberrations without calculating their net effect on their return on investment. A single significant loss can drag the return on your savings below the "Mendoza line"—the passbook savings rate—for the year. And one big loss can put a damper on your return for a decade or more. Ask one of the thousands of investors who had 25 percent of their savings in limited partnerships.

The bottom line: *If you avoid big losses, you can preserve your savings dollars just fine without big gains.*

TEN TIPS FOR AVOIDING STRESSFUL INVESTMENTS

1. *Don't let it out of your sight.* The easier it is to watch an investment, the less the room for stressful surprises. You don't have to keep a round-the-clock vigil, but when you want to check on it, it should be easy to do so.

Ideal situation: You can find the current value in your local paper or the *Wall Street Journal.*

Must avoid: Steer clear of investments for which the only source of price information is the person who sold it to you.

2. *Never buy a new investment.* We live in a world where "new" is almost synonymous with "better." But while there is nothing at risk if you are lured into trying that new kind of potato chip (even if it tastes like cardboard, your life remains intact), forking over your savings for a new investment is fraught with potential financial stress. No matter how good a deal looks on paper, reality has a nasty habit of finding hidden faults and then tossing that "good" deal into the scrap bin of lousy investments.

Always remember, investments are not created for your benefit. They are created because someone thinks you (or your neighbor) can be induced to buy them.

From your position, there is no compelling rational reason to buy a brand-new investment. If an investment turns out to be a good one, you'll have plenty of opportunity to take advantage of it after you've had a chance to watch it tested in the real world. Even if you have to pay a little more for it as a result of waiting (as might be the case with a company offering stock for the first time), you'll preserve far more savings in the long run than if you gambled that each new investment was perhaps "the one."

The one big exception when your new investment merits serious consideration: when the company you work for is going public and you can buy stock below the offering price.

3. *Stay near the phone.* Stick to investments that you can get out of immediately with a single phone call or branch office visit.

Sometimes your needs change—either over time, as your life unfolds, or suddenly, in response to an unexpected event or opportunity—and your investment requirements shift. And other times, you realize that you've got a turkey on your hands and you just want to get rid of the darn thing.

In any case, once you've decided to make a change, you want to be able to move swiftly and not have to wait days or weeks while you search for a buyer. The longer you have to wait between the decision to sell and the actual sale, the more stress you'll have.

Note: Real estate and other tangible assets take time to sell. So even though they may prove to be an excellent investment over time, you want to be sure you have some money you can get your hands on quickly.

4. *Don't invest just to save on taxes.* Sure, you don't like to pay taxes. Nobody does. But that doesn't mean you have to throw caution, let alone any semblance of rational thought, out the window when you see phrases like "tax-free" or "tax-advantaged."

At worst, you might not only be throwing your money away, but also sending out an invitation to the IRS to make you even more miserable. Although Congress has moved in recent years to tighten loopholes and close tax shelters, there are still connivers who believe they can find the invisible holes in the tax code. Avoid these operators and their schemes at any cost—unless you want financial stress of the highest order.

On the other hand, there are quite legitimate investments whose primary appeal is saving taxes—municipal bonds and annuities among the most popular. So even with chicanery out of the question, ask yourself, "If it weren't for the prospect of saving taxes, would I be comfortable making this investment, let alone even consider it?" For many first-time investors, the answer to this question is "no," but it never gets asked.

In answer to any howling, here are some of my reasons for not wholeheartedly recommending municipal bonds: increased financial pressures on states and municipalities, fallibility of bond ratings (could your county be the next Orange County?), lack of information on and understanding of specific issues (most brokers sell based solely on rating), potential for brokers to charge hefty hidden fees when buying and selling in the form of spreads, the low interest on short-term bonds negating almost all tax advantages, and the high fees and expenses of many municipal bond funds.

A wish for the future: that all of the time, effort, and resources that are applied to avoiding taxes be directed instead toward simplifying our tax code.

5. *Never make an investment based on hope.* An investment based on hope is an investment with high financial stress potential. The word "hope" should have no place in your investment lexicon, as in:

I hope this investment keeps going up.
I hope that story I heard is true.
I hope I get my money back.

You should never invest based on hope, always on reasonable expectation. That requires concrete knowledge rather than a leap of faith:

Based on what I know, I expect my bank to pay me back.
Based on what I know, I expect the Big Stack Corporation's earnings to continue to grow for the foreseeable future.
Based on what I know, I expect that property values in my area will rise over the next decade.

If, when you say, "Based on what I know," you hear the voice of Sgt. Schultz in *Hogan's Heroes* saying, "I know nut-tink!," then you are making an investment based on hope—and the return may well be financial stress.

6. *If you can't explain it, don't buy it.* Before you make an investment, always complete the following exercise. Sit down with your spouse (or a teenager) and cogently explain to him or her how the investment under consideration actually works. In other words, what is going to happen to your money after you turn it over and what has to take place for you to get back more than you handed over?

The explanation might be straightforward and simple, as with a Treasury bill. But when you start trying to explain an investment whose description includes a word like put, call, derivatives, collateralized, short, convertible, futures, short sales, mortgage-backed, leverage, currency, or hedge, then you might not be able to make it through the first sentence without coming to a screeching halt amid a flurry of "What??s" and "Huh??s"

Here's the real question: How come you'd invest your money in something when you don't even know what it really is? Stick to plain-vanilla investments whose purpose and structure can be really understood.

7. *Don't get suckered by titles.* Titles are to the financial world what packaging is to frozen dinners: No matter what's inside, the box always looks boffo. Sales reps are "financial consultants" or "portfolio

managers." Everyone is a vice president of some sort (the most exclusive title on Wall Street being N.A.V.P.—Not a Vice President).

Even the sleaziest of gutbucket operations have names that imply an upper-crust pedigree that can be traced back to contemporaries of J. P. Morgan. And mutual funds seem as if they are named by a computer that randomly assembles words like value, growth, appreciation, special, preservation, diversified, and capital into names that act as a cover for "whatever the heck we feel like doing."

As a rule of thumb, you should ignore the title of any financial entity—person, firm, or investment—put on your X-ray specs, and determine what's inside the packaging before you invest a dime.

8. *Never allow yourself to be sold an investment over the phone.* Never, ever, ever. You hear me? Never. Repeat after me. Never. Promise me. Never.

If you can follow this one piece of advice for the rest of your life, you'll avoid more financial stress than you'd ever want to know.

9. *If you don't want to own it forever, don't buy it in the first place.* Whether it's Elvis memorabilia, '50s lunch boxes, or graffiti art, there's always a collectible that appears to be an express ticket to Fort Knox. The truth is that the vast majority of the returns belong to people who developed a pure interest and quietly collected the item when few others cared. So unless you dearly love that rare *Scary Swamp Thang* comic book and wouldn't mind owning it your entire life, don't buy it.

10. *Walk away while you still can.* If you are ever the slightest bit unsure or uncomfortable with a prospective investment, you do have another option, and one that millions of investors wish they had grabbed for themselves: *You can walk away with all of your savings intact.* And even if it turns out that you did pass up a profitable investment, remember that there are still thousands of opportunities to make a profit. But there is no one who is willing to make up for your loss.

WORKSHEET: LOW-STRESS INVESTMENT

SAVINGS OBJECTIVE:

When do I anticipate exchanging my savings dollars for this objective?

Should I loan or own (Five-Year Rule of Thumb)?

What type of investment seems most appropriate for this objective from my perspective?

Can I set up a pipeline from my paycheck to this investment?

In everyday language, how does this investment work?

How can this investment make money?

How can this investment lose money?

How much can I lose (worst-case scenario)?

Can I live with that possibility?

Will my savings be readily available when/if I need them?

10

. . . And About Those Stress Symptoms

Now let's revisit the nine common symptoms of financial stress and look at some additional practical tips for addressing your particular symptoms:

FINANCIAL STRESS SYMPTOM #1: **You need a new job . . . yesterday.**

Set your mind back. Usually the "yesterday" in question wasn't, in fact, yesterday—it was months or even years ago. Yet with no big solution hopping into your lap, the days dribble by, and your sense of panic or futility mounts.

Relax for a moment, set your mind back six months, and then write down everything you could have started doing then that would have created a less stressful situation today. Use that list as a resource and mind-set for a series of methodical and purposeful decisions that will counteract your prevailing stress.

In retrospect, the past six months went by quickly, didn't they? Believe, then, that the time it will take to turn your situation around will seem just as short.

Start a new job tomorrow. Remember your first day at your current job? Probably it all seemed just right: the people, the place, your prospects. That was before the jerks identified themselves loudly and clearly, Ms. Chaos and Mr. Incompetency came back from vacation to resume management, and workers installed a metal ceiling right above your desk. As the bloom came off the rose, you muttered to yourself that your next job will be different. Or will it?

Your current job might seem truly odious, but it might have more to do with *you* than *them*. And it might be more of an opportunity than you give it credit for.

Approach going to work tomorrow with all of the energy and optimism that you had on the very first day. Leave all of your impressions and negative opinions at home. Separate the personality parade from the mission at hand. Concentrate on the essence of your craft. Only after you get out of your rut can you see the road ahead.

Don't get hung up on "what you're worth." Obsessing over perceived income inequalities is a futile, stress-creating waste of your life. Almost all of us can rattle off our personal litany of all the people who—in our own irrefutable estimation—make way too much money. Our lists range from the high-profile targets—"He's making two million bucks to sit on the bench all season"—to our neighbors and coworkers.

Why do some people get paid more than others? Much of the answer can be found in previously generated value. Maybe someone makes more because, once you consider how they've applied their energy and resources over time, *they deserve to make more*. What a concept! A brain surgeon might be paid $2,000 an hour for an operation. But what you're really paying for is what it took to gain the expertise that would make the surgeon's popping your top and rummaging around inside your skull an acceptable proposition.

This is not to deny that you can be paid far less than the value you generate and that your displeasure may be justified. But here's the key question: *Do you feel that you're underpaid as a member of a group or underpaid as an individual?*

If you look around you and see other people doing the same job with the same experience making approximately the same amount of money, it doesn't matter how unfair you think it is. You're going to be better off generating enough value to create opportunities elsewhere or increasing your satisfaction with where you are than waiting for your income to catch up with your perceived value.

One thing is certain: When you begin comparing your income to everyone else's, you're going to get stressed out. Try not to start.

Don't get jealous over hot air. There's no more annoying way to come down with Stress Symptom #1 than to get together with friends or family and then listen to some nimrod ramble on about how great his job is and how well he's doing at it, larded with not-too-subtle hints about his soaring remuneration. It gets to you: This guy is such a jerk, and yet here he is doing way better than you are. Or is he? El Jerko might be one step away from getting fired or declaring bankruptcy.

Ask yourself: How often have you ever heard the people whom you respect for their professional capabilities and good financial judgment run off at the mouth in blatant self-promotion? Probably never.

Start looking for a new job . . . today. The obvious—and most often ignored—solution.

FINANCIAL STRESS SYMPTOM #2: **You don't have enough money to pay your bills.**

Don't juggle—grab a chain saw. At the first signs of continuing shortfall, don't just juggle your bills to get through the month. Try to identify a major area of spending (an expensive habit, hobby, or possession)—better yet, several—that can be cut off immediately. Don't look at it as "giving it up"—look at it as a trade for reduced financial stress.

Get a grip on where it's going and apply the Exchange Standard. When you've got a healthy savings rate and are paying your bills, you don't have to be watching every penny. But if you're running a constant shortfall, then you should get obsessive for a few weeks and figure out just where all of your money is going.

In addition to expenditures with a paper trail—checks and charges—keep a daily diary of everything you spend money on to the nearest nickel or dime. After a couple of weeks (include at least two weekends), you'll have a much clearer picture of your actual expenditures.

Then it's time to apply the Exchange Standard—"What does this enable me to do and what can't I do without it?"—with all of your might. You could find that you will squeeze enough chud out of your budget to cover your deficit.

Look for ways to substitute value for money. Try to identify expenditures where you're 100 percent expecting money to do all of the work—entertaining yourself or the kids, for example—and substitute value instead.

Stop spending so much time—and money—in front of the mirror. If it weren't for maintaining an image, what expenditures would you cut out in a minute? Whether it's expensive cigars, a club membership, designer duds, or the latest electronic toy (does anyone want to guess what percentage of cellular phone calls are nothing more than an accessory to an act?), there may be some items that you wouldn't spend a cent on if you knew that no one was noticing. So unless the Joneses have offered to pay your bills, let your value be your image.

Get real help. Contact the Consumer Credit Counseling Service in your area (listed in the phone book or call 800-388-2227 for your nearest office) for free or low-cost credit counseling. They can help you determine the best ways to work through your quandary—and work with lenders. Your local United Way or community college might also offer a similar course or service. This is also a good time to go to the library and read all the books you can get your hands on that deal with getting out of debt. You'll find a wealth of additional tips.

Consolidate the freight. It's less stressful to deal with a single boss than many. If a consolidation loan—combining your debt into a single obligation through your credit union, bank, or mortgage company—makes sense economically (i.e., if the loan rate is lower than your various combined charge account rates), that strategy merits serious consideration. Make certain that you work with a reputable lender—there are a lot of sharks preying on desperate consumers. Don't pay for a credit repair service—they're rife with rip-off artists.

Hit it hard where it hurts the most. Target reducing those debts with the highest interest rates with a fast two-pronged attack.

First, pay as much as you can on those debts each month—even if it means paying the minimum on your lower-cost loans. Then, look for a way to raise a chunk of capital that can knock the debt down. Sell something you own of substantial value—boat, jewelry, collectibles, computer, lawn equipment, stock—that you can live without.

FINANCIAL STRESS SYMPTOM #3: **You can't control your spending.**

Give value instead of giving away money. Do volunteer work during the time that you typically shop. Not only will you be out of the stores, but the positive energy generated by the volunteer activity will likely diminish your spending urge.

Cut your access. The greater the access to a means of spending, the greater the temptation. Look at it this way: If you had to walk down ten flights of stairs and across a windy parking lot in subzero temperatures to get to the office pastry box or the ice cream in your freezer, that tasty treat might not look so inviting.

If your debts are causing you continual stress, cut up your charge cards and cancel all of your retail accounts. You can make do without them more easily than you think. You've already paid a huge price for the convenience. A little inconvenience now and then is a worthwhile price to pay for reduced financial stress.

Pay your day-to-day living expenses in cash only. Start on Monday morning (so you don't blow your allowance over the weekend) with a set amount of cash for the week: food, transportation, entertainment, and any other out-of-pocket expenses have to be covered by what's in your wallet. No exceptions.

I used this strategy to get through my first year living in New York City after I found myself severely monetarily understaffed. I remember having to stretch my last few dollars for the week for my Sunday dinner, but it was fun. If you approach it as a game, you'll find ways to win.

Stay out of stores. There is a direct relationship between how much time you spend in stores and how much money you spend. If you want to "just look around" somewhere, go to a museum or go on a hike. But walk into a store only if you're getting something you previously identified as a need, buy it, and then walk out.

Change the company you keep. Part of your inability to control your spending may be traced to the company you keep—relationships that center on consumption. Maybe you have some friends with whom your main activities are shopping or talking about going shopping. Or maybe your circle of buddies centers on playing with toys or hanging out in places where it takes cash to fuel the fun. You don't have to suddenly ditch your friends, but take a pass on some of the costly get-togethers and propose alternative low-cost activities at other times. You may even find out who your real friends are.

Appreciate what you already have. Part of our inability to control spending stems from a belief that we are just a string of purchases away from nirvana. This is when you need to step back and consider where you stand—from a perspective of creature comfort—on the entire spectrum of past and present human existence: on the ninety-ninth floor of a one-hundred-story building, trying to cram your way into the penthouse.

Think about the fellow on the fiftieth floor who looks up and believes you live in heaven. Be thankful.

FINANCIAL STRESS SYMPTOM #4: **You're constantly fighting with your spouse or partner about money.**

Lead by example—without a chip on your shoulder. Don't expect someone else to do what you haven't done yet. Change your currency from money to value and let the results speak for themselves. A holier-than-thou attitude is not an inspirational tool.

Look at the family or household as a "value unit." A partnership does not necessarily mean equal or identical contribution in every aspect of financial life, but rather equal satisfaction with the overall results. The key is to respect value generated toward common goals and objectives, not just money. If there's increasing friction under your roof over who pulls more weight, it's time to discuss the overall value objectives of the household and how each member of the family can best contribute, including lightening one anothers' load.

Agree on what you agree on. Although it may seem as though you and your spouse are at financial odds everywhere you turn, you probably agree on far more than either of you realize. Next time tensions flare, instead of doing battle with verbal grenades and emotional flamethrowers, try sitting down and agreeing on what you agree on. Reinforce your common needs, objectives, and vision. Discuss how you can work together to solidify these common bonds. The greater your shared positive experience, the greater the chance that your differences will be resolved or fade away.

Compromise on the rest. A household is not a hamburger stand: You can't always have it your way. Be prepared to meet your spouse halfway. For example, instead of debating new curtains versus new golf clubs, replace the downstairs curtains and get new drivers now— replace the upstairs curtains and get new irons later. Sometimes "a little of both" offers a better solution than "either/or."

Practice mutual spending deescalation. Do you need to cut back on household spending but are instead battling over who spends the most money in a totally idiotic and wasteful fashion? Then it may be time for mutual deescalation: matching spending cuts. It works like this: You identify a spending habit you are willing to forgo: "I'll cut my on-line charges by eighty dollars a month." In turn, your spouse has to match your amount: "I'll cut my lunch tab by eighty dollars a month," and then can put another cut on the table for you to match: "I'll cancel two magazine subscriptions." Even a few steps of mutual deescalation can lead to big savings.

Stop shooting at the messenger. In many relationships, one person takes on the role of accountant and the other person disassociates from the reality of the numbers. And just like the Hollywood star who fires his accountant for saying "You can't afford it" too often, the household bookkeeper takes it on the chin because two plus two doesn't equal five and four minus four doesn't equal three.

If you're not the bookkeeper in your house, stop shooting at the messenger just because you don't like the message. And bookkeepers, be fair—don't adjust the outlook to fit your agenda.

Find low-cost things to do together that you both enjoy. A couple who can have fun together—actively enjoying each other's company— without spending much money is a couple that will likely have less financial stress throughout their lives.

FINANCIAL STRESS SYMPTOM #5: **You're leaving the back door open to financial disaster, and deep down you know it.**

Don't invite Uncle Sam for a visit. Don't try harebrained tax dodges like writing off paying your kids to wash the family dog (who's listed as an employee in your gardening business that cares only for your yard). The best tax strategy is paying your proper amount of taxes on time—ask anyone who's ever been in trouble with the IRS.

Make a will. There seems to be no limit to our collective fascination with death as entertainment. But when it comes to making provisions for our own inevitable demise—could be tomorrow—we stick our heads in the sand. You probably already know an attorney (who handled your house closing?). If you don't—or don't have confidence in the ones you know—then ask someone you trust for a referral. Pick up the phone and make an appointment. This should take ten minutes at the most to get started—and no more than several hours of your time to generate a legal document that will save your heirs untold headaches and heartaches.

Cut it out. In case it didn't sink in the first time (page 157), stop doing the one big stupid thing that could really wreck your life.

Get at least some insurance: Any amount is better than none. Maybe you just can't insure yourself to all of the recommended levels throughout your life. But insurance isn't an all-or-none proposition.

If you get run over by a truck tomorrow, your family isn't going to be upset if your life insurance equals one year in salary and represented your true best effort. But your spouse and kids should be cursing you like the dog you are if you have zippo life insurance and you spend one dollar a day on any combo of cigarettes, alcohol, soda, lottery tickets, videos, junk food, or any of the other countless ways to toss four quarters down the drain. Ditto for health, liability, property and casualty, and disability: Whatever you can do is better than nothing.

Don't borrow on the good times. A lot of economic life works in cycles: good times, bad times, so-so times. But a stretch of the good times can cause you to believe that they'll last forever. Optimism is healthy; borrowing on a best-case scenario is hazardous to your financial health. When business slows down, happy-time commitments become nightmares.

One of the best ways to avoid financial stress is to borrow based on the middle—not at the edge—of your possible range of income. If you're buying a house, for example, if you borrow at least 25 percent less than you qualify for, you'll have at least some breathing room should your household income decrease for any reason.

Don't bet the farm on someone else's horse. There are rare times in life when you have to roll the potato and pick up the pumpkin, so to speak. In other words—put the present on the line for the future. That might be the sober and rational thing to do when you're growing your own business—one that you understand inside and out—and it requires a major commitment of capital to get to the next level. But to bet your life's savings—as is all too often done—on someone else's horse is insane. Ol' Bessie might look well groomed and ready to go the distance, but far more often than not, she's a few breaths away from the glue factory.

Dennis Jewell, my accountant, tells me that the biggest problem he sees with individuals who come into a lump sum of money is their insistence on buying a business (often a franchise) based solely on financial projections.

These prefab entrepreneurs ignore the possibility that past success in one field may not translate into future success in another completely unrelated field. What seemed like "a good thing to get into" can quickly vanish like a mirage or turn into a nightmare of marathon hours to stay afloat. The "next McDonald's" can turn out to be a greasy slide into the Dumpster, right alongside The Burger Boss, Captain Bunk's Seafood, and Chick-N-D-Lish.

Dennis offers good advice that is all too rarely heeded: If you're thinking of buying a business, go to work in a similar business for six months—even at minimum wage—and pay yourself what you think you're worth out of your savings. One of two things will happen: (1) You'll know the business from the ground up and have a better understanding of what it will take to make it, or (2) you'll decide that it's not for you and still have the bulk of your money.

Remember this: If real life mirrored sales pitches to any degree, we'd be a nation of millionaires.

Refrain from hitching your cart to a single horse. A corollary of the previous advice. You can steer clear of major financial stress if you refrain from hitching your financial well-being to a single win forever or lose big situation, whether it's a job you're expecting to carry you through life, a hefty mortgage on a house that you expect to soar in value, or that "perfect" investment for your entire savings.

FINANCIAL STRESS SYMPTOM #6: **You can't part with money, even if it's for your own darn good.**

First, a few words on this symptom. Just because you have money doesn't mean that you are obligated in any way to either spend it or give it away. You should never feel the slightest bit guilty about having and holding on to money that you earned through honest means and saved through diligence.

What you should want to avoid, however, is a situation in which:

The time, energy, and resources that you apply toward hanging on to each cent are of no net benefit beyond your dollars-and-cents bottom line; i.e., all you've got to show for your trouble is money.

By pinching pennies you waste time and energy and destroy resources that could otherwise be used to generate value in your life.

People who are unable to use their money for their own good usually fail to recognize that they have the problem. They don't see the trail of people—family, former friends, and business associates alike—who want nothing more to do with them as a result of their haggling and niggling. They fail to recognize the joys and opportunities they've missed out on, all for a couple of bucks that wouldn't have been missed. They don't know how miserable they are to be around because they've made themselves so miserable.

If you feel that you may be suffering from this symptom, my recommendations are brief and direct:

Consult with your doctor. You may be suffering from at least a mild case of depression.

Get out of your shell and help others who are less fortunate. Whether it's by spending time with folks in a retirement home who otherwise never have a visitor or by working with unwed mothers, you would be well served by serving others.

Give your money a job. If you have more money than you truly need, consider your money as a clone of yourself—a body of value ready to do a job. What job are you going to give it? Sending inner-city kids to private school? Supporting an arts program? Advocating a cause you believe in? Starting a business? The decision should be yours, not your heirs'.

Try to get wealthy with a different currency. Start with the first component of True Wealth—changing your basic currency from money to value—and then try all out to get wealthy. Value can't be hoarded—it has to be generated.

FINANCIAL STRESS SYMPTOM #7: The words "future" and "savings" turn your stomach into a knot and shut your brain down.

Break the glass. Imagine that you're caught in a fire and there's a fire extinguisher in a glass case. You'd certainly summon up the will to break the glass in any way possible. In a similar sense, you may have put your most powerful stress extinguishers out of reach. Whether it's by consciously boosting your value generation or putting aside some money for the future, you have to break that glass. Now.

Pressure your elected officials to deal with Social Security honestly. In not that long a period of time, we've gone from Social Security being considered as a rock-solid source of retirement income to being a bureaucratic pipe dream that will have gone up in smoke by the time all of the baby boomers have joined the party. It's common to hear people across several generations dismiss any possibility of receiving a dime in Social Security as cavalierly as if tossing a used Kleenex.

But stop for a moment and consider three things:

1. Even though you've been told not to expect anything back, you are pumping up to 15 percent of your income (I know that your employer supposedly pays half, but whose pocket do you think it ultimately comes out of?) into the "trust" (an inappropriate name if there ever was one). If that doesn't make you get off your tail and do something, what does?
2. Maybe the real solution lies somewhere in the middle—between bankruptcy and bonanza.
3. The sooner we address the problem in a practical and forthright manner, the more likely we are to find an equitable solution.

So here's what you can do right now: Write each of your elected national officials—house representative, senators, and president—and encourage them to start discussing openly and honestly the problems that face Social Security.

And then write any and every public figure who uses the issue as a demagogic scare tactic to frighten voters and thereby makes reasonable discussion impossible. Demand that these scuzzballs cut it the @#*$ out RIGHT NOW.

Keep an emergency line of credit. If you don't have a sufficient financial reserve—or even if you do—it is worthwhile to have a line of credit that can be accessed by check. A credit line serves in effect as a preprocessed at-the-ready loan—that needn't ever be used except in the case of true emergency. The fifteen- or twenty-dollar annual fee is worth the peace of mind that knowing you have some backup brings.

Watch your health. It makes no sense to worry about having to spend all of your money on health care in the future, if you don't spend any time or effort taking care of your health in the present. If you've got enough money to eat today, you've got enough money to be healthy. If you've got enough money to eat junk food or smoke cigarettes, you've got enough money to cover your future health care expenses.

Preserve the ties that bind. The future may be a scary place, but it's a lot scarier if you are all alone.

Find peace in the present. You can never be comfortable with the future until you are able to find peace in the present.

FINANCIAL STRESS SYMPTOM #8: **You're overwhelmed and intimidated by the prospect of making an investment decision.**

Make a split decision. Sometimes you arrive at a logical conclusion that you should invest a portion of your money in a certain manner. But, because the particular investment will be a new experience for you, your emotions hold you back from acting on your decision. Remember, investing is not an "either/or" situation. You can invest 25 percent of the amount under consideration and make a one-year loan with the remaining dollars. Your overall risk exposure will be minimal, and you'll learn through experience what's best for you.

Don't stick your head in the sand. Some people are like ostriches. Every once in a while they pull their heads out of the ground, look around at their investment options, decide they can't deal with the prospect of making any decisions, and stick their heads back in the sand.

There's nothing wrong with just saying "no" to a prospective investment. But it shouldn't be a cover for maintaining outright ignorance. Refusing to deal with any aspect of preserving your savings dollars can leave you stuck with a needlessly small return. If you have thousands of dollars in a passbook savings account, for example, you should wake up and get with it.

But there is a danger even greater than forgoing easy dollars. People who stubbornly refuse to learn anything about investing are among the ripest candidates to do something absolutely stupid with their savings. I've witnessed people go right from savings accounts to options trading, penny stocks, and limited partnerships (all with predictably disastrous results) at least partially because they lacked even the basic knowledge that might have helped them sniff out the dangers ahead.

When you know nothing, you can be sold anything.

Read the personal finance pages. One of the best ways to broaden your financial knowledge is to make it a habit to read the personal finance columns in your daily newspaper. This reporting covers not only investments but a wide range of consumer issues, and it tends to be cautious, evenhanded, and practical.

You'll want to take any article that says anything to the effect of "Now might be a good time to invest in XYZ, say experts" with a grain of salt. But the articles on how to deal with nuts-and-bolts issues like insurance and retirement planning and how to avoid rip-offs will prove to be quite useful. And if you read a little each week, the information is easier to absorb.

Helpful hint: Clip and keep a file of articles that you believe will be useful in the future.

Absolute must read: the columns of Jane Bryant Quinn.

Always have an exit strategy. Everyone talks about when to buy, but there's a second half to the question: When do you sell? That's a subject that remains underexplored.

Buy and hold forever might be fine in academic theory, but in real life there comes a time when people want to use their money. When you make an investment, you should give at least some thought as to when and what might cause you to sell. Otherwise, you'll eventually hear yourself saying "Now? Uh, I'll wait. Okay, now? Uh, maybe I'll wait. . . ."

There are no hard-and-fast rules on when to sell, but here are several guidelines:

Sell your big gains. It's never a profit until you put it in your pocket. When you have a big gain in an investment, consider selling the amount of the gain over your original investment and then moving the profit to firmer ground like a Treasury bill or your money market fund. Your original investment will remain at work, but even if the price of your investment goes right back to where you bought it, you'll still have at least some profit. Bernard Baruch once noted that he'd never lost a dime selling too soon.

As you approach a targeted objective, set up a schedule to sell. You know your kids are going to college when they are eighteen. Do you sell their stocks when they turn thirteen? Of course not. But what you should do is set up a schedule to sell over a five- to seven-year period—plan to sell a fixed percentage of their overall holdings each and every year—so that by the year each tuition payment is due, the money is at the ready in a short-term loan. Ditto for any other long-term objective with a known time frame.

Think about when you'll cry "uncle." Although we're in a time when all losses are seen as temporary dips on an eternal upward arc, there are times when a loss stays a loss and becomes a bigger loss, and you can neither wish nor will it away. Consider setting a pain threshold on the downside—a percentage loss that if the investment hits it, then you'll quit it. It hurts to take a 25 percent loss—but not as badly as living with it night after night if it's grinding away at you or it turns into a 40 or 50 percent loss.

FINANCIAL STRESS SYMPTOM #9: **You're losing money on the investments you've already made.**

Don't let the person who put you in the hole throw dirt on you. Be extra careful about allowing the person who put you into an investment mess try to "make it up to you."

If you can honestly say that you were "sold" the investment rather than logically bought it, allowing the seller to try to undo the damage could be very well like expecting a mugger to turn into a physician. When you start hearing phrases like "This should get it back for us," "This one should do the trick," or "I've got something that looks a lot better," then it's time to take your money and head for the door.

Go back to why you made the investment. If the fundamental reasons for your investment remain unchanged, then you'll do well just to be patient. If you invested in Swerve Electronics because it was the industry leader, and nothing has changed in the interim, then stay with it. If the underlying premise for the investment is no longer valid, then it's probably time to sell. A simple reminder that circumstances can change and leaders can fall behind: Wang Computer.

Is your boat the only one sinking? In an investment market, a rising tide lifts most boats. If your boat is sinking while most of the other similar-type boats are floating right along, that's an indication of trouble at the helm or a hole in the hull. Either way, a change is likely warranted. For example, if most international stock funds are going up but yours is heading down, that means the manager is making a lot of bad decisions. It's time to find a boat with a competent skipper.

Did you buy at the top? When you look back at when you purchased an investment, is it increasingly apparent that you got in at the top? Then you either have to sweat it out or take the loss. Several things to keep in mind:

The greater the frenzy and mania at the peak of an investment, the further it will fall and the longer it will take to come back. The more people love something, the more they can end up hating it, and it takes longer for the bad feelings to subside and the love affair to renew.

You should evaluate if the underlying source of value of the investment is deteriorating—or can deteriorate—in value. A stock that falls from eighty dollars to ten dollars a share has no chance of coming back if the company itself is losing money and has no new competitive products. But the source of the value of a choice piece of antique furniture—the design and the craftsmanship—will remain unchanged for decades to come, no matter what the near-term trend in price.

Consider it tuition—but don't repeat the class. Sometimes for all the fretting and sour feelings, it's just better to get a loss out of your life and be done with it. Consider the loss a tuition payment in the school of investing. Learn the lesson—how did it happen?—etch the lesson in your mind, and vow never to repeat the class again.

AND WHAT IF YOU STILL NEED HELP?

When it comes to financial matters, almost all of us need some form of professional help—and not necessarily the variety oft recommended by Ann Landers.

The possibilities fall into four general categories: accountant, attorney, insurance agent, and investment adviser (stockbrokers and financial planners). And although the trend is toward one-stop shopping, with firms offering every possible investment and service under one roof, I believe you should have a separate adviser in each area to serve as a system of checks and balances.

If you hand all of your financial decisions over to a single individual or even a single firm, and that choice proves to be ill advised—whether through incompetence or outright fraud—your financial life could become a nightmare. Any one of these four areas is complex enough to merit full-time concentration by a specialist. Don't work with a handyman—and never work with an accountant, lawyer, or insurance agent who also sells investments.

Now let's conclude by looking at a few tips relating to each type of adviser:

Accountants. Even if you're a do-it-yourselfer, have your tax returns prepared by a professional every few years—especially when your personal situation changes—if for no other reason than to confirm that you're doing the right thing. Look for a C.P.A. (either independent or with a small firm) who specializes in working year round with individuals and small businesses.

Avoid part-time seasonal tax preparers who cannot provide you with a sense of continuity and consistency in the advice you receive.

Attorneys. A will or estate is a legal document that cannot be altered from the grave. Use an experienced attorney—one who bills by the hour. There are a lot of convoluted estate-planning schemes for dodging taxes that look perfect on paper but in practice have serious drawbacks. You want someone who knows the drawbacks and knows from experience what works—and will talk you out of legal tricks, not promote them.

Insurance agents. Buying life insurance on your own is no problem. But when you get into the nuances of property, casualty, and liability insurance, you want to work with someone who can scope out your entire situation for any cracks or flaws in your armor. For example, you may not think you need liability coverage for business purposes in your home—until the person delivering a business-related overnight package slips and falls on your icy sidewalk.

Insurance companies will pay only in accord with the exact language of the policy. Make sure your policies fit your needs exactly.

Investment advisers. There are well over a half-million individuals registered to sell securities in the country. Almost all of them look and act sharp. Most of them are well intentioned. But we're talking about your money—and therefore only the best of advisers should be considered good enough.

Here are the criteria I would use in selecting an adviser to handle my money—or yours. The ideal investment adviser:

○ *Has been in the business at least ten years* (fifteen or twenty would be preferable). Time and experience are the best teachers. You don't want to be piloted through a bear market by a first-time flyer.

○ *Has worked for no more than two firms.* The more a broker hops from firm to firm, the greater the chance that his eyes are glued to the commission chart—not his clients' bottom line. One switch in a career is fine—in fact, often it's necessary for a broker to find the right working environment. Beyond that, buyer beware.

○ *Lives a lifestyle more modest than what she could afford.* The internal culture of the financial industry is largely one of conspicuous consumption—spend what you make to show that you've made it, and try to make more. Brokerage firm parking lots, in fact, often look more like luxury car dealerships. You don't want a broker pressed by a big mortgage and fancy cars—the temptation for her to churn your account, however subtly, is too great. As a rule of thumb, I'd steer clear of the broker with the Porsche and ride with the one who drives the equivalent of a Camry.

○ *Has the courage and the clout to tell his manager to get lost.* No matter what financial services firms say to the contrary, they do exert pressure on their representatives to sell certain products. The deciding factor behind the push: increased profits for the firm, but not necessarily for the client. Your adviser is your line of defense against the garbage coming out of headquarters, but unfortunately few reps have the courage and the clout (generally a function of time in the business—newer reps have little clout) to tell their superiors to leave them alone. One tip-off to a rep who will push whatever's placed in front of him: lots of geegaws around his office—mugs, paperweights, plaques, and so on—from investment sponsors.

○ *Is not number one in sales.* Look around a prospective adviser's office for sales awards. If you see signs that he's number one in sales in his training class, office, region, or firm, you are looking at either an extraordinarily focused individual who can deliver superior investment results with a greater degree of efficiency than any of his cohorts, or someone who's a good hustler. All too often, the answer is the latter.

○ *Has an interest in the craft and history of investing that extends beyond his desk.* A publisher once told me flat out, "Brokers don't read." Unfortunately, he's right. Few investment professionals read anything outside the everyday stream of information that keeps them in their little loops. But some of the best and most timeless advice lies well outside the river of "what." I'd want a broker who reads every book by John Train and read *The Intelligent Investor* a long, long time ago.

The eternal question is: How do you find a trustworthy and knowledgeable professional? There's a simple four-step process that will help steer you in the right direction:

1. *Ask for recommendations.* Think of all of your family, friends, and cohorts. Whom among them do you admire for their competence, restraint, and sober judgment? Ask them if they would recommend the professional(s) with whom they are currently working—and why they would recommend them.

2. *Interview several candidates.* Don't just hand the job over to the first name that comes your way. Interview several candidates—especially if you're choosing an investment adviser. Ask for references and a track record of recommendations. Communication is the key to any successful relationship, and you should feel comfortable expressing your thoughts and concerns to someone who's going to deal with an important part of your life. You don't want to work with a bully who's going to intimidate you into doing something you don't want to do.

3. *Check with the authorities.* Before making any investment, check out the adviser's disciplinary and complaint record with both the

National Association of Securities Dealers (800-289-9999) and your state securities regulator (call the NASD general information line at 301-590-6500). Your state's insurance department may also be able to give you the lowdown on a prospective agent.

4. *Trust your common sense and judgment.* It's your money and your life.

Epilogue:
If Money's
the Answer, Change
the Question

WE'VE NOW come full circle—generate, exchange, preserve—and covered a lot of ground along the way. So let's return for a moment to our initial quandary: "How do I make this stress go away?"

While trying to finish this book, I received some good advice: that writing the definitive statement about money and stress was an impossibility. Rather, it was suggested, I should seek to advance a set of useful and effective ideas that might also serve as the basis for a continuing examination and discussion of financial stress.

So I'd like to wrap things up with a thought that acts as both the period at the end of this discussion and the jumping-off point for the next one:

Whatever your financial stress, if money is the answer, change the question.

If you'd like to be part of the ongoing dialogue, visit my home on the Internet: **www.valuefirst.com.**

Appendix A:
For Further Reading

EVERY HOUSEHOLD should have *two* (one serving as balance against the other) personal finance reference books.

I recommend *Making the Most of Your Money* by Jane Bryant Quinn (Simon and Schuster, 1997). Recently updated, it deserves to be the cornerstone of your home financial library. *The Wall Street Journal Lifetime Guide to Money* (Hyperion, 1997) is the best of the remaining money guides.

Either of these two books would be an excellent foundation for a personal financial library. Helpful tip: If you live near a college campus, you might be able to buy a used personal financial planning textbook in the bookstore. I've purchased several such books over the years and find that they make good backup reference guides.

In addition, *The Wall Street Journal Guide to Understanding Personal Finance* (Lightbulb, 1997) is an excellent concise overview of its subject.

If you do want to become an active investor, you'll find that there are hundreds of books about investing. Most offer *either* a repackaging of material in the public domain *or* the only surefire way to get rich, which is just as the author purports to have done it. Very few attempt to develop and convey a viewpoint—how to think—that will serve the reader well over time.

I highly recommend the works of John Train to anyone contemplating an active investment program. Begin with *The Craft of Investing* (HarperBusiness, 1994) and then read the rest, including: *Preserving*

Capital and Making It Grow, The Midas Touch, The Money Masters, and *The New Money Masters.*

Andrew Tobias's *The Only Investment Guide You'll Ever Need* (Harcourt Brace, 1996) is an excellent companion to Train's work.

Bogle on Mutual Funds by John C. Bogle (Dell, 1994) is essential reading for fund investors. As the founder of The Vanguard Group of mutual funds, Bogle is the chairman of the board of low-cost, no-load mutual fund investing—including index funds.

I'd also like to mention my favorite financial writer of all, James Grant. His books, including *The Trouble with Prosperity* (Times Books, 1996), will reduce your stress to the extent that you enjoy sophisticated, literate, and wry financial analysis of the highest order.

You shouldn't immediately buy books on getting out of debt for a simple reason: If you need to read them, you really don't have the money to buy them. Your local library will have a number of books on the subject. Borrow and read every one of them. The Consumer Credit Counseling Service can also provide you with all the information you need to get out of the red. After you've absorbed these available resources, you'll be in a position to determine what, if any, books you should buy. *Cut Your Bills in Half* (Smithmark, 1993) by the editors of Rodale Press is a nonhysterical guide to cost cutting.

Read the personal finance pages of whatever newspaper you're in the habit of reading. The writing should be easy to understand and usually errs on the side of caution. Over time, you'll absorb a lot of information without really trying. If your local paper is lacking in coverage, *USA Today* offers a good, widely available alternative.

The Wall Street Journal regularly covers personal finance issues, as well as other topics of interest. The "Managing Your Career," "Work & Family," and "The Front Lines" columns contain a wealth of stress-reducing ideas.

Forbes magazine is not a personal finance magazine per se, but it contains excellent articles on personal finance and investing, including mutual funds. It is the one magazine I couldn't do without. Don't miss the annual mutual fund survey, as well as updates throughout the year.

There's a personal finance/investment magazine for everyone—from novices to daily traders. I prefer *Kiplinger's Personal Finance Magazine* for nuts-and-bolts personal finance coverage and *Smart Money* for feature articles, but I suggest that you review the options at your library (or doctor's waiting room) before you plunk down money for a subscription. Consumer warning: Magazines that feature a lot of articles with titles like "Five Hot Stocks for the Next Year" or "The Best Investment for Right Now" can actually raise your financial stress.

Appendix B:
Products and Services
Mentioned in This Book

THE FRANKLIN COVEY seminar on time management is second to none. Phone: 800-977-1776 for information on seminars in your area.

The McElfresh Map Company's works of historical art are available through bookstores or direct from Earl and Michiko. Phone: 800-308-3702. Fax: 716-372-8090.

Quaker Boy Inc. sells a wide variety of game calls (including the same championship turkey calls used by Dick Kirby and his son Chris), hunting videos, and accessories. Phone: 716-662-3979. Fax: 716-662-9426.

Motivational speaker Jonas Gadson is available to fire up your next meeting. He can be reached at 716-251-1186.

To learn more about the "700% Solution," write financial planner Richard Vodra at 6827 Montevideo Square Court, Falls Church, VA 22043, or call 703-538-4888.

Jazz bassist Ray Drummond can be heard on numerous fine recordings, including his recent *Vignettes* and *1-2-3-4* (Fall 1998) on the Arabesque label.

The Teaching Company offers a wide variety of full-length college courses—taught by top professors—on audio- and videotape. A great way to expand your horizons at your own pace. Phone: 800-832-2412.

Appendix C:
The "700% Solution"

TO GET AN approximate idea as to how much you need to save for retirement:

EXAMPLES:

Bob is forty years old, has $60,000 in savings, and earns $50,000 a year.

Aimee is twenty-five years old, has $20,000 in savings, and earns $80,000 a year.

1. Divide your retirement savings to date (don't include savings earmarked for college or other goals) by your annual income.

   EXAMPLES:
   Bob: $60,000 savings / $50,000 income = 1.2
   Aimee: $20,000 savings / $80,000 income = .25

   ANSWER = _____

2. Multiply the answer from step 1 by the multiplier below that corresponds most closely to the number of years remaining until your retirement:

YEARS TO RETIREMENT:

10	15	20	25	30	35	40

MULTIPLIER:

1.22	1.35	1.49	1.64	1.81	2.0	2.21

EXAMPLES:
Bob: 1.2×1.64 (25 years to retirement) = 2.0
Aimee: $.25 \times 2.21$ (40 years to retirement) = .55

ANSWER = _____

3. Subtract the answer from step 2 from 7.0.

EXAMPLES:
Bob: 7.0 minus 2.0 = 5.0
Aimee: 7.0 minus .55 = 6.45

ANSWER = _____

4. To calculate your savings rate, you'll need a financial calculator. Plug in the following values:

Number of payments = Number of years until retirement (be sure to use the same number you used in answering step 2)
Interest rate = 2.0
Present value = 0
Future value = Answer to step 3 above
Payment = Your percentage savings rate

This is the *percentage* of your annual income you need to save (along with your employer's contributions) and continue to save until retirement to reach the "700% Solution" target. Note: As your income rises, your percentage saving rate stays the same, increasing the amount of actual dollars saved.

EXAMPLES:
Bob: To save 5.0 times his current income by retirement date in twenty-five years, his savings rate should be 16 percent.
Aimee: To save 6.45 times her current income by retirement date in forty years, her savings rate should be 11 percent.

5. To determine how much more money you'll need to save this year, multiply the answer to step 4 by your current income.

Notes

22 "In his terrific book . . . money and happiness ends." David G. Myers, Ph.D., *The Pursuit of Happiness* (New York: Avon Books, 1992), pp. 31–46.

22 "Examining the relationship . . . differences in income." Dan Seligman, "Does Money Buy Happiness?," *Forbes*, April 21, 1997, pp. 394–396.

27 "Extensive research . . . nonmillionaire neighbors." Thomas J. Stanley, Ph.D., and William D. Danko, Ph.D., *The Millionaire Next Door* (Marietta, GA: Longstreet Press, 1997), p. 3.

28 "A sound bite . . . and nonfinancial." Joe Dominguez and Vicki Robin, *Your Money or Your Life* (New York: Viking Penguin, 1992), pp. 4, 231.

28 "Allow me to blunt . . . 'Man must work!'" Hans F. Sennholz, "Man Must Work," pamphlet (Irvington-on-Hudson, NY: Foundation for Economic Education).

29 Sennholz, op. cit.

29 "But do you . . . own forks." Elaine St. James, *Living the Simple Life* (New York: Hyperion, 1996), p. 145.

31 "The same is true . . . why she did it." Amy Dacyzyn, *The Tightwad Gazette* (New York: Villard Books, 1992), pp. 3–5.

40 "Tragically, a subsistence . . . expertise in recycling." Raju Narisetti, "Manufacturers Decry a Shortage of Jobs While Rejecting Many," *The Wall Street Journal,* September 11, 1995, p. A1.

49 Sennholz, op. cit.

56 "My local newspaper . . . get lost." "Savings Pave Way for Early Retirement," Richard Schroeder, *The Buffalo News,* October 24, 1995, p. B1.

79 "What's the most effective way . . . alcohol abuse." Agnes Palazetti, "Parental Monitoring Vital to Child-rearing, Study of Drug, Alcohol Abuse Finds," *The Buffalo News,* October 25, 1995, p. B1.

80 "Yet despite . . . are rare." Gilbert Fuschberg, "Taking Control," *The Wall Street Journal,* September 10, 1993, pp. R1–4.

105 "In his book . . . tragic universe." David Yount, *Growing in Faith* (New York: Penguin Books, 1994), p. 6.

105 "A study . . . attorney fees." Dawn Blolock, "For Many Executives, Ethics Appear to Be a Write-Off," *The Wall Street Journal,* March 26, 1996, p. C1.

106 "When I began . . . into contact." Daniel Goleman, *Emotional Intelligence* (New York: Bantam Books, 1995), pp. 33–126.

108 "I begin . . . responsible." John Rosemond, *A Family of Value* (Kansas City: Andrews and McMeel, 1995), pp. 121–231.

112 "To be culturally . . . modern world." E. D. Hirsch, Jr., *Cultural Literacy: What Every American Needs to Know* (New York: Vintage Books, 1988), p. xiii.

141 "Here's some . . . probably do too." Bill Gates, *San Diego Union,* February 21, 1995, as reprinted in *The New York Times,* January 14, 1996, p. E7.

214 "Recently . . . foundation for True Wealth." Susan Sheehan, "Ain't No Middle Class," *The New Yorker,* December 11, 1995, p. 82.

225 "That common cost . . . in tuition." "That Tuition Monster," *The New York Times,* September 29, 1996, p. C2.

252 "This strategy . . . a good return." "The Lessons of History," *The Wall Street Journal,* May 17, 1996, p. C1.

255 "Indeed, immediately . . . ownership possibilities." Floyd Norris, "Friday the 13th: The Bull's Birthday," *The New York Times,* September 15, 1996, p. C1.

266 "Make the future . . . an inopportune time." Carole Gould, "Hedging Risk/The Right Asset Mix," *The New York Times,* April 7, 1996, p. F17.

Index